This book is dedicated to my mother, Inez, the wind beneath my sails, a kind soul whose guiding hand and gentle manner will live on forever.

About the Author

Doug Sahlin (Lakeland, Florida) is an author, graphic designer, and Web site designer living in Central Florida. He is the author of 10 books on graphic design, including *How To Do Everything with Adobe Acrobat 5*. Sahlin's articles and product reviews have appeared in national publications such as *Computer Graphics World*, *3D Magazine*, *Video Systems*, and *Corel* Magazine. His tutorials have been featured at numerous Web sites devoted to graphic design.

How to Do *Everything* with

Macromedia® Contribute™

Doug Sahlin

McGraw-Hill/Osborne

New York   Chicago   San Francisco   Lisbon
London   Madrid   Mexico City   Milan   New Delhi
San Juan   Seoul   Singapore   Sydney   Toronto

The McGraw·Hill Companies

McGraw-Hill/Osborne
2600 Tenth Street
Berkeley, California 94710
U.S.A.

To arrange bulk purchase discounts for sales promotions, premiums, or fund-raisers, please contact **McGraw-Hill**/Osborne at the above address. For information on translations or book distributors outside the U.S.A., please see the International Contact Information page immediately following the index of this book.

How to Do Everything with Macromedia® Contribute™

1234567890 FGR FGR 019876543

ISBN 0-07-222892-X

Publisher:	Brandon A. Nordin
Associate Publisher & Editor-in-Chief:	Scott Rogers
Acquisitions Editor:	Margie McAneny
Project Editor:	Jennifer Malnick
Acquisitions Coordinator:	Tana Allen
Technical Editor:	Denise Laurent
Copy Editors:	Emily Rader, Darren Meiss
Proofreader:	Susie Elkind
Indexer:	Claire Splan
Computer Designers:	George Toma Charbak, Tara A. Davis
Illustrators:	Melinda Moore Lytle, Michael Mueller, Lyssa Wald
Series Design:	Mickey Galicia
Cover Series Design:	Dodie Shoemaker
Cover Illustration:	Greg Scott
Cover Photographs:	Jim Craigmyle (man), Nora Good (earth), both © Masterfile

This book was composed with Corel VENTURA™ Publisher.

Contents at a Glance

Contents

Acknowledgments

An author sits alone at his or her computer, typing, proofreading, and creating screenshots, hour after hour, day after day, often on weekends, and sometimes into the night. When the book is finally published, the author's name appears on the cover, which somehow doesn't seem fair because the author would never have gotten the job done without the support of many. And this author received heaping spoonfuls of support from an impressive array of individuals.

First and foremost, I'd like to thank the wonderful team at Osborne. Thanks to the ambitious and blonde Margie McAneny, for making this opportunity possible. Thanks to Tana Allen, for making sure my chapters and screenshots got to the proper parties at the proper time. Thanks to Project Editor Jenny Malnick, for your words of encouragement and witty asides, and for filling my inbox with edited chapters to review. Kudos to the lovely and talented copyeditor extraordinaire Emily Rader, for polishing my text to perfection. As always, thanks to the lovely and very blonde Margot Maley Hutichson for being the best literary agent an author could hope for.

Special thanks for my friend and fellow author Bonnie Blake. Your friendship, support, and upbeat attitude is greatly appreciated. Best wishes for success with your online endeavors.

As always, thanks to my friends, family, and mentors—life would indeed be difficult without you. Special thanks to my cousin Ted (aka Tedster) and my loving sister Karen.

Introduction

Welcome to *How To Do Everything with Macromedia Contribute*, a brand-new book about a brand-new software package. While the software may be new, Macromedia, the company that created the software, is a seasoned veteran in the graphic and Web design software market. When you begin using Contribute, you'll see that it's a well-thought-out program that makes it possible for you to edit Web pages without knowing a thing about HTML.

First and foremost, you should know that Contribute cannot be used to create a Web site. What you can do with Contribute is easily edit an existing Web site. You can edit text with ease, change images on your Web site, and much more. Whether you're looking to manage a small business Web site or a personal Web site, Contribute provides you with the tools to edit Web pages to perfection. If in the past you've considered editing Web pages but let out a gasp of despair when you saw the underlying HTML code that displays your Web pages, fear not. You don't need to know how to edit the HTML code; Contribute takes care of that daunting task with admirable efficiency. All you have to do is edit the content for the Web pages and Contribute takes care of the rest.

While you don't need to know HTML to edit Web pages with Contribute, you do need a basic knowledge of Web pages and how they are designed. You also need to know about the images incorporated in the pages you are editing. In this book, you'll gain a basic knowledge of Web pages, images for Web pages, as well as what you can and cannot edit with Contribute.

 *The first iteration of Contribute is for the PC. Macromedia is working on a version for the Macintosh that will be released in 2003. This book covers the PC only.*

About this Book

This book is divided into five parts. The chapters in the first part of the book familiarize you with Contribute and what you can do with it, the middle chapters of the book show you how to edit elements in your Web pages, and the final chapters of the book show you how to administer a Contribute Web site. The parts of the book are as follows.

Part I: Introducing Contribute

In Part I, you'll get a general overview of Contribute. You'll learn some essential nontechnical information about Web pages and how they are created. You'll gain a working knowledge of the Contribute workspace and learn which items you can and cannot edit with the software. You'll see an example of typical Contribute workflow and learn how to set up the application to suit your working preferences. You'll also learn how to create a connection to the Web site you'll be editing with Contribute.

Part II: Editing Web Page Elements

The second part of the book will get you up and running with Contribute. Here you'll learn how to use Contribute as a Web browser to navigate to sites that you edit and other Internet Web sites. You'll also learn how to put Contribute through its paces as a Web page editor. You'll learn how to choose a page to edit by navigating to it, or choosing it from a folder on your Web server, and how to add elements such as Word and Excel documents to the pages you edit. In addition, you'll learn how to create new Web pages, set Web page properties, and test your pages in a Web browser prior to publishing them. The last chapter in this part covers the important topic of working with text in the Web pages you edit.

Part III: Working with Hyperlinks, Tables, and Frames

The chapters in Part III show you how to deal with some of the more advanced Web page elements. You'll learn how to create links from the pages you edit to other Web pages in your site, and how to create a link and a new Web page at the same time. Another technique you'll learn is how to specify whether a linked page opens in the same window as the page that calls it, or in another window. You'll learn how to organize the elements of your Web pages with tables, modify tables, and edit tables already existing in the pages you edit. Chapter 9 instructs you how to edit frame-based Web pages, as well as how to create links from frame-based Web pages.

Part IV: Working with Images and Publishing Web Pages

Part IV shows you how to work with the images in the Web pages you edit with Contribute. You'll learn how to add images to Web pages, edit image properties, and more. If you own third-party image-editing software, you'll learn how to launch the image editor from within Contribute, edit the image, then publish the image to your Web site. If you have access to Macromedia Fireworks MX, you'll learn how to use this software to optimize images for Web pages, apply special effects to images, and roundtrip edit from Contribute. Chapter 13 shows you how to publish the pages you edit.

Part V: Administering Web Sites

If you use Contribute to edit Web pages for your organization, and you are appointed to administer the Web site, you'll learn everything you need to know in Part V. You'll learn how to become site administrator, administer the Web site, set up permission groups, and specify which Web page elements members of user groups have permission to edit. You'll also learn how to send encrypted connection keys to members of user groups. Connection keys make it possible for users to create a connection to a Contribute Web site. Once the connection is made, users can edit Web page elements according to the permissions granted to their user group.

Conventions Used in this Book

As of this writing, Contribute is only available for the PC. Therefore, you will not see any cross-platform conventions. Throughout the book, you'll see tips, notes, and words of caution separated from the main text, which contain information designed to streamline your workflow and warn you of any potential problems you may encounter while editing Web pages. You'll also find Did You Know and How To sidebars sprinkled throughout the book, which contain useful information related to the topic of discussion.

When you see instructions to execute a menu command, the path to the menu command will be formatted as follows: choose Insert | Image | From My Computer. This set of instructions requires that you choose Image from the Insert menu and then choose From My Computer from the Image submenu.

In Closing

My goal is to provide you with a book that you can use as a standalone reference for editing Web pages with Contribute. In addition, I have provided information that you will not find in the program manual, such as how to optimize images for Web pages, add special effects to images, and other useful tidbits. After you read this book, keep it within arm's reach for an instant refresher course on a particular topic. You can also use the inside back cover (or Appendix B) as a handy reference to the most popular Contribute keyboard shortcuts.

Part I

Introducing Contribute

Chapter 1

Getting to Know Contribute

How To...

- ■ Connect to a Web site
- ■ Navigate to a Web page
- ■ Edit a Web page
- ■ Edit images, text, and links
- ■ Create a new Web page
- ■ Publish a Web page

When you surf the Internet, you may wonder how the Web pages you are viewing were created. The design of a Web page is often the result of collaboration between client and designer where the client outlines his or her needs and the designer advises which Web design techniques or objects would be best suited to bringing the vision to fruition on the Internet. Armed with this information and other items such as the client's logo and any images the client wants displayed on the site, the designer goes to work and creates content. Often, designers are faced with clients that don't have a clue as to what they need or should have on their Web site. Then the task of creating a knockout Web page weighs on the shoulders of the designer who begins experimenting with color schemes, graphics, and different layouts. After a bit of creative play, a design begins to take shape and a Web site is born.

After the site is created and launched, designer and client breathe a sigh of relief and wait for the faithful to visit the site en masse. But the only thing consistent in this world is change, and if the Web site so carefully crafted by the designer doesn't change, the faithful audience becomes unfaithful and the site loses popularity; not a good result, especially for the client. When a site needs updating, a client can hire the site's designer to do the work and hope the designer has time to fit it into his or her schedule. Most designers prefer to do new design work because it's more lucrative, so they tend to work revisions into their schedule during slack periods. The Web site owner now has an alternative to hiring a designer, however: Macromedia Contribute. While Contribute won't do away with Web designers, it will free them up to do what they like to do best—design. What Contribute offers the Web site owner is a way to update Web site content without having to know a thing about HTML (Hypertext Markup Language) and Web page design. In this chapter, you'll learn how Web pages are created and how they can be edited with Contribute.

About Contribute

1

When the Internet was in its infancy, Web pages were dark and dreary text-only creations. Initially, the Internet was used predominantly by government agencies and industries for displaying and exchanging information. As the Internet evolved, companies like CompuServe and Prodigy brought the Internet to the masses. In the early days, viewers used crude facsimiles of Web browsers that were capable of displaying text and icons with a limited color palette.

As computers became more powerful and less expensive, Web sites took advantage of the increased processing power of computers. As a result, Web pages became more sophisticated, with full-color images and animations. As the Internet became more popular, companies hired professional Web designers to design their sites and take advantage of the latest Web technologies. Like everything else in the world, the companies that display their corporate and product information on the Internet are in a constant state of flux. As products and services change, Web sites need to be updated. The code used to create a Web page can be quite complex, and even the simplest revision to a Web site generally used to require the services of a Web designer. The revision timetable was dependent upon the Web designer's workload. This all changed with the release of Macromedia Contribute.

The fact that you have this book in your hands means you want to use Contribute to manage the content of your Web site. Whether you already own the software or intend to purchase Contribute in the near future, know that you can use the software to easily manage the content of one or more sites. You can use Contribute to change text and images, to create new pages, and much more without having to know HTML, the programming language used to format text and images in an HTML document that is displayed as a page on a Web browser. The Contribute workspace shown in Figure 1-1 has a look and feel similar to word processing software.

You manage the content of your Web pages by following these four steps:

1. *Set up a connection to your Web site.* You accomplish this easily using a connection wizard.

2. *Navigate to the page you want to edit.* This part of the process is similar to using your favorite Web browser. If you have already set up a connection to the site, you can edit the page you want as soon as it loads into the Contribute browser.

3. *Edit existing pages or create new pages.* In this phase of the process, you can edit text, replace images, create new pages, and more. You can edit

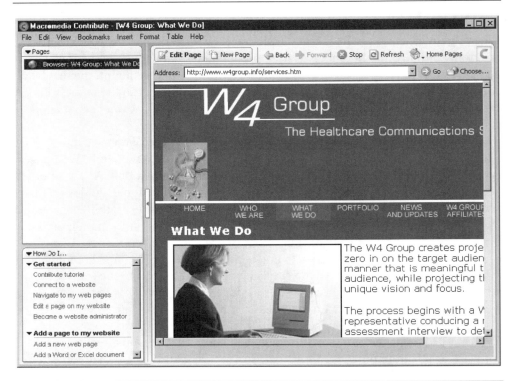

FIGURE 1-1   Contribute combines a Web browser and powerful editing features in an easy-to-use interface.

online or save a draft of the page for offline editing. When you work in Edit mode, you use a toolbar that features icons you are already familiar with from the software you use in your daily work. If you're entering or editing text, you can spell check the document before publishing it. You can add links, images, and tables to a page.

4. *Publish the page.* After you've modified the page or created a new page, you can publish the page to your site with the click of a button.

As the name implies, you use Contribute to contribute or manage content on your Web site. If you work in a large organization, you may have several members who are contributing content to a site. When this is the case, the Web site administrator sets up site-wide permissions, creates permission groups, and defines other parameters that can be edited within your Web site. If you work in a team environment, you can e-mail a copy of a page revision to other team members for review.

Contribute also saves previous iterations of a page. If you are not satisfied with an edited page, you can use the Rollback (that's Contribute terminology for going back to a past version) feature to revert to a previous iteration of the page. The Web site administrator can specify the number of rollbacks available when defining site permissions. Another powerful Contribute feature allows team members to check a page in and out. When you edit a Web page, contribute checks out in your username; other team members know you are editing it. After you finish editing a page, Contribute checks it back in and it's available for editing by other team members. This feature prevents another team member from accidentally overwriting the page you are editing.

Before Macromedia created Contribute, the only alternative to editing a Web page was using a word processor such as Windows Notepad to manually edit the code, or using a WYSIWYG (*what you see is what you get*) HTML editor such as Macromedia Dreamweaver or Microsoft FrontPage. Both of these programs have fairly steep learning curves and require basic knowledge of HTML.

The nice thing about Contribute is that it gives you all the necessary features to edit your site without destroying the Web designer's work. You cannot overwrite the underlying code, and this prevents you from wiping out the Web designer's formatting.

Another important feature of Contribute is that you are in control. You edit the pages according to your schedule instead of trying to squeeze the edits into your designer's schedule. Contribute enables you to maintain your Web site and keep the content fresh and up-to-date. As I'm sure you're well aware, people return to your site if they can be assured they will see new or updated content, not the same material displayed the last time they visited the site.

How Are Web Pages Created?

When you visit a company's Web page, you see information about that organization's products or services bundled for delivery over the Internet. The success or failure of the design rests squarely on the shoulders of the Web designer (unless of course the site owner requested certain items that made the HTML file excessively large, causing the page to load slowly, especially for viewers with modem connections). Most Web designers will steer their clients clear of any potential design flaws. The process begins when client and designer meet and exchange ideas.

After the client contracts the designer's services, the designer begins piecing together the home page. Every designer uses different techniques: some prefer creating freehand sketches, some create storyboards using a software package like Macromedia Freehand, and some begin the design process by creating the graphic elements for a page using a program like Macromedia Fireworks MX. After creating the content for the home page, the designer begins assembling the pages with an HTML editor such as Macromedia Dreamweaver MX or Microsoft FrontPage. Compare the Dreamweaver MX interface shown in Figure 1-2 with the Contribute workspace previously shown in Figure 1-1. You'll notice the Contribute workspace is not as cluttered as the Dreamweaver workspace and looks more like software you're already using.

Web designers organize elements within a Web page by positioning them precisely within tables. After positioning the elements, designers can add links and *behaviors*—effects used to spice up a design—to their work. They can also format the text and other page elements using Cascading Style Sheets (CSS). A Cascading Style Sheet is code created in a document that is linked to a Web page, or embedded within the Web page. It doesn't matter which program a designer uses to create content for a Web site; the end result is always the same: a document with HTML

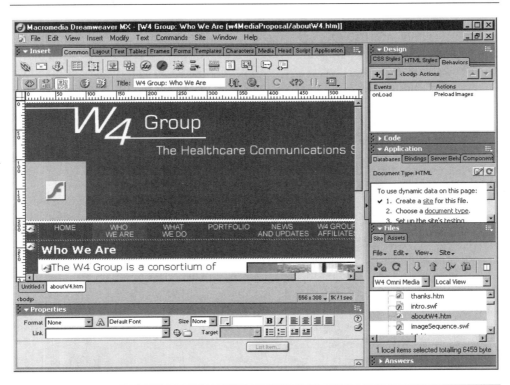

FIGURE 1-2   Web designers use programs like Dreamweaver MX to create and edit Web pages.

code that instructs the browser what to display and how to display it. Designers worth their salt know how to manually edit HTML code to achieve certain effects. The underlying HTML code of a document looks like hieroglyphics to most people. Figure 1-3 shows the HTML code associated with the HTML document used to display the Web page previously shown in Figure 1-1.

As you can see, HTML code is rigidly structured. If someone tries to manually edit HTML code without being familiar with the language, the results can be embarrassing (the Web page doesn't display correctly) and costly (a Web designer must be hired to correct the errant code). Many Web designers may be tempted to put a warning in the <head> section of their designs: "Caution, no user serviceable parts!" And when you think of it, you shouldn't be tampering with the designer's code. After all, you wouldn't want a Web designer tampering with the products you sell at your Web site, would you? Fortunately, you don't have to tamper with the designer's code. When you edit a page with Contribute, the software updates the underlying HTML code as you work.

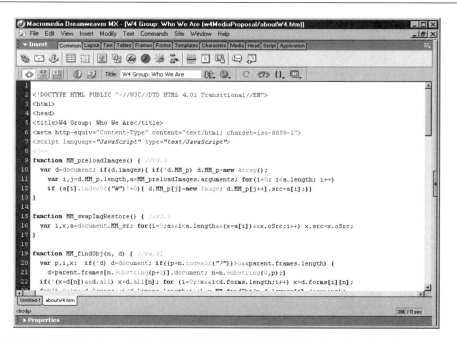

FIGURE 1-3   Web browsers interpret HTML code to display a Web page.

Does this mean that Contribute does away with the Web designer? Absolutely not. You still need the designer to create the fundamental design and update any of the highly technical code that may be present in your Web pages. But instead of having to shoehorn the editing of your Web site into a designer's hectic schedule, Contribute allows you to edit the basic elements of your site according to your schedule.

Now that you have a basic idea of how Web pages are created, you'll learn how to modify them with Contribute. The balance of this chapter gives you an idea of what you can accomplish with Contribute. It also gives you a general overview of the type of workflow you'll experience with Contribute.

About the Site Administrator

If you are the only person responsible for maintaining the Web site, a site administrator is not necessary. However, when a company assigns a team of employees to maintain a Web site, a site administrator can be appointed to manage the work. The site administrator specifies which elements of the Web site can be edited as well as the amount of editing each team member can perform, and also sets site-wide permissions.

A large corporation generally has an Information Technology (IT) or Information Services (IS) department. The IT or IS department head usually becomes the site administrator or selects a staff member for this task. The site administrator can set up and modify the editable parameters of a Web site. The site administrator also creates user groups, assigning permissions to those groups. The site administrator is responsible for defining the editable parameters of site documents. By specifying global permissions for the site, the administrator can control the continuity and look of the site's pages and images. The site administrator also functions as the liaison to other team members.

Even though the assigning of a site administrator is one of the first actions taken when using Contribute to edit a Web site, the site administrator documentation appears in Part V of this book because not every Contribute user will need this information.

Connecting to a Site

Before you can edit a site with Contribute, you must establish a connection to the site. If you are connecting to the site as an administrator, you send connection settings to the other members of your team in the form of an encrypted e-mail message. If you are a team member and you receive a connection setting, double-clicking the file will enable you to connect to and edit the site according to the permission settings defined by the site administrator. If you are the first person to establish a site connection with Contribute or you are working without a site administrator to guide you, you create a connection by following the steps in the Connection Wizard, shown next. The wizard prompts you for the information needed to establish a connection to the site. After a connection is established, pages within the site are available for editing. In Chapter 3, you'll find detailed instructions that show you how to connect to a site.

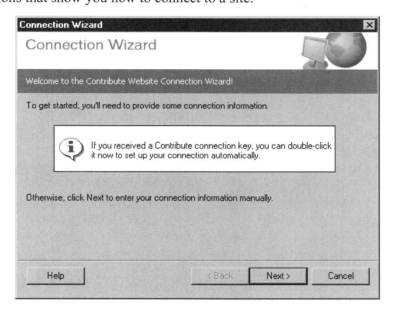

Using Contribute to Browse Web Pages

If you've experimented with Contribute prior to reading this chapter, you know that you can use the software to browse Web pages. When you use Contribute as a Web browser, you can navigate to any public Web site and bookmark Web sites as you would with Netscape Navigator or Internet Explorer. The Contribute interface has the familiar Web browser buttons: Back, Forward, Stop, and Refresh. When you navigate to a page to which you have not established a connection, Contribute displays a warning dialog box to that effect. You can create a connection to the site by clicking the Create Connection button and then following the Connection Wizard prompts. Note that you can only create a connection to a Web site when you have a valid username and password recognized by the Web site hosting service. Your site administrator can provide this information. You also have a Home Pages button you can use to connect to sites to which you have created a connection. Figure 1-4 shows the Contribute interface when used as a Web browser. In this figure, the side panel has been collapsed in order to maximize the browser viewing space.

Browser toolbar

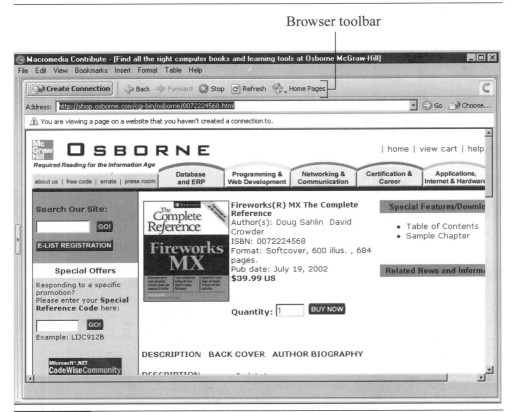

FIGURE 1-4   You can navigate to any Web page with Contribute.

Using Contribute to Modify Web Pages

When you navigate to a Web page in a site to which you have created a connection, the Edit Page button becomes available. You can edit the page by clicking the button. After you click the button, Contribute downloads the page and all of the necessary images, animations, and so on to your system. After Contribute downloads the page and elements, you can begin editing. As noted previously, you will not be able to manually edit the underlying HTML. Your permissions level as specified by your site administrator may also limit the type of edits you can perform. When you attempt to edit an object you do not have permission to edit, or an object that cannot be edited using Contribute, Contribute displays a warning dialog box prompting you to contact the site administrator for additional information. When you use Contribute in Edit mode, the editing toolbar appears at the top of the workspace, as shown in Figure 1-5.

You'll also be able to edit your pages by working with Microsoft Word and Microsoft Excel documents. You can add the contents of either document type to a page you are editing. Another option you have available is creating a link to a Word or Excel document. If you format your Word documents using tables, Contribute

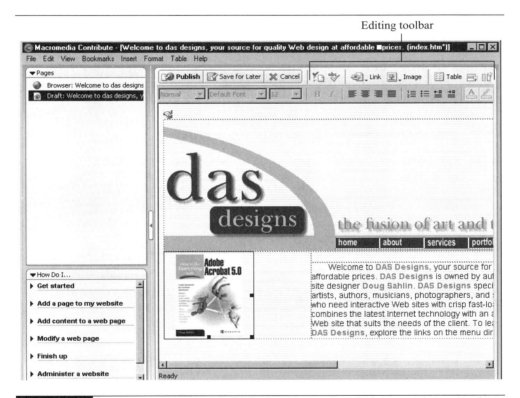

FIGURE 1-5   You can edit pages to which you or your site administrator has created a connection.

converts the Word tables to HTML tables when you add the document to a page you're editing. You can also edit Word or Excel documents from within Contribute.

When editing a page, you can work online, or if you prefer, you can save a draft of the page and perform your edits offline. You can also transfer the draft and associated files to another computer. This option is handy when you need to use a laptop computer to edit pages from a different location.

As you navigate to and edit pages with Contribute, you can use the panels on the left side of the interface to get information about specific topics quickly, or to access the page currently open in the browser or a previously saved page draft. In Chapter 4, you will learn to use Contribute to browse and edit Web pages.

Editing Text

Text appears in many different formats in Web pages. Text can be part of a Flash movie or an image, or it can appear in the body of the Web page. When working in Edit mode, you can use Contribute to edit text that appears in the body of an HTML document. You have different options available for adding text to a page. You can:

- Type the text directly into the page you are editing.

- Copy text from another application and then paste it into the page you are editing.

- Drag selected text from another application and drop it directly into a page you are editing.

You can add, delete, or reformat selected text, whether it is a single letter, a word, several lines, or several paragraphs of text. Editing text with Contribute is similar to editing text with your favorite word processing program. The icons and buttons on the toolbar have a familiar look. With a few clicks of the toolbar, you can perform any of the following formatting tasks:

- Change the font, font color, or font size, or apply a font style such as Bold or Italic.

- Modify the alignment of a selected block of text.

- Create tabs by indenting or outdenting selected text.

- Create bulleted lists, numbered lists, definitions lists, and sublists.

■ Stylize selected text using a preset style from the default Contribute style sheet, or choose a style added by the site administrator or the designer who created a Cascading Style Sheet for the Web site.

When working with text, you can locate specific text by using Contribute's powerful find and replace feature. Before publishing an edited page you can spell check your work.

Editing Images

Images are an important feature in any Web site. The images displayed at a Web site portray information about a company's products and services. You can use Contribute to edit the properties of photos linked to your Web pages. You can use Contribute to add images to your Web pages, resize images, separate images from other content by adding a horizontal rule, and more. Figure 1-6 shows Contribute being used to edit the properties of an image from a Web page.

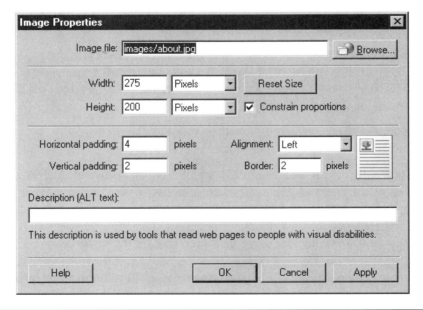

FIGURE 1-6   You can edit the properties of your Web site images with Contribute.

In addition to editing images, you can also insert or replace images on the pages you edit. You can insert image files from your computer or from directories residing at the Web site whose page you are editing. After inserting or replacing an image, you can further modify the image by changing the following properties:

- **Image source** You can change the directory or folder from which the image is loaded into the document you are editing. Invariably this means you're inserting a different image in place of the image displayed on the page before you chose the Image Properties option.

- **Size** You can modify this image property to change the size of the image as it appears in the Web page. You can resize the image proportionately or enter different values for the width and height. When you change the size property, you do not change the physical size of the image. When you publish a Web page with an image whose size property you have changed, Contribute rewrites the HTML code so that the image is displayed at the desired size when the page is loaded in a Web browser.

- **Padding** When you modify the padding around an image, you change the amount of space between the image and adjacent objects on the page, such as text. You can modify horizontal padding, vertical padding, or both.

- **Alignment** You can modify how the image is aligned to the page or how the image is aligned to a table cell in which it resides. This property determines how an image is placed in relation to other items in the page or table cell where the image is displayed.

- **Border** You can specify whether or not to place a border around the image, as well as the width of the border in pixels.

- **Description** You can enter a description (also known as ALT text) for the image. ALT text is displayed when someone is viewing your Web page in a browser that does not display images or in a browser with properties modified by the user so as not to display images. Certain browsers display ALT text as a tooltip when users move their cursors over the image.

There are certain aspects of image editing that the site administrator can specify, such as the maximum file size of images inserted into a Web page. You'll learn how to manage the image assets within your Web pages in Chapter 10.

If you have image-editing software at your disposal, you can choose to edit a selected image using that software. When you edit an image in an external editor, you have total control over the image's appearance within the Web page. For example, you can optimize the image to create a smaller file size. Image file size has become less of a concern with the advent of blazingly fast broadband Internet connections. However, if your intended audience will be viewing your pages using a dial-up modem, image file size becomes an issue. You'll learn how to edit images using an external editor in Chapter 11.

Many corporations have digital cameras available for archiving images of company meetings, picnics, and so on. Digital photographs are a perfect source for Web page content. However, digital images must also be resized and optimized for viewing on the World Wide Web. You may also have a scanner available for creating digital files from printed images. Again, this is an excellent source for Web page content, but the end result is generally the incorrect resolution for Internet viewing. Chapter 12 shows you how to work with digital and scanned images, and it features advanced image-editing techniques using Fireworks MX.

Inserting Tables

Web designers use tables to format the content of the Web pages they design. Tables are divided into rows and columns. Tables are not only an efficient way of sorting text data such as information about upcoming events, they can also be used to house images. If you've ever been to a Web site where small images (also known as *thumbnails*) are neatly arranged, you've seen a table at work. Tables in a Web page are similar to the tables you create with your word processing software. Figure 1-7 shows a table being used to organize thumbnail images. Each thumbnail image is linked to a larger version of the image.

You can insert a table in any document you are editing. When you insert a table, you specify the number of rows and columns. The individual elements of a table are known as cells. You can specify how the data is placed within the cell and whether or not the cell has a visible border.

Editing Tables

If you are editing a page with tables, you can change the data within the tables. For example, if you're editing a page where images are organized in the table, you can replace the images with different ones; if the table data is text, you can enter new text or edit the existing text. When editing a table, you can select data from cells and copy and paste cell data. You can insert rows and columns as needed to enlarge the table, or delete rows and columns. You can also merge or split selected cells.

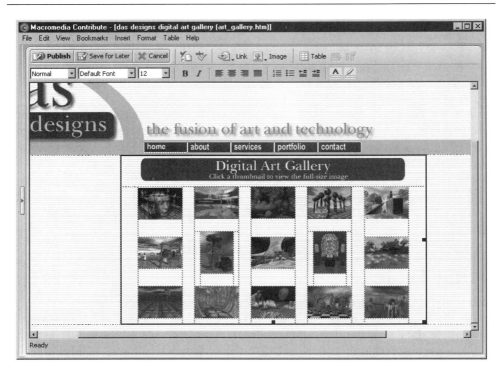

FIGURE 1-7   You can use tables to arrange images and other data.

You can change the look of a table by changing its properties. After selecting a table, you can modify the following properties:

- **Table alignment**   You can modify how the table is aligned within the HTML page or table in which it resides.

- **Table width**   You can specify the table width in pixels or as a percentage of the HTML page or table in which it resides.

- **Border thickness**   You can specify the thickness of the table border in pixels or choose a value of 0 for a table with no border.

- **Cell padding**   You use this option to specify the amount of space between the cell's content and its border.

- **Cell spacing**   You can specify the amount of space in pixels between adjacent cells.

- **Border color** If your table has a border around each cell, you can specify the border color by selecting a color from a pop-up palette.

- **Background color** You can modify a table's default background color (the background color of the document) by selecting a color from a pop-up palette.

Another option you have available is to select individual cells and then modify one or more of the following properties:

- **Horizontal alignment** You can specify how the data is aligned horizontally in the cell.

- **Vertical alignment** You can specify how the data is aligned vertically within the cell. This option is useful when you have a table with text data that causes the cells to have different heights. You can align the data to the top, middle, or bottom of the cell.

- **Background color** You can change the background color of selected cells by choosing a color from a pop-up palette.

- **Row height** You can "shrink-wrap" the cell to conform to the data contained within or specify a height value in pixels.

- **Options** You can choose to wrap the text to a new line when it exceeds the boundary of a cell or convert the cell to a header, in which case the cell adopts the default header style for the document.

You can also sort tabular data. This option comes in handy when you've been given a large amount of data to enter into a table but the data has not been previously sorted. You can enter the data into the table in any order, select the table, and then sort the data by column.

You'll learn how to add tables to your Web pages and edit them in Chapter 8.

Inserting Flash Movies

If you have a Flash guru working on your team, or your Web designer supplies you with Flash content, you can insert a Flash movie in any page you are editing. Flash movies are animations published in the SWF (Small Web File) format. After you insert a Flash movie in a Web page, you can specify the movie alignment and modify the movie properties. Figure 1-8 shows a Flash movie inserted into a Web page.

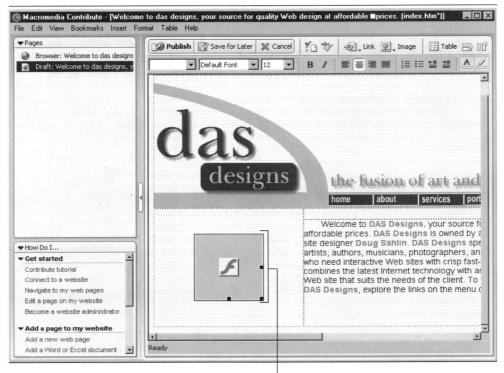

Embedded Flash movie

FIGURE 1-8   You can insert a Flash movie into a new or existing Web page.

Adding and Editing Links

When your Web site was created, the designer created links so that visitors to your site could navigate to different pages within your site and perhaps outside of your site. You can modify existing links or add new links to pages you are editing. You can create a link by selecting an image or block of text as the *anchor object*. After selecting the anchor object for your link, you can navigate to a document on your computer, at your Web site, or browse the Web to find the Web page to which you want to link. You can also use a link to create a new page. When you create a link, you can specify whether it appears in the same window as the document that calls the linked page or within a new window. You'll learn how to create and edit links in Chapter 7.

Editing Pages with Frames

If your site was designed with frames, the content of your site is divided into windows. For example, in a Web site designed with frames, the navigation menu may appear in a window along the left side or at the top of the document. Other information about your site, such as the name of your Web site and company logo may appear in a window at the top of the document; this is also known as a *header*. The contents of the navigation menu window remain static; however, the content window for your site changes when a viewer clicks one of the navigation links. The image displayed in the header window may change as well to reflect the name of the page. You'll learn how to edit Web sites with frames in Chapter 9.

Creating New Web Pages

As your Web site grows and evolves, you may find it necessary to create new pages. You may also want to create a new page when the amount of data you're displaying on a single page necessitates that your viewers scroll through a lot of text. You can create a new Web page by starting with a copy of a page from your site that you are currently viewing. You can also create a new Web page by choosing one of the Contribute preset templates or by using a template provided by your Web designer. If you use Contribute to edit multiple sites, you can choose a page from one of your other sites as the basis for your new page. Figure 1-9 shows a new page being created with one of the Contribute preset templates.

After you create a new page, you can use any of the previously discussed methods for adding content to the page. Creating new Web pages will be covered in detail in Chapter 5.

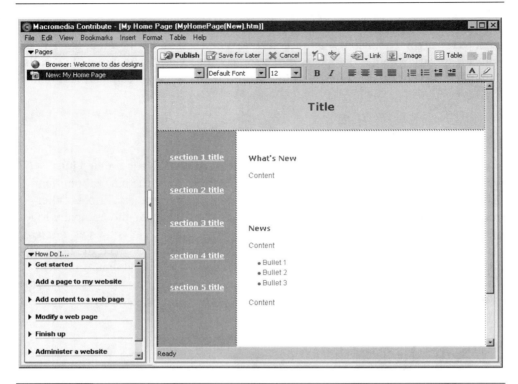

FIGURE 1-9 You can create a new Web page from a template.

Publishing an Edited Page

After you create a new Web page or edit an existing one, you preview the page
using your system's default Web browser, as shown in Figure 1-10. If you're
satisfied with the results of the page, you can publish the page to your Web site. If
you feel the page needs a bit of tweaking or you need to add elements not currently
available, you can save the page for future editing, which places a copy of the page
on your hard drive. You can edit a saved page offline and publish it when you're
online. If you're part of a team using Contribute to manage a Web site, you can
e-mail the revised page to other team members for review. You'll learn how to
publish Web pages in Chapter 13.

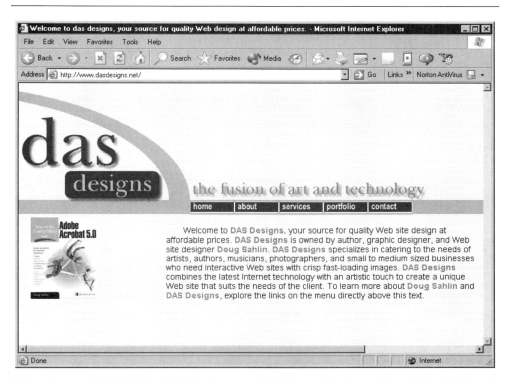

FIGURE 1-10   You can preview Web pages in your default browser prior to publishing them.

Summary

In this chapter, you were introduced to Contribute and the wide diversity of features you can use to edit pages from your Web site. In the next chapter, you'll get an in-depth look at the Contribute workspace you'll use to perform these tasks.

Chapter 2

Exploring the Contribute Workspace

How to...

- Navigate the workspace
- Use the Contribute panels
- Use Contribute in Browse mode
- Use Contribute in Edit mode
- Set Contribute preferences

When you use a new application for the first time, there's bound to be a bit of a learning curve. Every application has its own unique nomenclature, buttons, and toolbars. Contribute is no exception. However, you will find icons and menu commands that bear a striking resemblance to those found in software you already use. This is because you use Contribute to perform many of the same tasks you currently perform when creating and editing documents with your word processing software, except you're performing these tasks on Web pages. Likewise, when you use Contribute to browse to Web pages, you'll find buttons and windows similar to those found in most popular Web browsers.

The icons and buttons you have available when using Contribute differ depending on the task for which you're using the software. In this chapter, you'll learn what tasks you can accomplish with the available buttons. You'll also learn to set Contribute preferences to suit your working style and specify which external file editor is used to edit Web page elements such as images and text documents.

Launching the Application

The designers of Contribute have designed the software to be as user friendly as possible. Often when applications launch, the user is confronted with a vast array of options, but when you launch Contribute, a welcome screen appears, as shown in Figure 2-1.

After the welcome screen appears, you can choose one of the following options:

- **Take a quick tour Of Contribute**   If you're connected to the Internet, you'll be redirected to Macromedia's Web site where you'll find more information about Contribute.

- **Take the Contribute Tutorial**   This choice launches the Contribute tutorial.

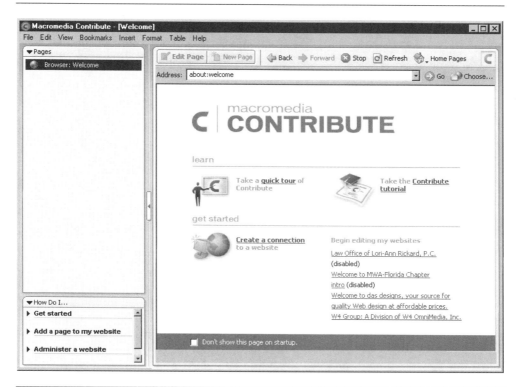

FIGURE 2-1   When you launch Contribute, a welcome screen appears.

■ **Create a connection to a Web site**   This option launches the Connection Wizard, enabling you to create a connection to a Web site to which you have the proper information.

■ **Begin editing my Web sites**   This option opens the home page of your Web site. If you use Contribute to edit multiple sites, they will be listed below the menu command. Click the name of a Web site to begin editing its pages. When you open a Web site for editing, the home page is displayed in Browse mode. You can edit the page by clicking the Edit Page button shown in Figure 2-2, or use the site navigation to display another page that you want to edit. The Contribute sidebar in Figure 2-2 has been collapsed to display the entire Web page.

Edit Page button

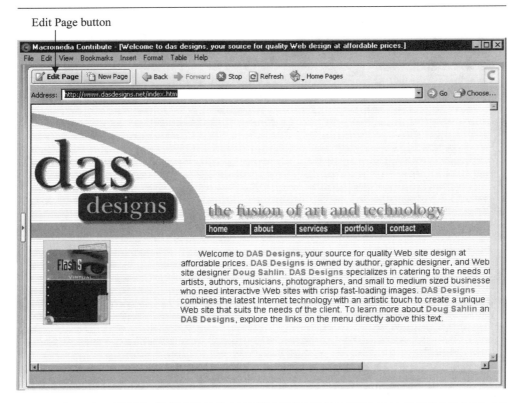

FIGURE 2-2   After you navigate to one of your Web site pages, click the Edit Page button to modify the page.

Navigating the Workspace

The Contribute workspace is divided into two windows: the document window and the sidebar. The document window displays the Web page you are viewing or editing. The sidebar is composed of two panels: the Pages panel and the How Do I… panel shown in Figure 2-3.

The interface shown in Figure 2-3 contains several common elements in both Browse and Edit modes. You'll find menu command groups across the top of the interface. Many of the available commands are also carbon copies of buttons. To access a command from a menu group, click the menu command group's name.

Document window

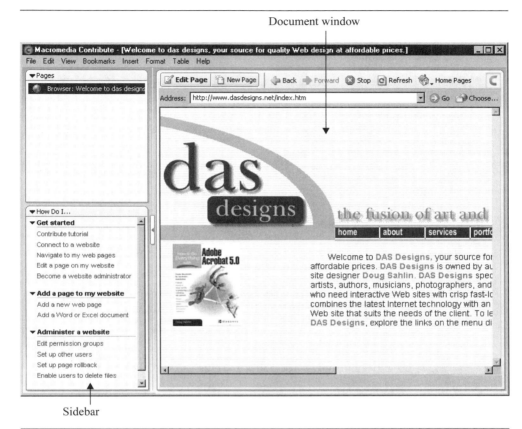

Sidebar

FIGURE 2-3   The Contribute Workspace is divided into two windows.

When you are using Contribute in Browse mode, menu commands pertaining to editing pages are unavailable. You can choose commands from the following command groups:

- **File** Contains menu commands pertaining to file maintenance, editing pages, creating new pages, publishing pages, and saving pages. This menu group also contains commands for setting up pages for printing, saving pages as drafts, and rolling back to a previous version of a page.

- **Edit** Contains commands you use to cut, copy, and paste elements from a page you are editing. Here you'll also find commands to modify preferences and edit your connections.

- **View** Contains commands for navigating to Web sites, going to home pages of sites to which you have created connections, and viewing pages you have recently published. You also have commands you can use to navigate to a Web site by manually entering the site's URL (universal resource locator) in a dialog box.

- **Bookmarks** Contains menu commands for bookmarking the URL of a Web site you frequently visit, as well as accessing the list of URLs you have already bookmarked. A *bookmark* is a menu command that you use to navigate to a site without typing the site's URL in the Address window.

- **Insert** Contains commands for inserting images, links, documents, and other elements into a Web page you are editing.

- **Format** Contains commands for formatting selected text in a Web page you are editing. In this group, you'll also find a command for spell checking your work.

- **Table** Contains commands for inserting a table into a Web page, as well as the necessary commands for editing tables in your Web pages.

- **Help** Contains commands for getting help while using Contribute. You'll also find commands for launching the Contribute tutorial, visiting the Contribute Support Center at Macromedia's Web site, and registering your software.

Using the Contribute Sidebar

On the left side of the Contribute workspace you'll find the sidebar. The sidebar is divided into two panels: Pages and How Do I…. The Pages panel displays the title of the page you are currently viewing in Browse mode, as well as the drafts of any pages you are editing. The How Do I… panel contains links to useful information about Contribute.

You can modify the way the sidebar is displayed by doing one of the following:

■ To collapse the sidebar, click the left-facing arrow in the middle of the sidebar's right border. Collapsing the sidebar expands the document window so that it fills the width of the workspace.

■ To restore the sidebar to its original width, click the right-facing arrow in the middle of the collapsed sidebar.

TIP   *You can also expand or collapse the sidebar by pressing* F4.

To expand the width of the sidebar, follow these steps:

1. Move your cursor over the dividing line, making sure it is above or below the arrow.

2. When your cursor becomes a double-headed arrow, click and drag to the right to increase the width of the sidebar, or click and drag to the left to decrease the width.

NOTE   *You cannot shrink the sidebar to a dimension less than its default width.*

To the left of each sidebar panel's name, you'll find a triangle that you can click to expand or collapse the panel. When a panel is expanded, the triangle points toward the bottom of the interface; when it is collapsed, the triangle points toward the document window.

If the contents of a sidebar panel exceed the available space, a scrollbar appears on the right side of the panel. Click and drag the scrollbar to view the hidden contents of the panel.

Using the Pages Panel

You use the Pages panel to open drafts of pages you are editing or to view the page currently displayed in the browser. If you have saved drafts of several pages, they will be listed in the panel, as shown next.

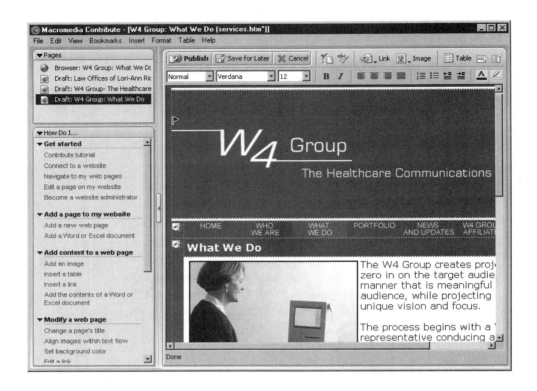

You can select a page draft by clicking its name, or you can view the page currently displayed in the browser that has become hidden while editing or viewing an open draft by clicking its name. After doing either of the preceding, the document window refreshes to display your selection.

Using the How Do I... Panel

When you are not sure how to perform a certain task, you can use the How Do I... panel to get the necessary information quickly. The How Do I... panel, shown previously, is divided into several topics. Each topic contains links that you can click to get more information about a specific task related to the topic. You can select the first task under a topic, and when you're done brushing up on that task, you can click a link to instructions on how to perform the next task. You can use the How Do I... panel in conjunction with this book, or as an alternative when you don't have this book available. To use the How Do I... panel, follow these steps:

1. Move your cursor over the topic about which you want to learn more. Your cursor becomes a hand.

2

2. Click the topic title. The topic is displayed in the How Do I... panel, as
shown next.

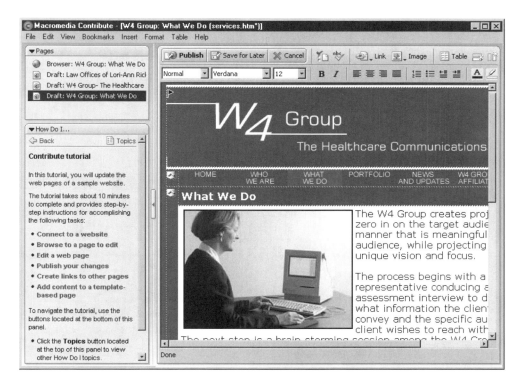

3. Click the Next button that looks like a triangle pointing to the right, to read
the next page. Alternatively, you can click the Back button to read the previous
page or click the Topics button to display the titles in the How Do I... panel.

Working in Browse Mode

As mentioned previously, you can use Contribute as a Web browser. When working
in Browse mode, you can use Contribute as you would any other Web browser. In
Browse mode, you can use Contribute to perform the following tasks:

■ Navigate to a Web site by entering its URL in the Address window

■ Click links on the Web page you are currently viewing to navigate to other
pages within the Web site

■ Navigate to previously viewed pages using the Forward and Back buttons

- Bookmark Web sites and manage bookmarks

- Navigate to the home pages of sites to which you have created a connection

- Stop a page from loading

- Refresh (known as *reload* in some browsers) the current page

- Choose a file from a Web site to which you have created a connection

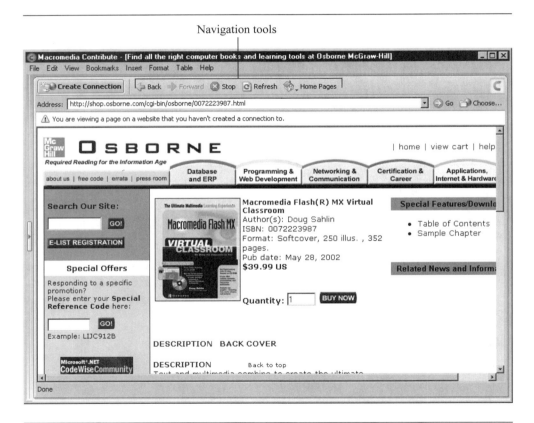

FIGURE 2-4   Contribute contains all the features you need to navigate to Web sites.

Did you know?

Understanding URLs

A Web page's URL consists of the Web site domain name (for example, www .mydomain.com), followed by a forward slash and the document name of the page (for example, www.mydomain.com/allaboutme.htm). If you enter the name of a Web page incorrectly or enter an invalid URL, your Web browser refreshes and displays a page with an error message to the effect that the page cannot be found. When you receive this error message, check for misspelling. If the URL is spelled correctly, try entering a different extension (for example, *html* instead of *htm*).

The Web site's home page can be accessed by entering *www.* followed by the domain name (for example: www.mypages.com). You do not need to enter the filename of the site's home page because most browsers will automatically load a page that begins with *index* or *default*.

You'll find detailed information on how to use Contribute as a Web browser in Chapter 4. Figure 2-4 shows Contribute being used as a Web browser with the sidebar collapsed.

Note the warning message in the figure below the Address window. A connection has not been made to this site; therefore, the page cannot be edited. In order to edit this page, you click the Create Connection button and use the Create Connection wizard to create a connection to the site. You will need a valid username and password in order to connect to the site successfully. Contact your site administrator if this information is not available to you.

Working in Edit Mode

Contribute's main function is to edit Web pages. If you are viewing a Web page to which you have made a connection, Contribute displays the Edit Page button, as shown in Figure 2-5.

After navigating to a Web site to which you have made a connection, you can navigate to the page you want to edit using the navigation menu your site's designer created. After navigating to the page, click the Edit Page button, and Contribute downloads the page and any other elements such as images and Flash movies to

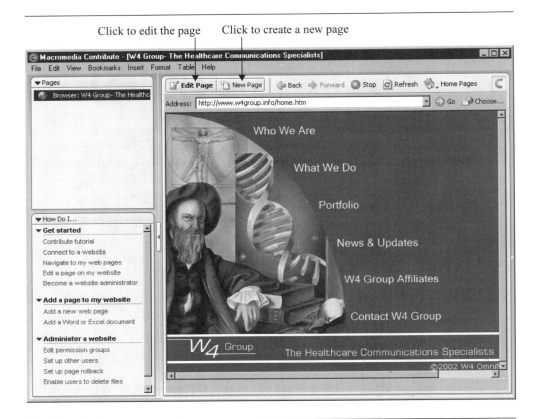

FIGURE 2-5   You can edit a page from a Web site to which you have made a connection.

your hard drive. After the download is finished, Contribute reconfigures your workspace as shown in Figure 2-6.

After you switch to Edit mode, you can use the tools and menu commands to perform the following tasks:

■   Enter new text or edit existing text. When you edit text in Contribute, you can specify the font style, font type, and alignment. You can create bulleted lists, numbered lists, and sublists. If your Web designer used a Cascading Style Sheet (CSS) to define styles used for the text elements of your site, you can use any of the designer's CSS styles to format text. If desired, you can also change the text color or assign a highlight color to the text.

Web page editing tools

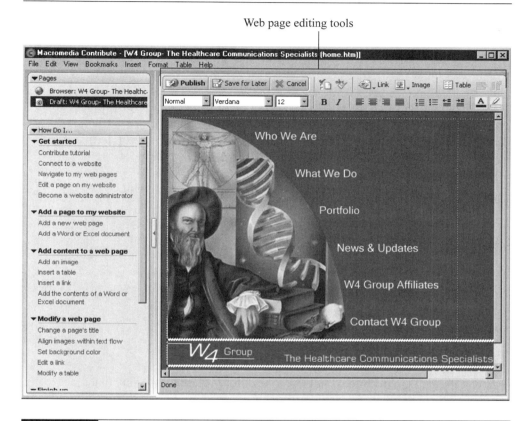

FIGURE 2-6   When you work in Edit mode, you have a different toolset to work with.

- Spell check your work.

- Edit existing images or insert new images.

- Edit existing tables or insert new tables.

- Insert all or part of a Microsoft Word or Microsoft Excel document into the page.

- Edit existing links or create new links. You can specify whether the linked page opens in the target (current) browser window or in a new browser window.

- Create links to Microsoft Word or Microsoft Excel documents.

- Modify the page's properties. This option enables you to change the page background color, change the title of the page, change the page margins, and more.

You can insert some objects by dragging them from other applications and dropping them into the page you are editing. If you prefer, you can use menu commands to insert objects, or you can click the appropriate button to insert the desired object. Editing pages will be covered in detail in Chapter 4.

After you edit a Web page, you can perform any of the following tasks:

- Cancel the edits you have applied to the page

- Preview the edited page in a Web browser

- Publish the edited page to your Web site

- Save a copy of the document for future editing

- E-mail a copy of the revised page to a colleague for review

Setting Contribute Preferences

You can modify Contribute to suit your working preferences. Contribute preferences are divided into four sections: General, File Editors, Firewall, and Invisible Elements.

To modify General preferences, follow these steps:

1. Choose Edit | Preferences. The Preferences dialog box appears, as shown in Figure 2-7.

2. In the Editing Options section, choose Faster Table Editing (the default), and Contribute will not redraw the table continually as you edit it. If your computer has a slow processor, this might enable you to work faster when editing large tables. To redraw a table when you have this option enabled, click anywhere outside of the table. Also, Contribute will always redraw the table when you publish the page or switch to another page draft.

3. Click the triangle to the right of the Spelling Dictionary field and choose the language used in the pages you are editing. If you are editing pages published in multiple languages, you can switch to different dictionaries as

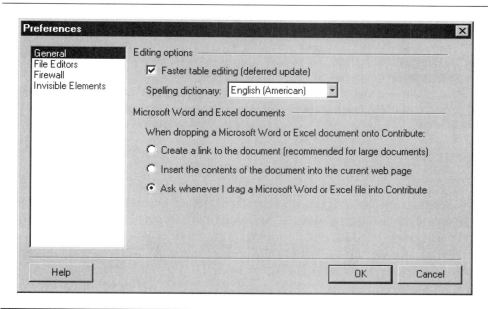

FIGURE 2-7   You use this dialog box to edit General preferences.

needed. You can choose a spelling dictionary from the following languages: Danish, Dutch, English (American), English (British), English (Canadian), Finnish, French, German, Italian, Norwegian (Bokmal), Portuguese (Brazilian), Portuguese (Iberian), Spanish, or Swedish.

NOTE   *You can only have one dictionary active at a time. If your pages have two languages in the same document, you'll have to choose the applicable dictionary to spell check one language, then change preferences to another dictionary to spell check the other language.*

4. In the Microsoft Word and Excel Documents section, choose one of the following options:

■ **Create a link to the document**   Choose this option, and the document will not be displayed in the page. When a viewer clicks the link, the document will be displayed in the viewer's browser. This option is recommended for large files.

■ **Insert the contents of the document into the current web page**
Choose this option, and Contribute will automatically insert the
contents of the file at the current cursor position.

■ **Ask whenever I drag a Microsoft Word or Excel file into Contribute**
Choose this option (the default), and when you drag a file into a page,
Contribute will display a dialog box prompting you to choose whether
the document will be linked to the page or displayed in the page.

5. Click OK to apply the changes. Alternatively, you can click Cancel to void
the changes, or you can choose another preference title.

When you edit Web pages with Contribute, you can edit elements of the pages
in external editors. When you installed Contribute, the install utility scanned your
system and determined the default file editor for the files you can edit externally.
For example, the default file editor for Excel .xls documents is Microsoft Excel.
Many software installations are fairly invasive; the software's install utility
automatically assigns the software as the default viewer and/or editor for file types
associated with the software being installed. If this is undesirable, you can use
your operating system's utility to modify the default viewer and editor. Another
option you have available is to specify a different file editor for Contribute by
following these steps:

1. Choose Edit | Preferences. The Preferences dialog box shown
previously opens.

2. Choose File Editors. The dialog box is reconfigured as shown in Figure 2-8.
The left window displays the extensions you can edit, and the right window
displays the editors you can use to edit these file types.

3. Select a file extension from the left window. The default editor is
displayed in the right window. If desired, you can add extensions to
the list by following step 8.

4. To add an editor for the selected file type, click the button that looks like a
plus sign (+). The Select External Editor dialog box appears.

Add extension

Delete extension

Add editor

Delete editor

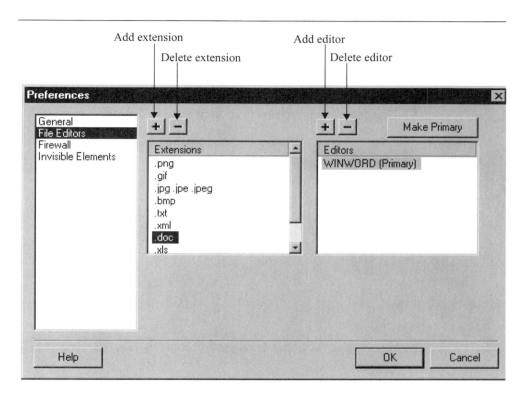

FIGURE 2-8 You can specify which file editor is used to externally edit Web page elements.

5. Navigate to the directory where the .exe file for the editor resides.

6. Select the editor's .exe file and click Open. The Select External Editor dialog box closes, and the editor's name is added to the list of available editors for the selected file type. When you have more than one editor for a file type, you can designate the primary editor by following step 7.

7. To designate the primary file editor for the selected file type, select the desired editor and then click Make Primary, as shown next.

Make Primary button

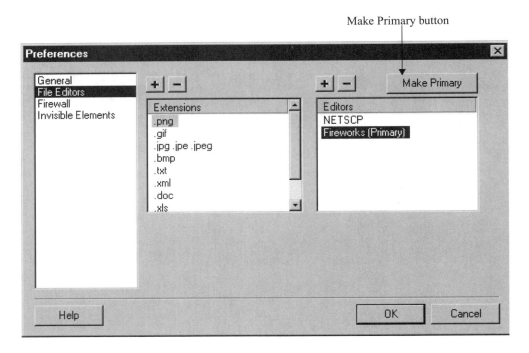

8. To add an extension, click the plus sign (+) in the Extensions window. A blank field appears at the bottom of the Extensions list.

9. Enter the file type. When you enter the file type, be sure you type a period (.) before you enter the file's extension. For example, to add the Cascading Style Sheet (CSS) extension you would type *.css*. After you add an extension, you can specify the external editor by following steps 4–6.

10. Click OK to close the dialog box and apply your changes. Alternatively, you can click Cancel to void your changes, or you can choose another preference title.

TIP *You can remove an extension from the list by selecting the extension and then clicking the minus sign (–) in the Extensions window. You can remove an editor from the list by selecting the editor and then clicking the minus sign (–) in the Editors window.*

If your Web site has a firewall, you can specify the firewall settings by changing preferences. If you are not sure whether your site has a firewall, check with your Web hosting service or your system administrator. To specify Firewall settings, follow these steps:

1. Choose Edit | Preferences. The Preferences dialog box shown previously appears.

2. Choose Firewalls. The Preferences dialog box is reconfigured as shown next.

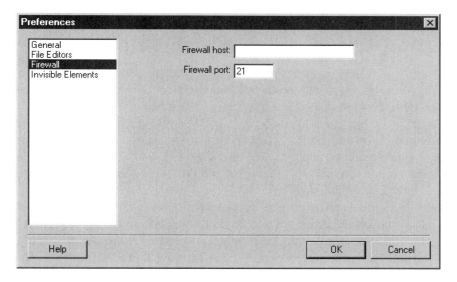

3. In the Firewall Host field, enter the name of the Firewall host.

4. In the Firewall Port field, enter the Network port through which File Transfer Protocol (FTP) access is enabled.

 If you are not sure of the name of your Firewall Host or which port is used for FTP access, contact your site administrator or a member of your Web hosting service's technical support team.

5. Click OK to apply the changes. Alternatively, you can click Cancel to void the changes or change another preference to edit.

The Firewall

A firewall is software that prevents unauthorized access to your Web site and network. The software prevents hackers from gaining access to and maliciously altering your Web pages. Home computer users who use cable modems that are connected to the Internet whenever the computer is in use also use firewall software. In this case, the home user is protected against unauthorized access to personal files such as online bank records and credit card information that may be stored on the computer.

Many Web designers include invisible elements in their designs. An example of an invisible element is a *named anchor*—a link destination within the Web page, such as the top of a long Web page. You can create a link to a named anchor. For example, if you add text to a page that causes a user to scroll to the bottom of a page, you add a named anchor at the top of the page. At the bottom of the page, you create a link to the named anchor that enables viewers to jump to the top of the page by clicking the link.

Invisible elements are displayed by default and are designated by an icon that looks like a triangular flag on a post, similar to the ones you see sticking out of holes on golf courses. You can specify whether invisible elements are displayed or not by modifying your preferences. To modify Invisible Elements preferences, follow these steps:

1. Choose Edit | Preferences. The Preferences dialog box shown previously appears.

2. Choose Invisible Elements. The dialog box is reconfigured as shown next.

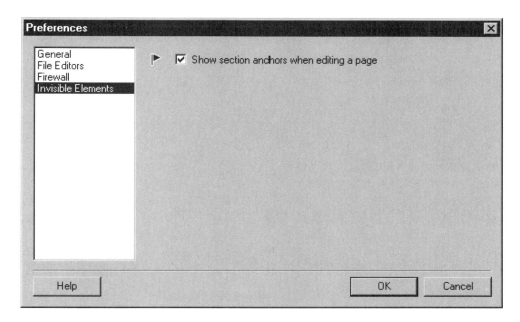

3. Invisible elements are displayed by default. To hide invisible elements, click the Show Section Anchors When Editing Page check box to deselect the option.

4. Click OK to apply the changes. Alternatively, you can click Cancel to void the changes, or you can choose another preference title.

NOTE   *You can display hidden invisible elements by performing steps 1 and 2 and then clicking the Show Section Anchors When Editing Page check box.*

Summary

In this chapter, you learned about the tools you can use to browse Web pages and edit Web pages. You also learned how to modify Contribute preferences to suit your working style. Now that you're armed with this knowledge, it's time to roll up your sleeves and get to work. In the next chapter, you'll learn to create connections to the Web sites you are going to edit with Contribute.

Chapter 3

Creating a Connection

How to...

■ Connect to a Web site

■ Use the Connection Wizard

■ Import a connection file

■ Connect over a network

■ Manage your connections

■ Work offline

When you decide to use Contribute to manage and edit the content of one or more Web sites, you must first establish a connection to the site. When you want to establish a connection to a site, certain information is required. You will need to know the proper username and password in order for the site's Web hosting service to allow you access to the site files. If the Web page files are stored on your network server, you will need to know the proper path to the server in order to create a connection. After you establish a connection to a Web site, Contribute recognizes the site's home page; you can then use Contribute in Edit mode to make changes to the Web site's pages. If your company owns, or you own, multiple Web sites, you can establish connections to these sites provided you have the proper usernames and passwords. When you establish multiple connections, you can manage your connections.

In this chapter, you'll learn to establish a connection to the Web site or sites you'll be editing with Contribute. If you're using Contribute as a member of a team, you'll learn how to connect to a site using a connection key that was sent to you by the site administrator or another team member. You'll also learn how to create a connection by importing a connection key from your local server. Another task you'll learn is how to manage your site connections.

Connecting to a Web Site

The method by which you connect to a Web site varies depending on your working situation. If you're the system administrator, or the only person using Contribute to maintain a Web site, you must create the connection. If you are working as a member of a team responsible for maintaining your company's Web site, you can create your own connection, or you may have received an e-mail containing a connection key to your Web site.

The Contribute Connection Wizard makes creating a connection a fairly straightforward process. The wizard prompts you for information and then creates the connection to the site. Once you create a connection to a site, you can begin editing Web pages. Before you create a connection to a site, have the following information available:

- **Your username and e-mail address**   Your username and e-mail address identify you to other members of the Web team. When you edit a page, Contribute checks out the page in your username and prohibits other members of the team from simultaneously editing the page.

- **The Web address of the site**   Your site's Web address (also known as its uniform resource locator, or URL) is the link to the Web hosting service computer that stores the Web pages you'll be editing. A Web site URL is formatted as follows:

  http://www.myCompany.com

- **The network path to your Web site**   If you edit pages for a corporate intranet, or your pages are stored on a local network prior to deploying them to your Web hosting service, you'll need to know the path to the computer and directory where your Web pages are stored. The path to your Web pages on a network server might look something like this:

  \\corporate01\c\inetpub\wwwroot

  where *corporate01* is the server, *c* is the drive, *inetpub* is the main directory, and *wwwroot* is the directory where the files are stored.

- **Your site's FTP information**   You'll need this information if the Web pages you'll be editing are stored at a Web hosting service, in which case you'll access the files over the Internet using the File Transfer Protocol (FTP). You may also use FTP to connect to a corporate network server if you're editing Web pages on a computer outside of your corporate network. In either case, you'll need a valid username and password to gain access to the directory where the files are stored.

Using the Connection Wizard

Contribute's Connection Wizard makes it possible for you to quickly and easily establish a connection to a Web site that you want to edit. The Connection Wizard is a collection of screens that prompt you for the information needed to create a connection. You navigate between screens using Next and Back buttons.

You can create a connection to a site provided you have the username and password issued by the service that hosts the Web site to which you are creating a connection. If you are creating a connection to Web pages hosted on a network server, you need the path to the directory where the files are stored. If you do not have this information, contact your system administrator or a member of your Information Technology (IT) or Information Services (IS) team. To connect to a Web site, follow these steps:

1. Launch Contribute.

2. Navigate to the Web site to which you want to create a connection. To do this, enter the URL of the site's home page in the Address window and click the Go button. The home page of a site is usually named *index,* or *default,* followed by the file extension. An example of a URL for a site's home page is http://www.mySite/index.htm.

   After you navigate to the site's home page, Contribute displays a warning telling you that you are viewing a Web site to which you have not made a connection, as shown next.

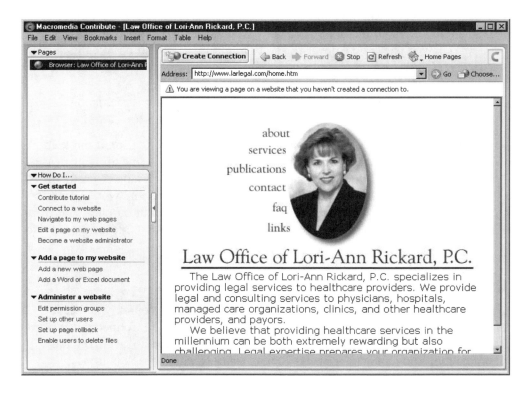

3. Click the Create Connection button. The Connection Wizard opens, as shown in Figure 3-1.

4. Click Next. The User Information screen appears.

5. Enter your name and e-mail address. This contact information is used to identify you when you are editing a Web page. Contribute will not allow more than one user to edit a Web page at a time.

6. Click Next. The Website Home Page screen appears. If you are creating a connection while viewing a site's home page, enter the URL as shown next.

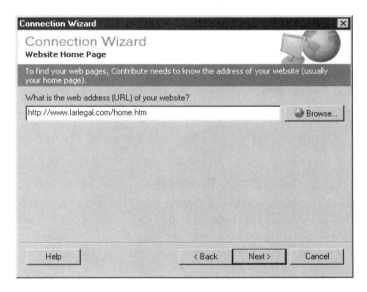

7. Click Next. The Connection Information screen appears.

8. Click the triangle next to How Do You Connect To Your Web Server and choose one of the following options. The option you choose determines how files are transferred between your computer and the Web site.

- ■ **FTP**   Choose this option if a Web hosting service hosts your site. If you choose this option, the dialog box is reconfigured as shown in Figure 3-2. Proceed to step 10.

- ■ **Local/Network**   Choose this option if your Web site files are stored on a local computer prior to uploading to a host or if your site is hosted on a network server. Proceed to step 9.

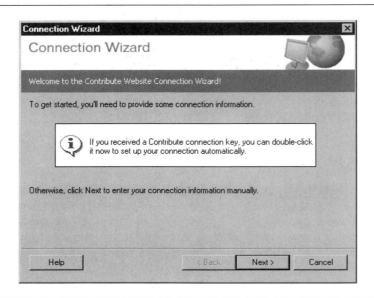

FIGURE 3-1 The Connection Wizard makes it easy to create a connection to a Web site.

9. If you are familiar with the directory structure of your local machine or network, enter the path to the directory where the files are stored. Alternatively, you can click the Choose button to open the Select Website Path dialog box. Navigate to the folder where your Web site files are stored and click Select. This is the safest option because it ensures that the path will be stored correctly when you complete the connection. If the files are stored on a network, the path will be to another computer in the network. If you're using the Windows operating system, you can click My Network Places in the Select Website Path dialog box and then navigate to the host computer directory where your Web site files are stored. A typical path to Web site files on a server might be \\myCompany001\c\inetpub\wwwroot.

If you are unsure of the path to the computer storing your network files, contact your site administrator or a member of your IT or IS staff. After entering the path to your Network server directory, click the Next button and proceed to step 13.

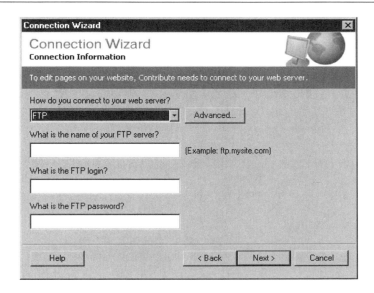

FIGURE 3-2   You can connect to your Web site via FTP.

10. If you choose the FTP connection option, the screen in Figure 3-2 appears. Enter the following information in the appropriate fields:

- **Name of your FTP server**   The actual address of your FTP server varies depending on the service used to host your Web site. Some Web hosting services use the actual address of the Web site, such as www.mySite.com, while other hosting services require you to enter the domain name of the site preceded by *ftp,* such as ftp.mySite.com.

- **FTP login**   This is the username assigned by your Web site's hosting service. If you are not sure of your site's FTP login, contact your system administrator or a member of your company's IT or IS team.

- **FTP password**   This is the password assigned by your Web site's hosting service. If you are not sure of the password, contact your system administrator or a member of your company's IT or IS team.

TIP   *If during any stage of the connection process, you make a mistake or want to confirm previous entries, click the Back button to navigate to screens you've already filled in.*

11. If the Web site to which you are making a connection does not use a standard FTP connection or if it uses a firewall, click the Advanced button to set advanced FTP options. The Advanced Connection Settings dialog box shown next appears.

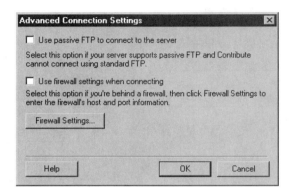

Select one or both of the following settings:

■ **Use passive FTP to connect to the server**   Choose this option, and Contribute will initiate the connection rather than relying on the remote Web site host. If you choose this option, the site's firewall must be configured to allow the client (in this case, Contribute) to initiate the FTP connection.

■ **Use firewall settings when connecting**   Choose this option, and you can specify the firewall host and port through which the FTP connection is made. When you select this option, you can click the Firewall Settings button to open the Firewall section of the Preferences dialog box. You can then specify the firewall host and port numbers. Note that these are global settings for Contribute, and you cannot specify different settings for different sites.

12. Click OK to close the Advanced Connection Settings dialog box, and then Click Next. After you click the Next button, Contribute attempts to connect to your Web site host. If the connection is successful, the Administrator Information screen appears, as shown next.

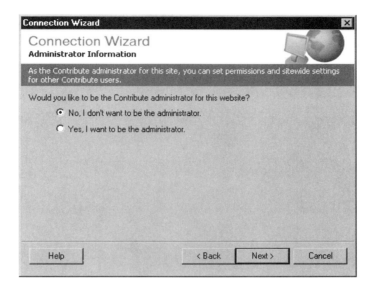

CAUTION *If you enter an invalid username or password, or you incorrectly enter any of the other needed information, Contribute displays a warning dialog box telling you the connection was unsuccessful. When this dialog box appears, click the OK button to exit the dialog box and return to the Connection Information dialog box. Reenter the required information and click the Next button. Note that this information is case-sensitive. If you enter an uppercase character for a password or username when it is actually lowercase, you will not be able to create a connection. If the dialog box reappears, contact your system administrator or a member of your IT or IS staff to obtain the correct connection information.*

13. In the Administrator Information screen, choose whether or not to become the site administrator. The administrator can specify sitewide settings. If you choose to become the administrator, the Administrator Information screen is reconfigured and prompts you to enter a password. For more information on administering a site with Contribute, refer to Part V.

14. If you select the administrator option, enter a password and then confirm the password.

15. After completing the Administrator Information screen, click Next. The Summary screen appears, as shown next.

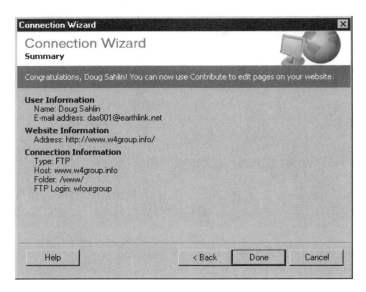

16. Review the connection settings. If everything is in order, click Done to complete the connection. Alternatively, click the Back button to navigate to an earlier screen and change a setting, or click Cancel to void this connection operation.

After you click Done, Contribute registers the information. The Create Connection button on the site home page changes to an Edit Page and a New Page button, and the site appears on the Home Pages pop-up menu on the browser toolbar.

Using a Connection Key

Companies with multiple locations find that it's easy to maintain corporate communications via e-mail. If you work in such an environment, you may have received a connection key via e-mail from your site administrator. Contribute connection key files use the title of the site's home page followed by the .stc filename extension. Your Web site connection key file attachment might look something like this: corporateWebsite.stc. To connect to a Web site using an e-mail attachment, follow these steps:

1. Open the e-mail containing the connection key file.

Did you know?

FTP vs. E-mail

File Transfer Protocol (FTP) is the fastest method of transporting large files from a user's computer to a directory on a computer that is not on the user's network. FTP is much faster than e-mail because it does not have to go through an Internet service provider's network. FTP goes directly from the user's computer to the specified directory at the remote computer.

There are several programs available for sending files via the Internet using FTP; however, they all require you to set parameters and specify the folder on the remote computer to which the files are uploaded. You also have to enter the proper username and password to gain access to the remote computer's folder. You have to specify a username and password with Contribute as well, but Contribute automatically searches for and selects the proper directory on the remote computer that contains your Web site files.

2. Double-click the connection key file. Double-clicking the file launches Contribute, and the Import Connection Key dialog box appears. Your name and e-mail address are already filled in, as shown next.

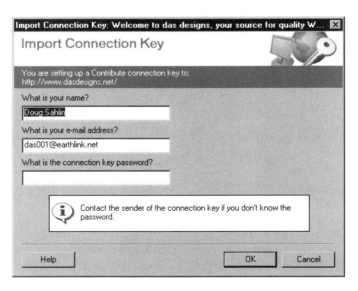

3. Accept the name and e-mail entries as displayed, or enter different data. The name and e-mail information is how Contribute identifies you when you edit a page.

4. Enter the password. The person who sent you the connection key created the password. If you don't know the password, contact your site administrator or the person who sent you the e-mail.

5. Click OK. The connection is made. Contribute launches the site's home page, and you can now begin editing the site's pages.

Using a Network Setup File

Many organizations will store a connection key file in a directory on the main network computer. In lieu of e-mailing you the connection key file, your system administrator or a member of your IS or IT team may send you the link to the connection key file. In order to create a connection by importing a connection key file, follow these steps:

1. Choose Edit | My Connections. The My Connections dialog box opens, as shown in Figure 3-3.

2. Click Import. The Select Connection Key dialog box opens, as shown next.

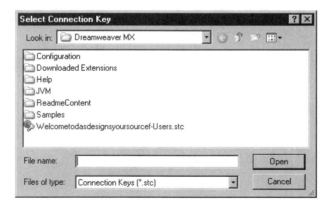

3. Navigate to the directory where the connection key is stored. Contribute connection keys have an .stc file extension. If you are on a network server, the path to the connection key file may be to a different computer in your network.

4. Select the file and click Open. The Import Connection key dialog box shown previously opens.

5. Enter the connection key password and click OK. Contribute logs the information with the Web server.

6. Click Close. The My Connections dialog box closes. The site to which you created a connection is added to the Home Pages pop-up menu on the browser toolbar. You can begin editing the site by clicking the Home Pages button and then choosing the site from the pop-up menu.

Managing Connections

If you're using Contribute to edit several Web sites, you can manage your connections. When you manage your Web connections, you can perform the following tasks:

- Remove an obsolete Web site that you no longer edit with Contribute.

- Edit a connection when the Web site URL has changed or when the server information (the FTP connection, the directory the files are stored in, and so on) has changed.

- Rename a connection. You can rename a connection when you need to differentiate it from other sites you are editing.

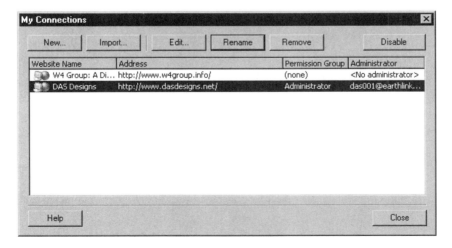

FIGURE 3-3   You can edit your connections using this dialog box.

■ Disable a connection. You can disable a connection to temporarily disconnect a Web site that is not accessible or is not currently being edited. You can improve the performance of Contribute by disabling a connection, which reduces the number of connections Contribute has to maintain.

■ Enable a connection. You can enable a previously disabled connection.

Removing a Web Site Connection

You can remove an obsolete or unused Web site connection at any time. When you remove a Web site connection, you alleviate clutter in the My Connections dialog box and in the Home Pages menu. To remove a connection from your computer, follow these steps:

1. Select any open draft pages from the site and click Cancel or Publish. You can open draft pages by clicking their names in the Pages panel. Contribute will not remove a connection to a site when you have unpublished draft pages from the site.

2. Choose Edit | My Connections. The My Connections dialog box (Figure 3-3) opens.

3. From the connections list, select the Web site you want to remove.

4. Click the Remove button. Contribute opens a dialog box asking you if you're sure you want to remove the connection.

5. Click Yes to remove the connection. Alternatively, you can click No to void the operation and retain the connection.

Editing a Web Site Connection

You can edit a Web site connection whenever necessary. When you edit a Web site connection, you can modify any of the connection parameters if they have changed—for example, if the network location of the Web site files has moved or the site URL has changed.

If you edit a Web connection you created using a connection key, you can change only your username and e-mail address. To edit a Web site connection, follow these steps:

1. Select any draft pages to the Web site you are going to edit, and then publish them or cancel them. This step is only necessary if you are changing your username or e-mail information. You cannot change your user information

when you have open drafts because Contribute checks the pages out according to a user's information. You can, however, update your username and password as it appears on the server, even if you have unpublished page drafts.

2. Choose Edit | My Connections. The My Connections dialog box (Figure 3-3) opens.

3. Select the Web site whose connection information you want to edit.

4. Click Edit. The Connection Wizard (Figure 3-1) opens.

5. Click the Next button to navigate through the various Connection Wizard screens shown previously in this chapter. Make the necessary edits in each screen.

6. When you've finished editing connection settings, click the Next button until you navigate to the Summary screen.

7. Verify your new settings. If necessary, click the Back button to modify settings in previous Connection Wizard screens.

8. While in the Summary screen of the My Connections dialog box, click the Done button to apply the new settings.

> **NOTE** *When you change connection settings, you do not have to send a new connection key. Settings are updated when users launch Contribute and the software synchronizes with the server. The only time you need to send a new connection key is when you move a user to a different group. For more information on creating a connection key, see Chapter 16.*

Renaming a Connection

You can rename a connection at any time. When you create a connection, Contribute uses the title of the site's home page for the connection name. You can specify a shorter name or a name that makes more sense to you, such as the site's URL. When you rename a site, the new name appears on the Home Pages menu, in the My Connections dialog box, and in the Administer Websites submenu. To rename a connection, follow these steps:

1. Choose Edit | My Connections. The My Connections dialog box (Figure 3-3) appears.

2. Select the Web site whose name you want to change.

3. Click the Rename button. The Web site name is highlighted.

4. Enter a new name for the site. Choose a meaningful name that describes the type of site you are editing. Remember, if you choose a long name, it may be truncated in the My Connections dialog box.

5. Press ENTER to apply your changes.

6. Click the Close button to exit the My Connections dialog box or select another Web site whose parameters you need to modify.

Disabling a Connection

When you launch Contribute, the program verifies a connection for each Web site to which you have made a connection. If a Web site is unavailable or you are working offline, Contribute displays a warning dialog box to that effect. If you know a site is going to be offline for an extended period of time or you are going to work offline, you can disable a connection in order to avoid the warning.

If you have connections to multiple Web sites, Contribute's performance may suffer while maintaining multiple connections. You can improve performance by

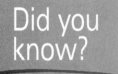

What's in a Domain Name

When the Web site(s) you are editing with Contribute were in the planning stages, the site owner and designer decided on a domain name. When the site owner and designer chose a domain name, they probably used an acronym or abbreviation of the business name or the owner's name. If they have done their job well, they decided on a name that is short, in case users have to manually enter the domain name in their browser address window.

Domain names are followed by an extension such as: .com, .net, .org, .info, and so on. In the past, .org was reserved for universities and government entities. However, with the Internet growing at an unprecedented rate, this extension is now available for all Web site owners, and other extensions are being created to keep up with the demand.

Domain names are linked to the IP address where the Web site's pages are stored. Therefore, each domain name must be unique. After a domain name is selected, the site owner or designer checks to make sure the domain name hasn't already been registered. Domain names are registered for a minimum of one year through services such as VeriSign. If the registration lapses, the domain name again becomes available.

3

temporarily disabling connections to sites you will not be working with. To disable a connection, follow these steps:

1. Choose Edit | My Connections. The My Connections dialog box (Figure 3-3) appears.

2. Select the Web site you want to disable temporarily.

3. Click the Disable button. Contribute displays a dialog box informing you that the site has been disabled.

4. Click OK to close the dialog box. A red slash mark appears over the icon to the left of the site's name.

5. Click the Close button to exit the My Connections dialog box. Alternatively, select another Web site whose connection parameters you need to modify.

After you disable a Web site, Contribute no longer maintains a connection to the site. If you select a disabled site from the Home Pages menu, Contribute displays a warning to that affect. You will not be able to edit pages from the site until you enable the connection to it.

Enabling a Connection

You can enable a connection to begin editing a Web site that you have previously disabled. To enable a Web site you have previously disabled, follow these steps:

1. Choose Edit | My Connections. The My Connections dialog box (Figure 3-3) opens.

2. Select the disabled Web site you want to enable. Disabled sites are signified by an icon with a red slash through them, next to the site's name.

3. Click Enable. Contribute reestablishes a connection with the site.

4. Click the Close button to close the My Connections dialog box. You can now edit the site pages as needed.

TIP *If you are viewing a Web site to which you have made a connection and Contribute disables the connection due to a server glitch, the Edit Page and New Page buttons are replaced by the Retry Connection button. Click the Retry Connection button, and Contribute attempts to reestablish the connection.*

Summary

In this chapter, you took your first steps toward editing Web pages: you created a connection. You learned to create a connection by importing a connection key that was e-mailed to you and to create a new connection by choosing Edit | My Connections. You learned to import a connection key from a folder on your network. You also learned to edit your connections and improve Contribute's performance by temporarily disabling unused connections. In the next chapter, you'll learn how to edit the HTML pages within the sites to which you have created a connection. You'll also learn how to incorporate new content in your pages by dragging and dropping Word and Excel documents into existing pages.

Part II

Editing Web Page Elements

Chapter 4

Working with HTML Documents

How to...

- Navigate to a Web site
- Bookmark a Web site
- Edit a Web page
- Work offline
- Work with text

Contribute is a diverse tool that you use to edit Web pages. When people view the Web pages you edit, they view a document containing code that instructs the browser how to display the images and text included with the document. The majority of the documents you will be working with will be Hypertext Markup Language (HTML) documents with either the .htm or .html extension. You may also encounter pages written with other extensions such as .asp (Active Server Pages) or .cfm (Cold Fusion Templates). Don't fret over strange-looking extensions. Contribute treats all editable pages the same way; you'll be able to navigate to any page created using current Web design technology. If you navigate to a Web page at a site to which you have made a connection, you'll be able to edit the page with Contribute.

In this chapter, you'll learn to navigate to Web sites. You'll also learn how to create bookmarks to the Web sites you frequently visit and how to use Contribute to edit your pages. You'll learn to add text from Word documents, as well as add spreadsheets from Excel documents. If you prefer to do your work when you are not logged on to the Internet, working offline is covered in this chapter as well. In addition to the tasks just mentioned, you'll discover how to modify properties of a page, such as the background color and other attributes. While you are reading this chapter, remember that your ability to perform some of the tasks may have been disabled when your site administrator specified sitewide settings for your user group.

Navigating to Internet Sites

When you use Contribute to edit sites, you can also use the software to navigate to any uniform resource locator (URL). This dual functionality comes in handy when you need to navigate to other Web sites while editing your pages—for example, when you need to link to a different Web site or navigate to another Web page to get information.

Navigating to Other Web Sites

When you use Contribute as a Web browser, there are several different ways you can navigate to a page. After you navigate to a page, you can view the page as you would in any Web browser, create a connection to the Web site whose page you are viewing if you have the connection information, and edit the page once you have made a connection to the Web site. To navigate to a Web page, do one of the following:

- Enter the site's URL in the Address window, and then click Go or press ENTER, as shown in Figure 4-1. When you type the URL, make sure you enter the URL in the following format: http://www.InternetWebsite.com/about.htm. This is standard nomenclature for a Web site URL. HTTP is an acronym for hypertext transfer protocol. A Web site URL begins with http, a colon, and two forward slashes, http://. This is optional with some Web browsers. WWW is an acronym for World Wide Web and is followed by the URL of the Web site to which you want to connect, a forward slash, and the filename of the page you want to view. If you want to navigate to the site's home page, you do not need to enter the page name; Contribute will search for the site's default home page, which in many instances will be index.htm.

- Click a link on a page you are already viewing to navigate to the linked page.

- Choose View | Go To Web Address to open the Go To Web Address dialog box. Enter the URL of the page to which you want to navigate, and then click OK.

When you use Contribute to navigate to Web pages, you can do the following:

- Click the Back button to navigate to pages you viewed before the page you are currently viewing.

- Click the Forward button to navigate to pages you viewed after the page you are currently viewing.

- Click the Stop button to stop a page from loading. This option is useful if you navigate to a page with a lot of animations and you don't want to wait for them to load.

- Click the Refresh button to reload a page.

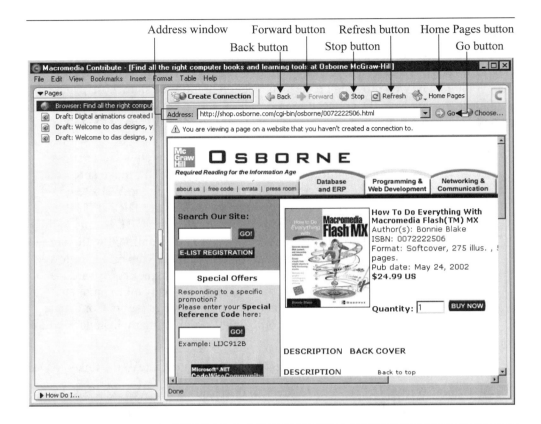

FIGURE 4-1 You can navigate to a Web page by entering a URL in the Address window.

If Contribute starts loading pages slowly or performs poorly after you've been using your computer for a while, save your work and reboot your computer.

Navigating to Your Home Pages

When you create connections to Web sites, you can quickly navigate to the site's home page. After you navigate to the home page, you can then navigate to any page in the site that you want to view or edit. To navigate to the home page of a site to which you have made a connection, click the Home Pages button or choose View | Home Pages, and from the submenu, select the home page to which you want to navigate.

 *You can hide icon labels from view by right-clicking any icon and deselecting the Show Icon Labels option.*

Working with Bookmarks

If you navigate to certain pages on a regular basis, you can bookmark those pages. When you bookmark a page, it is added to the Bookmarks menu. After you create a bookmark, you can navigate to the bookmarked page by choosing it from the Bookmarks menu. If you bookmark a lot of sites, you can organize your bookmarks into folders.

 When you installed Contribute, the install utility searched your default Web browser for bookmarked pages and added them to the Bookmarks menu. To navigate to a site you bookmarked prior to installing Contribute, choose Bookmarks | Other Bookmarks, and then choose the site's name from the submenu.

Adding a Bookmark

You can create a bookmark at any time. You can bookmark pages you visit frequently within other Web sites, or pages within a Web site you are editing. The latter option is useful when you edit sites with a lot of pages or you edit pages that open from links within a page instead of a site navigation menu. To bookmark a page, follow these steps:

1. Navigate to the page that you want to bookmark.

2. Choose Bookmarks | Add Bookmark. The Add Bookmark dialog box shown in Figure 4-2 appears.

3. Accept the default name for the bookmark or type a different name. Contribute uses a Web site's title as the default name for a bookmark. The Bookmarks menu expands to include the complete title of a Web site; however, you'll end up with a tidier menu if you replace a long Web site title with a shorter name.

4. Click OK. The Bookmark is added to the menu.

Creating a Bookmarks Folder

If you navigate to many different sites, you may find it helpful to organize your bookmarks into folders. You can add as many folders as you need. You can store

FIGURE 4-2 You can add a frequently visited Web site to the Bookmarks menu.

bookmarks to similar Web sites in a folder. You'll find it's easier to organize your bookmarks in folders rather than navigate through a lengthy menu to locate a bookmark to a favorite Web site. Figure 4-3 shows a bookmark folder as it appears on the Bookmarks menu. This folder has been opened to display the bookmarks within it.

To create a bookmark folder, follow these steps:

1. Choose Bookmarks | Add Bookmark. The Add Bookmark dialog box (Figure 4-2) appears.

2. Click New Folder. The New Folder dialog box shown next opens.

3. Type a name for the folder. Choose a name that makes sense to you and other people who may share your computer.

4. Click OK. The New Folder dialog box closes, and the folder's name is added to the Add Bookmark dialog box.

5. Click OK to add the Web page you are currently visiting to the new folder. If desired, prior to clicking OK, you can name the bookmark as outlined in the previous section. The page is bookmarked in the new folder. Alternatively, you can click Cancel to exit the Add Bookmark dialog box without creating a bookmark for the page you are currently visiting. The new folder will be available when needed for adding new bookmarks.

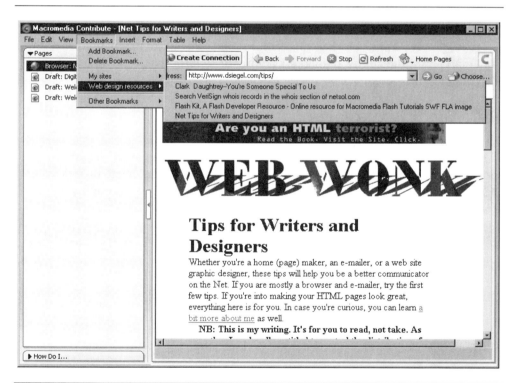

FIGURE 4-3   You can alleviate menu clutter by organizing your bookmarks into folders.

After you organize your bookmarks into several folders, you can add a new bookmark to any existing folder. To add a new bookmark to an existing folder, follow these steps:

1. Navigate to the site that you want to bookmark.

2. Choose Bookmarks | Add Bookmark. The Add Bookmark dialog box (Figure 4-2) appears.

3. Click the name of the folder to which you want the bookmark added. The folder opens.

4. Accept the default name for the bookmark, or type a different name.

5. Click OK. The Add Bookmark dialog box closes.

After you organize your bookmarks into folders, you can navigate to specific bookmarks by choosing Bookmarks, clicking the appropriate folder name, and then clicking the bookmark you want to view.

Deleting a Bookmark

The Internet is in a constant state of flux. Web sites come and go quicker than tenants in apartment buildings. When a bookmarked Web site no longer exists, or you no longer need to navigate to the bookmarked Web site, you can delete the bookmark. Deleting unused bookmarks makes it easier for you to navigate through your Bookmarks menu. To delete a bookmark, follow these steps:

1. Choose Bookmarks | Delete Bookmark. The Delete Bookmark dialog box shown in Figure 4-4 appears. If your bookmarks are organized into folders, each folder is open. The bookmark's name and URL are displayed.

2. Click the name of the bookmark you want to delete. Note that you can only delete one bookmark at a time.

3. Click Delete. The selected bookmark is deleted.

4. To delete another bookmark, select the bookmark and click Delete. Click Close to exit the Delete Bookmark dialog box.

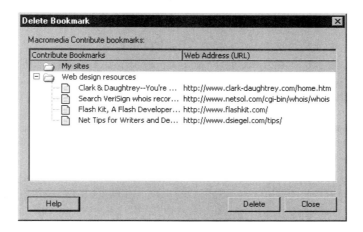

FIGURE 4-4   You can delete unneeded bookmarks.

Working in Edit Mode

When you navigate to a Web page to which you have made a connection, you have two options: you can edit the page or create a new page. You can edit any page that is linked to your site's home page and any files that are stored in your Web site's directory on the Host server, provided your site administrator has granted permission for your user group to edit files. When you edit a page, you can edit the page online and then publish the page, or you can save a draft of the page for future editing offline.

Choosing a Page to Edit

When you need to update a Web page on a site to which you have made a connection, you choose the page you want to edit. You can work on any available Web page—that is, any page that you have permission to edit provided that the page is not currently being edited by another team member.

One of the easiest and most intuitive ways to view a page is to navigate to the page using links on your Web site's navigation menu. However, the Contribute design teams realize no two people work alike. In this regard, they have provided different methods for you to connect to a page you want to edit.

To navigate to one of your Web pages, do one of the following:

- Choose View | Home Pages, and then choose a home page from the submenu.

- Click the Home Pages button and choose a home page from the submenu.

To navigate to a linked page within your Web site, do one of the following:

■ Click a navigation link on your site's home page.

■ Choose View | Go To Web Address. This opens the Go To Web Address dialog box. In the Web Address (URL) field, enter the URL of the page you want to edit, and then click OK.

■ Enter the URL to the Web page in the Address: field above the Contribute browser window.

Another option you have available is to go to a recently published page. When you publish a page, Contribute adds the page to a submenu so that you can quickly navigate to the page and perform additional edits. To navigate to a recently published page, choose View | Recently Published Pages, and from the submenu, choose the page you want to edit.

Many Web sites have pages that are accessed from text links within another HTML document, while other pages are linked to external Web sites. If the site you are editing has pages that are linked in this fashion, navigating to them from a Web link can be time consuming and counter-productive. One solution for this is to bookmark the pages and store them in a folder for easy retrieval. The other option is to choose the file directly from your site's directory on the Web server. You can choose a file from a Web site by doing one of the following:

■ Choose View | Choose File On Website.

■ Click the Choose button on the toolbar.

After doing either of the above, the Choose File On Website dialog box opens to the root folder of your Web site. Double-click the folder to open it and display all of the files and folders stored on your Web site, as shown in Figure 4-5.

To edit a file from the Choose File On Website dialog box, double-click it, and Contribute loads the file into the document window. If you select a file that cannot be edited with Contribute, a warning screen is displayed that prompts you to contact your site administrator. If you select a file that cannot be displayed in the Contribute browser, the warning screen shown in Figure 4-6 is displayed.

When you choose a file that cannot be displayed with the Contribute browser, the Edit button may be available. If so, you can click the button to edit the file in the default external editor for the file type of the selected file.

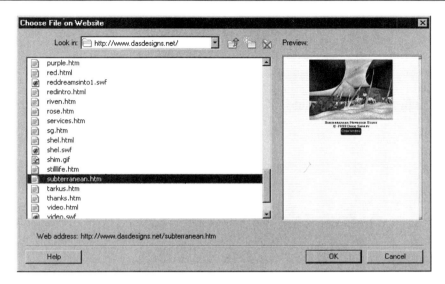

FIGURE 4-5 You can edit files by selecting them from your Web site directory.

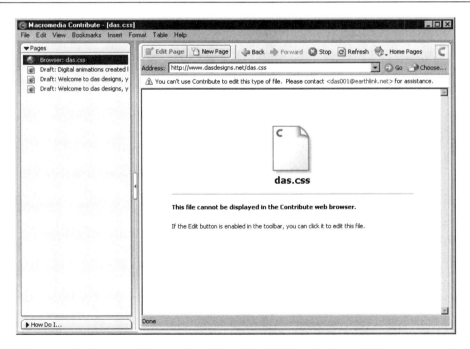

FIGURE 4-6 Some files cannot be displayed in the Contribute browser.

Editing a Page

After you navigate to a page at a Web site to which you've made a connection, your Contribute browser is reconfigured; the Create Connection button is replaced with Edit Page and New Page buttons, as shown in Figure 4-7.

To edit a page to which you have made a connection, you click the Edit Page button. After clicking the button, Contribute downloads the HTML document and any associated files to your hard drive. A draft of the page is also created, as shown in Figure 4-8.

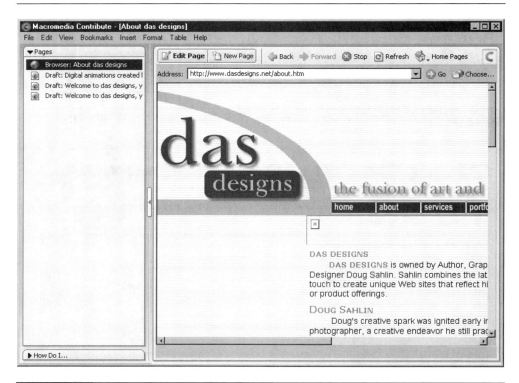

FIGURE 4-7 You can edit a page by clicking the Edit Page button.

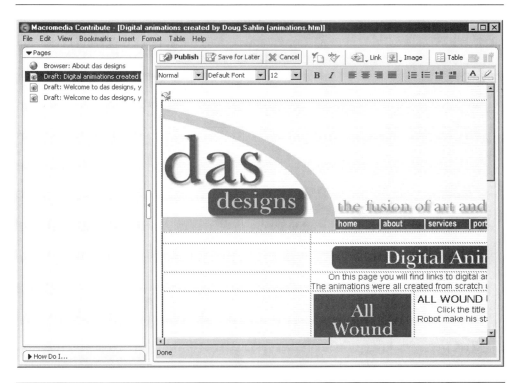

FIGURE 4-8   When you edit a page, Contribute creates a draft of the page.

Using the Editor Toolbar

When you choose a page to edit, the editor toolbar becomes available. You use the tools on this toolbar to edit elements in your pages, add elements to your pages, change page properties, and more. A close-up of the editor toolbar is shown in Figure 4-9.

To use a tool, click it. After you click a tool, a dialog box appears, giving you various options pertaining to the tasks you perform with the tool. Each tool will be discussed in detail when it pertains to an editing task. The following list gives a brief description of what you can do with each tool on the editor toolbar.

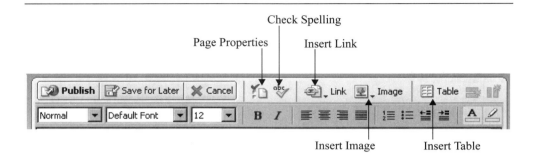

FIGURE 4-9 You use these tools to edit your pages.

- **Publish** Publishes the edited page.

- **Save for Later** Saves a draft of the page that you can edit offline.

- **Cancel** Cancels editing of the page.

- **Page Properties** Opens the Page Properties dialog box. You can change the page title, background color, background image, margins, and more.

- **Check Spelling** Spell checks selected text or the entire page.

- **Insert Link** Inserts a link to a Web page or a document.

- **Insert Image** Inserts an image at the position you choose.

- **Insert Table** Inserts a table into the document. You specify the number of rows and columns in the table, as well as other attributes.

- **Insert Row** Inserts a row into a table.

- **Insert Column** Inserts a column into a table.

- **Text styling tools** Formats selected text.

- **Text alignment tools** Aligns text to the document or to a table cell.

- **List tools** Formats bulleted or numbered lists.

- ■ **Indentation tools**   Indents or outdents text.

- ■ **Color tools**   Colors or highlights selected text.

Adding Word or Excel Documents to Web Pages

You can use Contribute to easily add text to any Web page. In addition to adding text to a page, you can add an existing Microsoft Word or Microsoft Excel document directly to a Web page. The beauty of inserting an existing document into an HTML page is the fact that Contribute preserves the formatting of the original document. For example, if you create a Word document with tables and images, you can insert the document into a Web page, and the embedded images are inserted with it. Compare this with having to re-create the table and then inserting the images, and you begin to see the amount of time you can save by inserting Microsoft Word and Excel documents into your Web pages.

There are two ways to add Microsoft Word and Excel content to your pages:

- ■ Insert the contents of the document into the page. This is the recommended method for documents with a file size of 300K or less.

- ■ Link the document to a Web page. This is recommended when a document's file size exceeds 300K.

Web-Friendly Fonts

When you insert a Word or Excel document into a Web page, Contribute attempts to format the text with the same font you used to create the original document. If the text is formatted with a specialized font, Contribute will revert to a Web-friendly font, and your document may not display as you intended. When you create a Word or Excel document with the intention of adding it to a Web page, make sure you stick to Web-friendly fonts: Arial, Courier New, Geneva, Georgia, Times New Roman, or Verdana.

Inserting a Word or Excel Document into a Web Page

You can insert a Word or Excel document into any Web page you are editing. The contents will be inserted where you place your cursor. To insert a Word or Excel document into an HTML document, follow these steps:

1. Choose the page you want to edit by using one of the methods discussed previously in the section "Choosing a Page to Edit." Alternatively, you can select a draft of a page you are editing or create a new page. For more information on creating a new Web page, see Chapter 5.

2. Place your cursor at the point where you want the contents of the document inserted.

3. Choose Insert | Microsoft Word Document to insert a Word document, or choose Insert | Microsoft Excel Document to insert an Excel document. The Open dialog box appears.

4. Navigate to the folder where the document is stored and select it.

5. Click Open. Contribute inserts the document at the insertion point you specified.

NOTE   *If you try to insert a document larger than 300K, Contribute displays a warning dialog box saying the document is too large to import. If you receive this warning, you can cut and paste parts of the document into the page you're editing or create a link to the document as outlined in the next section.*

You can also insert a Microsoft Word or Excel document by dragging and dropping the document into the page you are editing. To insert a Microsoft Word or Excel document into a page using the drag-and-drop method, follow these steps:

1. Select the Web page that you want to edit using one of the methods discussed previously in the section "Choosing a Page to Edit."

2. You can use the Windows Explorer to locate the Word or Excel file you want to insert. Resize Contribute so that you can view Contribute and your file navigation utility at the same time.

3. Locate the Microsoft Word or Excel file whose contents you want to insert in the page you are editing.

4. Drag the file into the Web page you are editing, and drop it at the point where you want the contents of the file to appear. Contribute displays the Insert Microsoft Word Or Excel Document dialog box shown next.

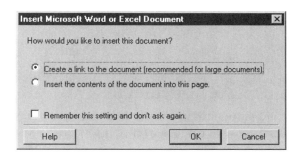

> **TIP**   *If you frequently insert Microsoft Word or Excel documents into the pages you edit, store the files in a folder on your desktop.*

5. Click the Insert The Contents Of The Document Into This Page radio button.

6. Click OK. Contribute inserts the document at the insertion point where you dropped the file.

Linking to a Word or Excel Document

If you have a large Word or Excel document you want to display on your Web site or a document that is updated frequently, you can create a link to the document. When you create a link to a document, a text link appears in the HTML document you are editing. When you publish the page, the linked document is uploaded to your Web site. When viewers click the link, the document is displayed in their browser. To link a Word or Excel document to your Web page, follow these steps:

1. Choose the page to which you want to add the document using one of the methods outlined earlier in the section "Choosing a Page to Edit."

2. Drag the document from its folder, and then drop it where you want the link inserted. The Insert Microsoft Word Or Excel Document dialog box appears, as shown.

3. Accept the default option to create a link to the document, and then click OK. Contribute creates a link to the file. When you publish the page, the linked document is uploaded to the Web site at the same time as the page. The linked document is stored on the Web site server in a folder named Documents.

To avoid seeing the Insert Microsoft Word Or Excel Document dialog box every time you drag a file into Contribute, choose the method of insertion you prefer (link the document or insert the contents), and then click the Remember This Setting And Don't Ask Again check box.

You can also create a link to a Microsoft Word or Excel document by using the Link tool. The Link tool is discussed in detail in Chapter 7.

Editing Word or Excel Documents

If you insert, copy, and paste or drag and drop the contents of a Microsoft Word document into a Web page, you can use Contribute's text-editing tools to edit the inserted text within the page draft. If you create a link to a Microsoft Word or Excel document, you can edit the document using the native Microsoft application, which is launched from within Contribute. To edit a linked Microsoft Word or Excel document from within Contribute, follow these steps:

1. Click the Choose button. The Choose File On Website dialog box (Figure 4-5) opens.

2. Navigate to and open the Documents folder.

3. Select the Microsoft Word or Excel document that you want to edit. Contribute displays the file in Browse mode.

4. Click the Edit button. Contribute downloads the file, creates a draft of the file, and opens the file in the native Microsoft application. Contribute displays the Editing Draft In Another Application screen, as shown in Figure 4-10.

5. Switch to the Microsoft application and edit the document.

6. After the document is edited, save and close the document in the Microsoft application.

7. Switch to Contribute and click the Publish button. Contribute uploads the edited document to the Web site server.

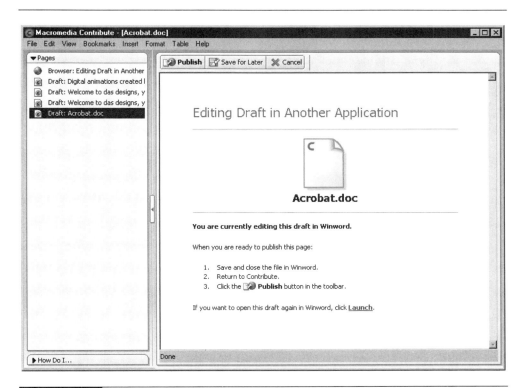

FIGURE 4-10   You can edit a Microsoft Word or Excel file from within Contribute.

Modifying Page Properties

When your Web site was designed, each page was given a title and other attributes, such as a background color or background image. When you are editing a page, you can modify page properties. To modify the properties of a Web page, follow these steps:

1. Choose the Web page whose properties you want to change.

2. Click the Edit Page button. Contribute creates a draft of the page for you to edit.

3. Click the Page Properties button shown previously (Figure 4-9). The Page Properties dialog box shown in Figure 4-11 opens.

4. Modify any of the following properties:

- **Title** Change the title to display a different title when the page is loaded into a browser. The page title appears in the title bar at the top of the user's browser.

- **Background image** Some Web designers use a tiling background image as a backdrop for the text and other images on a page. A tiling background image can be a GIF file, a JPEG file, or a PNG file. If the background image is a GIF or PNG file, parts of the image may be transparent, allowing the page's background color to show through. To modify the existing background image, click the Browse button and navigate to the folder where the image is stored. For more information on image file formats, see Chapter 12.

- **Background color** To change the background color of the page, click the color swatch and choose a color from the pop-up palette.

TIP *If the Web designer who created your site used a background image with transparent areas, you can change the appearance of the page by choosing a different background color. The background color will show through the transparent areas of the background image.*

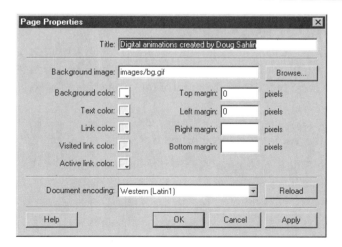

FIGURE 4-11   You can change the page properties to modify the look of a page.

- **Text color**   To change the color of text, click the color swatch and choose a color from the pop-up palette.

- **Link color**   To change the color of text links on the page, click the color swatch and choose a color from the pop-up palette.

- **Visited link color**   To change the color of visited links, click the color swatch and choose a color from the pop-up palette. A visited link is a link to a URL that the Web page visitor has already viewed.

- **Active link color**   To change the color of active links, click the color swatch and choose a color from the pop-up palette. This property determines the color of the links before users click them.

- **Top margin, Left margin, Right margin, Bottom margin**   These values determine how large the margin is between the Web page content and the edge of the user's browser. If you enter values of 0 for each margin, the content will be flush with the edge of the user's browser.

- **Document encoding**   Click the triangle to the right of this field, and choose an option from the pop-up menu. Select Western (Latin 1) if the language on the page is English or a Western European language. Other options include Central European, Cyrillic, Greek, Icelandic, Japanese, Traditional Chinese, Simplified Chinese, and Korean. If the language you want is not available, choose Other to edit the page using the encoding from your computer operating system.

5. Click Apply to preview the changes prior to closing the dialog box. Click Reload to view the page in its previous iteration.

6. Click OK to apply the changes. Alternatively, click Cancel to void all changes and exit the dialog box.

 *If you are editing a page based on a template, or if your site administrator has restricted you to editing only text, you can only change the page title.*

Undoing and Redoing Actions

To err is human; that's why designers of most software programs always give you a way to undo your last action. If you undo an action and later decide that you actually need the edit, you can redo the action.

- To undo an action, choose Edit | Undo.

- To redo the last action, choose Edit | Redo.

Deleting a Web Page

When you edit a Web site with Contribute, you can delete a page at any time if your site administrator has enabled deleting pages for your user group. If you have permission to delete Web pages, you can also delete other files such as documents and images from your Web site. To delete a page or file from a Web site you are editing, follow these steps:

1. Click the Choose button, and then select the file or page you want to delete.

2. Click OK. Contribute loads the file or page into your browser.

NOTE *You can also navigate to the page you want to delete. When you delete a page in this manner, you delete only the HTML file. Files linked to the page such as images and text documents will not be deleted. To delete these files, you must select them as outlined in step 1.*

3. Choose File | Delete Page. Contribute displays a warning dialog box telling you that deleting the page may cause broken links on the site.

NOTE *If you do not have permission to delete files, the Delete Page command will be unavailable and will appear grayed out in the File menu.*

4. Click Yes to delete the file. Contribute deletes the file and displays the last page you visited in the browser.

If your site administrator has given you permission to delete pages, use this option with extreme caution. Deleting a page permanently removes it from your server. It's a good idea to check with other members of your team and the site administrator prior to deleting a file or Web page.

Saving a Page Draft

When you click the Edit Page button, Contribute saves a draft of the page, which then appears in the Pages panel. Contribute also saves the page as you work. However, if you need to switch to another draft page or to the page currently displayed in the browser, you can save the draft you are working on prior to switching to another document. You can also save a draft in order to edit the page offline.

To save a draft of a page while you are working, choose File | Save.

To save a draft of a page you intend to edit offline, do one of the following:

- Click Browser in the Pages panel to switch to the page you last viewed in the browser. If the page you were viewing is the same page you are editing, Contribute displays a dialog box informing you that you have an unpublished draft of the page.

- Choose View | Browser. Contribute switches to Browse mode and displays the page you last viewed.

- Choose File | Save For Later.

- Click the Save For Later button.

Canceling Edits

If you're working on a page and you decide that you need additional information before publishing a page or saving it as a draft, you can cancel your edits. You can also cancel any drafts you have previously saved. To cancel a draft, follow these steps:

1. Select the draft from the Pages panel. (This step is not necessary to cancel edits in a page you are currently editing.)

2. Click the Cancel button or choose File | Cancel Draft. Contribute displays a dialog box asking you to confirm the operation.

3. Click Yes to confirm the operation. Alternatively, click No to save the page as a draft for future editing.

NOTE   *When you cancel a draft, you lose all changes you have made to the unpublished draft.*

You can also cancel a new page you are editing by clicking the Cancel button or choosing File | Cancel Draft. Contribute discards the new page.

Working Offline

If you prefer, you can edit Web pages offline. This option is useful when you need to edit Web pages at a different location, such as working at home or editing files while traveling on an airplane. When you are working offline, you will be able to edit page drafts, but you will not have access to the browser to locate other files or to preview your pages in a browser because Contribute needs to save a copy of the edited page on the server prior to displaying it in a browser. To work offline, follow these steps:

1. Launch Contribute without being connected to your network server or the Internet. Contribute displays the Connection Failure dialog box. You can choose between two options: Work Offline and Try To Reconnect Anyway.

2. Choose Work Offline.

3. Click OK.

Contribute displays the Working Offline page in the browser window. You can now choose a page draft to edit from the Pages panel. Contribute displays the page draft in the browser window, and the editor toolbar becomes available.

Editing Pages Offline

While you are working offline, you will not be able to navigate to a Web site or select a file from your Web site server. You can edit any page draft from the Pages panel, or you can create new pages. You cannot publish a page while working offline.

 While editing pages offline, it's a good idea to save your work periodically, especially if you're working on a battery-powered laptop. Saving your work prevents you from losing edits if you have a computer glitch or if your laptop computer exhausts its battery.

When you work offline, you can create a new page by choosing File | New Page. For more information on creating new pages, see Chapter 5.

Although you can edit page drafts offline, you cannot delete pages or cancel edits. Both options are grayed out in the File menu when you work offline, and the Cancel button is unavailable as well. You can, however, delete new pages you have created while working offline by clicking the Cancel button or by choosing File | Cancel Draft.

4

Switching Between Online and Offline

If you launch Contribute without a server connection and later establish a connection, Contribute will not recognize the server connection and will not try to establish a connection. You can manually establish the connection by doing one of the following:

- Click the Work Online button.

- Choose File | Work Offline. When you are working offline, a checkmark appears to the left of this menu command. Choosing the command again causes Contribute to attempt to connect to the sites to which you have established a connection and the checkmark is removed from the Work Offline menu command signifying you are now working online.

TIP   *If, for any reason, you decide to work offline while still connected to your server, you can do so by choosing File | Work Offline. When you do this, you are still online, but Contribute temporarily disables connections to the Web sites you are editing.*

Using the Pages Panel

When you save drafts of pages for future editing, they are added to the Pages panel, which appears to the left of the document window. You use the Pages panel to select pages you want to edit or view the Web page currently displayed in the browser.

You can use the Pages panel to do the following:

- While viewing a Web page, you can select a page draft to edit by clicking its name.

- While editing a page draft, you can switch to another page draft by selecting it. When you select another page draft, Contribute saves any changes you have made to the page draft you are currently editing.

- While editing a page draft, you can switch to Browse mode by clicking Browser in the Pages panel. When you do this, Contribute saves any changes made to the page draft you are currently editing and displays the Web page you were viewing prior to editing a page.

Exporting a Web Page

When you create a page draft, the information is stored within Contribute's Application Data folder. You can export the page to view it outside of Contribute. When you export a page, you export only the HTML. You will not be able to view any images or other files that are associated with the page if the page has already been published. If the page you are exporting is a draft of a new page, you will be able to view images and associated files because they are linked to a folder on your computer. The ability to export a Web page is useful if you decide to delete a page from your server but you want to archive a copy of the page. To export a Web page, follow these steps:

1. Select the page you want to export by doing one of the following:

   ■ Navigate to the page you want to export.

   ■ Click the Choose button and then choose a file from your server to export. Note that you can only export pages with the .htm or .html extension.

2. Click the Edit Page button. Alternatively, you can select a page draft for export by clicking its name in the Pages panel.

3. Choose File | Export. The Export dialog box appears.

4. Navigate to the folder where you want to export the file and then enter a name in the Filename field.

5. Click the Save button. Contribute exports the file.

Printing a Web Page

You can print to your local printer a copy of a page to which you have browsed or a page you are editing. You can print out for future reference a hard copy of a Web page you are visiting or print a copy of a page draft to view your changes. To print a copy of the Web page or draft you are currently viewing, follow these steps:

1. Choose File | Print. The Print dialog box appears. (The actual dialog box varies depending on the hardware you use to print, as do the options.)

2. Click Print. A copy of the page or draft you are viewing is printed to your local printer.

Previewing an Edited Page in a Browser

When you're editing a page, you don't see how your changes will look in a Web browser. The Contribute editor gives you a good idea of what the page will look like when published, but you still see dashed lines around table rows and columns, as well as markers for invisible elements such as named anchors. One way to know how your edited page will look in a Web browser is to publish it. You can, however, preview the page in a browser prior to publishing it by following these steps:

4

1. Select the page draft you want to preview in a browser. You can preview the page you're currently editing or choose another page draft from the Pages panel.

2. Choose File | Preview In Browser. Contribute displays a dialog box notifying you that a copy of the draft will be placed in a temporary folder on your Web site server. The file will be deleted when you publish the finished page.

3. Click OK. Contribute publishes a copy of the draft to a temporary folder. Your default Web browser launches and displays a copy of the draft you are editing. When you are finished previewing the page, close the browser window to return to Contribute.

Summary

In this chapter, you learned how to edit Web pages, how to add content from Microsoft Excel and Word documents to your pages, and how to modify the properties of a page. You also learned to save drafts of your pages for future editing or for editing offline. In Chapter 5, you'll learn to create new pages for the Web sites you edit with Contribute.

Chapter 5

Creating New Web Pages

How to...

- Create a new Web page
- Copy an existing Web page
- Work with document templates
- Set page properties
- Test pages

When the Web sites you edit made their debut on the Internet, the content displayed was determined by your Web designer. As the business or service for which the Web site was designed evolves, the content on the pages needs to be updated. You can edit the pages by adding content from Word or Excel documents, as outlined in the previous chapter, or you can edit existing elements such as text and images.

You can add as much content as you want to a Web page. However, at some point a Web page may become so large that it takes too long to load into a user's browser, or the page is so long, viewers have to scroll excessively to view the content. When a Web page gets to this point, you should consider creating a new Web page for the additional content.

You can also create a new Web page when you need to display information about a new product or service offered by your company or organization. In this chapter, you'll learn to add content to your Web site by creating new Web pages.

Creating New Web Pages

When you decide to create a new Web page, you can do so easily with Contribute. You can create a page that captures the look and feel of the other pages on the Web site, or you can start with a blank slate and let your artistic muse dictate the direction the new page will take. You can use any of the following as the basis for a new Web page:

- A copy of the page you are currently viewing
- A blank Web page
- A preset Contribute template

- A Dreamweaver template created by your Web designer
- A Web page from the site designated by the site administrator for use as a template

> **NOTE**   *Some of the preceding options may not be available if your site administrator has disabled them for your user group.*

Creating a Copy of a Web Page

You can use any Web page from your site as the basis for a new Web page. Creating a copy of an existing Web page is useful when the page is lengthy and you need to add more content to it. You can also create a copy of a page when you want the new page to have the look and feel of other pages in your site but you don't have a template from which to work.

When you create a copy of an existing page, you must link to it later. You can't create the copy and the link at the same time, you can't create a copy of a page from a different Web site, and you can't create a copy of a page draft. You must be viewing the page in Browse mode before you can create a copy of it. To create a new Web page by copying an existing page, follow these steps:

1. Navigate to the Web page you want to use as the basis for your new Web page. In lieu of navigating to a page, you can choose a page by clicking the Choose button.

2. Click the New Page button or choose File | New Page. Either method opens the New Page dialog box.

3. Choose Copy Of Current Page. Contribute refreshes the Preview window to show a smaller version of the current page, as shown in Figure 5-1.

4. In the Page Title field, enter the title for the new page. This is the title that viewers will see in their browsers when navigating to the page after it is published. This is also the working filename for the new page, which you can change when you publish the file.

5. Click OK. Contribute copies the associated files from the page to your hard drive and creates a draft of the page.

After you create a copy of the page, you can delete content from the copy and add new material as needed. After you create the page, you can publish the page.

Contribute preset templates folder   Dreamweaver template

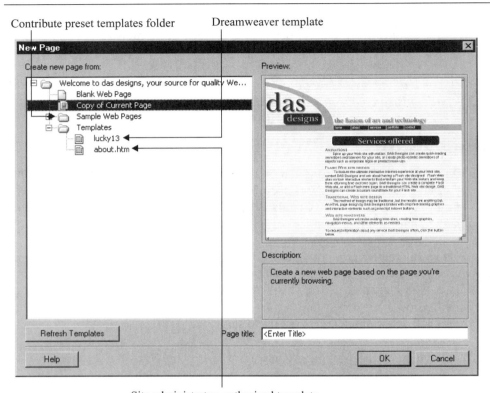

Site administrator–authorized template

FIGURE 5-1   You can create a new page by copying an existing page from your site.

After editing the page, click the Publish button to publish the new page to your
Web site. For more information on publishing Web pages, see Chapter 13.

Creating a Blank Web Page

When you create a blank Web page, you begin with a clean slate. When you create
a blank Web page, you can add content by typing text directly into the document,
adding images to the document, or adding Microsoft Word or Excel files to the
document. You can also organize the content of the page by using HTML tables.
As you create the Web page, Contribute writes all of the HTML code necessary
to properly display the page in a viewer's browser.

Working with a blank Web page gives you a tremendous amount of artistic
license. You can control the look and feel of the page by specifying page properties,

font styles, table properties, and more. The ability to create a new page from a blank page will not be available if your Web site administrator has disabled this option for your user group.

You have two methods by which you can create a blank Web page:

- Create a link from within an existing Web page and then create the new blank Web page. This is the recommended method for creating a new Web page.

- Create the new blank Web page and create the link after the fact. You can choose this method when you need to create a new Web page that will link to a page your Web designer or site administrator is creating.

5

Creating a Web Page While Creating a Link

The most reliable way to create a new Web page is to create the link first and then create the new page. When you create new pages in this manner, you eliminate the risk of creating an unlinked page. An unlinked page cannot be viewed from other pages in your site. The only way to view an unlinked page is to enter the absolute URL of the page in the address field of a Web browser. This is undesirable unless you only want certain individuals who know the absolute URL of the page to be able to view the content.

To create a Web page while creating a link, follow these steps:

1. Navigate to the Web page on your site to which you want to link the new page. You can use the site's navigation tools to navigate to a page, or you can click the Choose button and then select a Web page from your Web site directory.

2. Click the Edit Page button. Contribute creates a draft of the page.

3. To choose the point in the page where the link appears, do one of the following:

   - Place your cursor at the point in the document where you want the link to appear. Enter the text for the link when the Insert Link dialog box appears.

   - Select a block of text that you want to be the hyperlink.

   - Select an image that you want to be the hyperlink.

4. To create the link, do one of the following:

   ■ Click the Link button and then select Create New Page.

   ■ Choose Insert | Link | Create New Page.

   ■ Right-click and then choose Insert Link.

   After choosing either of these methods, the Insert Link dialog box shown in Figure 5-2 appears.

5. In the Link Text field, enter the text that will be the link to the new page. This option is grayed out if you selected text or an image as the basis for the new page link in step 3.

6. In the Create New Page From section, choose one of the following:

   ■ **Blank Web Page**   Choose this option to create a blank Web page.

   ■ **Sample Web Pages**   Choose this option to create a page based on one of the Contribute presets discussed earlier in this chapter.

   ■ **Templates**   Choose this option to create a Web page based on a template created by your Web site's designer or based on an existing page designated as a template by your Web site administrator.

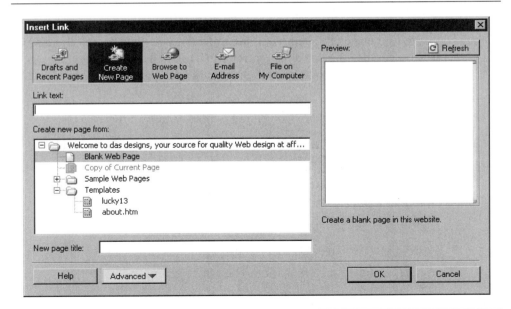

FIGURE 5-2   You can create a link and a new page at the same time.

7. In the New Page Title field, enter a name for the new page. This is the page title that is displayed in the user's browser while the page is being viewed. It also serves as the working filename while you are editing the page draft. You can choose a different filename when you publish the page. For more information on publishing Web pages, refer to Chapter 13.

8. Click the Advanced button to choose advanced linking options. For more information on advanced linking options, refer to Chapter 7.

9. Click OK. Contribute adds the link to the page draft you were editing when you created the link. A new page draft based on the option you chose in step 6 is created as well.

Creating a Web Page Without a Link

You can also create a new Web page without first making a link. This option is a little risky in case you forget to create a link to another page after you publish the new page. Of course you may have a perfectly legitimate reason for creating a page without a link to another page in your site: for example, a page that you only want certain clients or visitors to view. In this case, you'll have to supply the people you want to view the page with the absolute URL to the page, as there will not be a link within the site that can be used to view the page. To create a Web page without creating a link, follow these steps:

1. Navigate to any page within the Web site you are editing. You can navigate to a page by entering the URL in the Address: field, clicking a navigation link within the site you are editing, or choosing View | Go To Web Address and then entering the URL in the Go To Web Address dialog box.

2. Click the New Page button. Contribute displays the New Page dialog box (Figure 5-1).

3. In the Create New Page From section, choose one of the following:

■ **Blank Web Page**   Choose this option to create a blank Web page.

■ **Copy of Current Page**   Choose this option to create a new Web page based on the page you are currently viewing.

■ **Sample Web Pages**   Choose this option to create a page based on one of the Contribute presets discussed earlier in this chapter.

■ **Templates**   Choose this option to create a Web page based on a template created by your Web site's designer or based on an existing page designated as a template by your Web site administrator.

4. In the Page Title field, enter the text that you want displayed in a browser title bar when a visitor views the page.

5. Click OK. Contribute creates a draft of the new page, based on the option you chose in step 3.

Creating a Web Page from a Contribute Template

Contribute ships with a wide array of preset templates you can use to create Web pages. If your Web site administrator has enabled your permissions group to use the Contribute presets, you can use a preset from any of the following groups:

- **Business** The templates in this group, as the name implies, are geared toward business Web sites. You can use the templates to create a generic home page or to organize content into two columns, bullet lists, and more.

- **Personal** The templates in this group are geared toward personal Web sites. With the templates in this group, you can create photo albums and résumés. If you use Contribute for a business Web site, the photo album pages can be used to display images from company seminars and events.

- **Calendars** You can use the templates in this group to create an events page at your Web site. There are templates for each month of the year in 2003 and 2004.

- **Collaboration** You can use the templates in this group when you collaborate with other members of your team to create new Web pages. In this group, you'll find templates for creating presentations, displaying company reports, and more.

When you create a Web page from a Contribute preset, you are copying a template. When you work with a template, certain areas of the document may be locked and unavailable for editing. When a Web designer creates a template and locks areas such as page headers and section headers, this is done so that the look and feel of the site can't be changed by modifying the content of these areas. When you attempt to edit a locked region, your cursor becomes a circle with a diagonal slash.

You can create a Web page using a Contribute preset by doing one of the following:

- Create a link while editing an existing page, and then create a new page. This is the recommended method, as you do not run the risk of creating an orphaned (unlinked) Web page.

- Click the New Page button while editing an existing page, and then choose a preset from one of the Contribute preset categories discussed in the preceding section. Figure 5-3 shows an example of a Contribute preset being used to create a new page. The Contribute sidebar has been hidden in this screenshot to show the template.

5

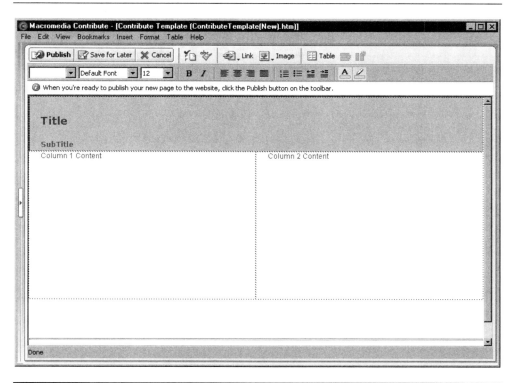

FIGURE 5-3   You can use a Contribute preset as the basis for a new Web page.

Creating a Web Page from a Web Designer or Administrator's Template

Your Web designer or site administrator may have created templates for the Web site you are editing with Contribute. A template is created to maintain a uniform appearance throughout a Web site. Your Web site administrator may have enabled access to templates that you can use to create new pages. Certain regions of the template may be locked, which means you cannot edit the content in those regions. When you move your cursor over a region that is locked for editing, your cursor becomes a circle with a diagonal slash through it. Many Web designers put sample content into a page, as shown in Figure 5-4.

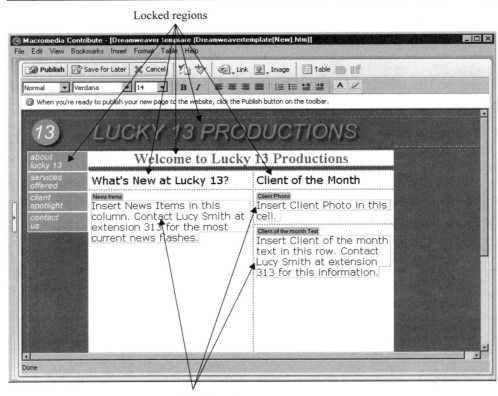

FIGURE 5-4 You can use a Dreamweaver template as the basis for a new Web page.

There are two types of templates you may encounter:

■ A Dreamweaver template created by your site's Web designer. Templates of this type will have both editable and locked regions.

■ A template created by your Web site administrator. When Web site administrators set up sitewide permissions, they can designate any page in the Web site as a template. These pages will not have any locked regions, unless, of course, the page was created from a template with locked regions; however, permissions for your user group may disable the ability to edit certain parameters of a page, such as applying HTML text styles to text.

You can create a new Web page using a template and one of the following methods:

■ Create a link while editing an existing page, and then create a new page. This is the recommended method, as you do not run the risk of creating an orphaned (unlinked) Web page.

■ Click the New Page button while editing an existing page, and then choose a template.

After creating a new Web page from a template, you can complete the page by altering the content in the following ways:

■ Deleting and replacing existing text

■ Modifying existing text

■ Deleting and replacing existing images in the template

 When you open the New Page dialog box, click the Refresh Templates button to get the latest versions of existing templates and to refresh the dialog box to show any new templates that may be available on the server.

Setting Page Properties

When you create a new Web page, you can define the page properties. When you set page properties, you determine how certain elements in the page appear; for example, you can set properties for background color, text color, link colors, page margins, and so on. To set the properties of a page draft you are editing, follow these steps:

1. To open the Page Properties dialog box shown in Figure 5-5, do one of the following:

   ■ Click the Page Properties button.

   ■ Choose Format | Page Properties.

2. Change the properties to suit the page you are creating. For detailed instructions on modifying page properties, refer to Chapter 4.

3. After modifying the properties of your new page, click OK. The Page Properties dialog box closes, and the changes are applied to the new page.

NOTE *If the page you are creating is based on a Dreamweaver template or if your user group is restricted to editing text only, you will be able to change only the page's title.*

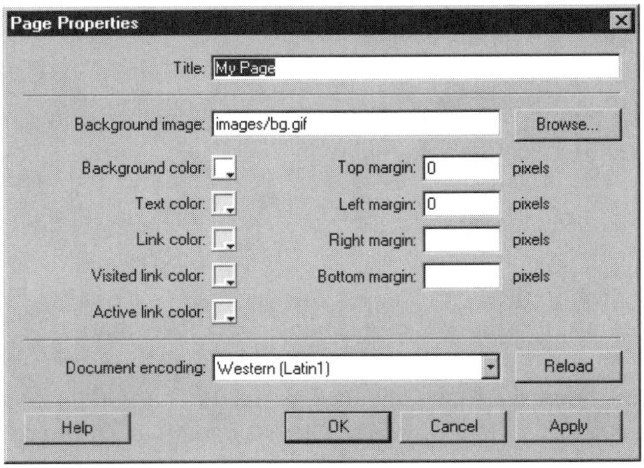

FIGURE 5-5 You can modify the look of your new page by changing the page's properties.

Adding Keywords to a Web Page

When the Web site you are editing was created, the site designer and the owner of the site collaborated to create keywords. Keywords are not visible to Web page visitors, but some search engines use them after your site is registered with a search engine and added to its directory. If a user types the same words or phrases as the keywords or keyword phrases in your site's pages, your site will be one of the sites returned in the search engine's results list. You can also modify a page's description. The page description is within the Head section of the HTML document and is also invisible when pages at your site are browsed. If your Web designer added a site description, it is displayed when a search engine displays your Web site in a results page. To add keywords or a description to a page you are creating or editing, follow these steps:

1. Navigate to the page or select the page draft to which you want to add the keywords.

2. Choose Format | Keywords And Description. The Keywords And Description dialog box appears, as shown next. If the page you are editing already has keywords and a description, they appear in the Keywords and Description fields.

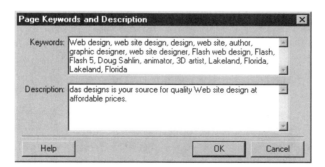

3. Enter new keywords or modify existing keywords. Keywords can be single words or phrases that visitors to a search engine might enter to find sites with information similar to your site. You must separate each keyword or keyword phrase with a comma.

4. Enter a new description or modify the existing one. The description should be a short sentence that describes the contents of the site, or the services your company or organization provides.

5. Click OK. The Keywords And Description dialog box closes and the new or edited keywords are inserted into the Head section of the document you are editing.

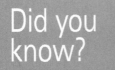

About Keywords, Meta Tags, and Search Engines

When a Web site has keywords, certain search engines such as Lycos (lycos.com) and Alta Vista (altavista.com) associate these keywords with the Web site. If the owner of a Web site wants to attract Web site traffic from a search engine, the site owner supplies the Web designer with a list of words or phrases he thinks visitors to search engines will enter to find sites with similar products or services.

Keywords and descriptions are known as *Meta tags*. Meta tags are not visible when the pages are browsed; they are stored in between the <head> and </head> tags in the HTML document. After a Web site is uploaded to a Web host, it is often registered with several popular search engines. Some Web site owners use search engine submission services to submit a site to several hundred search engines. When a Web site is submitted to a true search engine, the search engine scans the site's pages and records the information from the Meta tags before adding the site to the search engine's index.

Even though you can enter more than 100 keywords to an HTML document, most search engines use only the first 15 or 20 keywords when adding a site to their index. In that regard, it's important to choose the keywords you think people will most likely use to find your site. It's also important to keep your description short, sweet, and to the point. Most search engines check only the first 15 or 20 words of a description. You should also be aware that many search engines will not add a Web site to their index if you repeatedly use the same word as a keyword. Some search engines will also exclude a site if the word "Sex" is used as a keyword to attract visitors. Therefore, make sure you carefully choose keywords that are relevant to your Web site.

When a visitor enters a keyword or a phrase into the search field at a search engine, the search engine explores its index to find Web sites with keywords that match those entered. After the search is finished, the search returns a list of the Web sites with matching keywords or phrases. The first sites listed in the Web site queue contain the most relevant matches. Designers of Web sites often use a little chicanery to vault their sites to the top of the list. One technique is to repeat different variations of the keyword in both the keyword and description Meta tags, as well as in the first few lines of text on the site's home page. The results of a search using the Lycos search engine are shown next.

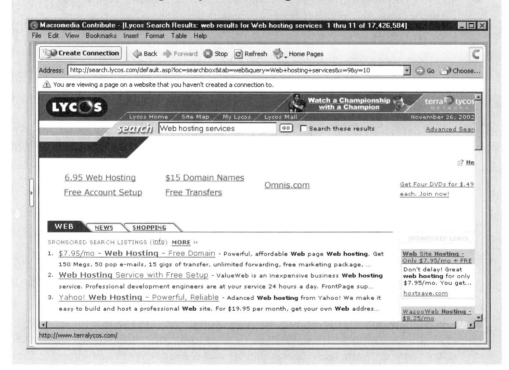

Tutorial: Creating a Calendar of Events

If the company or organization you edit Web pages for decides to make a calendar of events available for Web site visitors, you can easily create one using a Contribute preset. Another practical use for a calendar of events is on a corporate Intranet. When you create a calendar of events and update it every month, visitors will return to the Web site to view the latest information. To create a calendar of events, follow these steps:

1. Navigate to the page that you want to contain the link to your calendar of events.

2. Click the Edit Page button. Contribute creates a draft of the page.

3. Create the link using one of the techniques outlined in the "Creating a Web Page While Creating a Link" section of this chapter. The Insert Link dialog box (Figure 5-2) appears.

4. In the Create New Web Page From field, choose Sample Web Pages | Calendars, and then select the proper month and year from the pop-up menu.

5. If necessary, enter a title for the text link.

6. In the New Page Title field, enter a title for the new page, and then click OK. Contribute creates a copy of the calendar, as shown in Figure 5-6. Notice that the month is neatly laid out into little boxes. This is a good example of an HTML table at work. The individual boxes are table cells.

7. Click anywhere above the month and type a title for the calendar.

8. Select the text, click the triangle to the right of Normal, and then choose Heading 1. Contribute formats the text using a preset HTML style.

9. Click the Center button to align the text to the center of the page. This button looks just like the Center button in your favorite word processing application. Consider this your introduction to text editing in Contribute. You'll learn everything you need to know about editing text in Contribute in Chapter 6.

10. Click inside any of the date boxes and enter some text. Notice that if you type only a single word, the text is aligned to the center of the table. If you enter more text, the table cell expands, and the text eventually wraps to the next line.

11. Continue entering text for different dates. When you finish, you'll find that some text is aligned to the top of the cell and other text is aligned to the center of the cell. You can change the text alignment by right-clicking and choosing Table Cell Properties from the context menu to open the Table Properties dialog box. Click the triangle to the right of the Vertical field, and then choose Top.

This is just a small example of what you can do with the Contribute preset templates. It's also your first introduction to working with a table. You could have just as easily put a thumbnail image in a table cell instead of text. In Chapter 8,

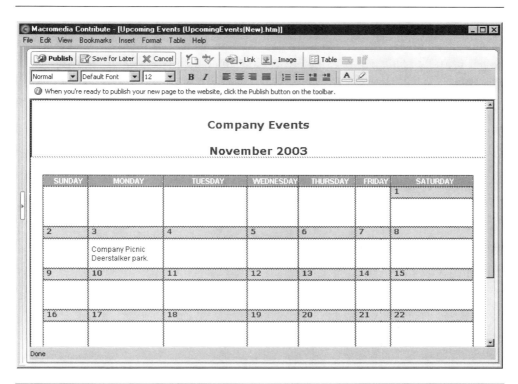

FIGURE 5-6   You can create a calendar of events by using one of the calendar presets.

you'll learn how to create your own tables and edit tables like the one in this preset. The Contribute sidebar has been hidden in this screenshot so that you may view the entire template.

Testing New Web Pages

As you create a Web page, you can see how the page looks within the Contribute editing environment. However, when you view a page in Edit mode, you see markers for invisible anchors, borders around images, borders around cells, and other visual editing aids that will not be seen when the page is displayed in a browser. The only way to properly preview a page is to preview it in a browser. You can preview a page you are creating in your system's default browser by choosing File | Preview In Browser or by pressing F12.

Summary

In this chapter, you learned to create new Web pages by creating copies of existing pages, creating blank pages, using preset Contribute templates, and using templates created by your Web designer. You learned to create new pages and links at the same time and to create new pages that will be linked after the page is published. You also learned to add keywords and descriptions to Web pages you are creating or editing. After you create a new Web page, you publish it to your Web site. Publishing Web pages is covered in Chapter 13. In the next chapter, you'll learn to create and edit text within the Web pages you edit.

Chapter 6

Working with Text

How to...

- Add text to a page

- Format text

- Create lists

- Spell check your work

- Find and replace text

- Work with styles

It's rare to find a Web page without text. The Web pages you edit with Contribute are probably no exception. When you edit text with Contribute, you'll be happy to know that the Contribute text-editing features and tools are similar to those you find in your favorite word processing software. When you format text in pages you edit, Contribute modifies the HTML code to display the text properly in a Web browser. When you create text in Contribute, you can format the text using any of the preset HTML styles or styles created by your Web designer using a Cascading Style Sheet (CSS). You can also add bullet lists, special characters, and symbols such as the copyright symbol to your Web pages.

In this chapter, you'll learn to add text to your Web pages, format and edit text in your Web pages, and more. You'll learn to work with preset HTML styles and any styles that your Web designer or site administrator may have made available through a CSS. You'll learn to spell check your work and use Contribute's powerful Find and Replace feature.

Adding Text to a Web Page

When you need to add text to a page you are editing, you simply click inside the document window and begin typing. Or if you prefer, you can drag and drop text from another application into the HTML document you are editing.

To add text to a Web page you are editing, do one of the following:

- Place your cursor where you want to insert the text and begin typing.

- Select a block of text in another application, then drag it into Contribute and drop it at the point where you want the text to appear.

 *When you drag and drop text from another application into Contribute, the formatting from the native application is preserved, and you may not be able to change this formatting in Contribute.*

■ Select a block of text in another application, then use the application's Copy command to copy the selected text to the clipboard. In Contribute, place your cursor where you want the text to appear, then choose Edit | Paste.

Typing within the Web page is the most direct method for adding text to a Web page. As you type, the text appears within the Web page, as shown in Figure 6-1. If you are typing inside a table cell that is formatted to a specific width, the text wraps to the next line when you reach the table cell border. When you're typing inside a cell, press ENTER to create a new paragraph. For more information on working with tables, see Chapter 8.

If you have images in the same area as text, you can flow the text around images. When you enter text beside an image that is already in the Web page, the

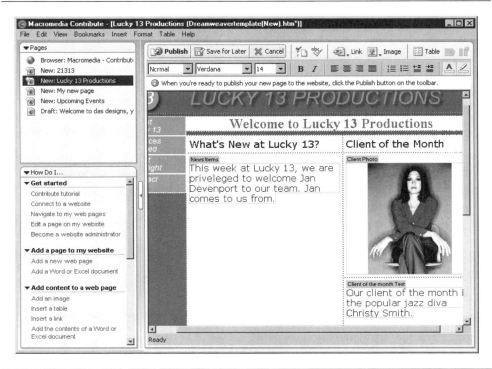

FIGURE 6-1   You can add text by typing directly in a page draft.

text appears at the bottom of the image. However, you can change this so that the text appears at the top of the image and to the left or right of the image. When you create a new line by pressing ENTER, or the text wraps to a new line when the end of a table cell is reached, the text flows around the image. You can specify the distance the text appears from an image, as well as which side the text appears on, by changing the image's properties. For more information on changing image properties, refer to Chapter 10.

Adding the Date to a Page

If you update your Web pages on a regular basis, it's a good idea to add the revision date to the page. This shows viewers that the content is up-to-date. To add the current date to a page, follow these steps:

1. Place your cursor where you want the date inserted. You may want to precede the date with other text, such as "Revised on."

2. Choose Insert | Date. The Insert Date dialog box appears, as shown next.

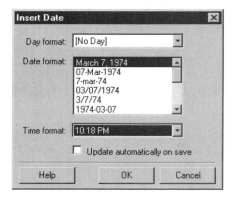

3. Click the triangle to the right of the Day Format field, and choose an option from the pop-up menu. The default option doesn't display the day; however, you can choose to display the day and select the formatting.

4. Click the triangle to the right of the Date Format field and choose one of the options from the pop-up menu.

5. Click the triangle to the right of the Time Format field and choose an option from the pop-up menu. The default option doesn't display the time. If you choose to display the time, you can choose the manner in which it is formatted.

6. Click the Update Automatically On Save check box to add the current date to the document each time it is saved.

NOTE   *If you need a Web page to display the date and time it is viewed, this requires JavaScript, which cannot be created or edited from within Contribute. If you need this feature on a page you are creating or editing, contact your site administrator or Web designer.*

Adding Special Text Characters

When you create text in Contribute, you can add special characters such as the copyright symbol (©) or an Em Dash (—) to a page draft. You can choose a character from a menu list or from within a dialog box. To add a special character to a page you are editing:

1. Place your cursor where you want the special character to appear in the draft that you are editing.

2. Choose Insert | Special Characters, then do one of the following:

- Choose a special character from the submenu.

- Choose Other, then choose a character from the Insert Other Character dialog box, as shown next. Click the character you want to insert, then click OK.

Contribute inserts the character in your page draft.

Formatting Text

When you create text for a Web page, you can format it. You can select a block of text and apply formatting to it, or choose formatting options that you want applied to the next block of text that you type. Using menu commands or the text tools shown in Figure 6-2, you can perform the following formatting tasks:

- Choose a font style.
- Choose a font type.
- Apply a style to text.
- Choose text alignment.
- Indent text.
- Choose a font color.

Applying a Style to Text

You can apply any HTML style to text or choose a style that your Web site designer or site administrator has made available by linking a CSS to the document. The default style for text you create is Normal. You can draw viewer attention to text by applying a style to it. As a rule, you generally apply one of the Heading styles (for example, Heading 1, Heading 2, and so on) to text that headlines a particular section of a Web page; there are other styles that you can apply to entire paragraphs of text.

> **NOTE** *If your Web site administrator has disabled HTML styles for your user group, those styles will not be listed on the Style menu.*

If your Web site designer has created styles using a CSS and your Web site administrator has enabled these styles for your user group, they will appear on the Style menu. If you are not sure of the purpose of a style from a CSS, contact your site administrator or Web designer.

> **NOTE** *Cascading Style Sheets cannot be linked to an HTML document from within Contribute. If you have ideas for styling text, or would like a CSS attached to new pages that you create, contact your Web site administrator.*

Style menu   Font size menu   Italic   Center ———   Right   Numbered list

Font menu   Bold   Left ———   Justify   Bulleted list

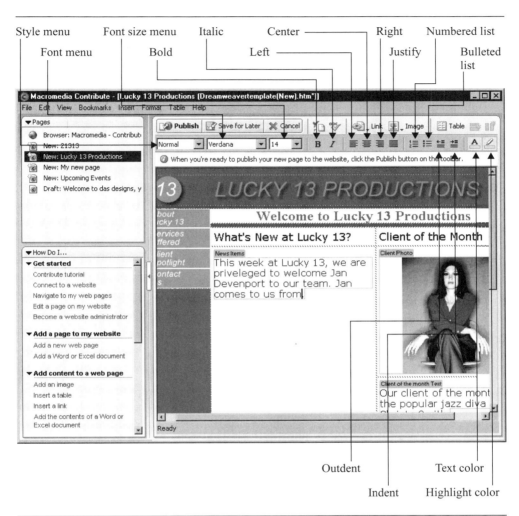

Outdent   Text color

Indent   Highlight color

FIGURE 6-2   You can format Web page text using these tools.

To apply a style to text:

1.   Select the text that you want to format or click within a paragraph to apply a style to the entire paragraph.

2.   Do one of the following:

■   Choose Format | Style and select a style from the submenu.

■ Click the triangle to the right of the Style field in the toolbar and select a style from the pop-up menu.

The style you select is applied to selected text.

Alternatively, you can choose the style before typing, and the style will be applied to all the text you type until you select a different style.

 If you select a single word and select one of the HTML styles such as Heading 1 or paragraph, the style will be applied to the entire paragraph, even if you have selected only a word or sentence from within the paragraph.

Changing or Removing a Style

After you apply a style to text and then preview the page in a Web browser, you may decide to change to a different style or remove the style entirely.

To change a text style, follow these steps:

1. In your page draft, select the text whose style you want to change, or place your cursor within the block of text.

2. Do one of the following:

   ■ Choose Format | Style, then choose the desired style from the submenu.

   ■ Click the triangle to the right of the Style field in the toolbar and choose the desired style from the pop-up menu.

   The new style is applied to the selected text.

 If you use one of the preset HTML styles such as Heading 1 to restyle text, the preset style is applied to the entire paragraph, even if you select only a word or sentence from within the paragraph.

To remove a style from text, follow these steps:

1. In your page draft, select the text whose style you want to change, or place your cursor within the block of text.

2. Select the style by doing one of the following:

   ■ Choose Format | Style | Normal.

■ Click the triangle to the right of the Style field in the toolbar and
   choose Normal from the pop-up menu.

The style is removed from the selected text.

*If you are a Web designer or site administrator and you create Cascading
Style Sheets for your Contribute sites, choose style names that can be
easily understood by members of user groups editing your pages who may
not understand HTML terminology.*

Changing Font Size and Type

When you create or edit text within a page draft, you can change the font size and type
to accent a single word or a line of text. You will only be able to choose a font size
from the pop-up menu. You cannot manually enter a different size in the Font field.

    To change the font size, follow these steps:

1. In your page draft, select the word or sentence to which you want to apply
   a different font size. The selected text is highlighted. (Note that you must
   manually select the text. You cannot place your cursor within a paragraph
   of text to change the font size.)

2. Select the text size by doing one of the following:

   ■ Choose Format | Size, then choose one of the presets from the submenu.

   ■ Click the triangle to the right of the Font Size field in the toolbar and
      choose one of the presets from the pop-up menu.

   The selected text is changed to the desired size.

    The font types available on the Contribute menus are common fonts that can be
rendered by most popular Web browsers. You can change the font type by following
these steps:

1. In the page draft, select the text whose font type you want to change. You can
   select a single letter, word, or paragraph. The selected text is highlighted.

2. To select a different font style, do one of the following:

   ■ Choose Format | Font, then choose the desired font from the submenu.

   ■ Click the triangle to the right of the Font field and choose the desired
      font type from the pop-up menu.

The selected text is changed to the desired font style.

Understanding Cascading Style Sheets

A Cascading Style Sheet (CSS) is used to modify preset HTML styles and create custom styles for Web pages. Cascading Style Sheets can be external and linked to an HTML document, or they can be embedded in the Head section of the HTML document. A Web designer can create a CSS that eliminates underlining of text hyperlinks. When modifying an HTML style or creating a custom style with a CSS, a Web designer can specify the font size, font style, font color, and more to create a custom look for a Web design.

NOTE   *The font size and font type menus are not available if your site administrator has disabled the ability to change font size or type for your user group.*

Modifying the Fonts List

If your Web site administrator has enabled changing font styles for your user group, you can edit the font list. When you edit the font list, you can delete font styles or add other font styles to the list.

To delete fonts from the font list, follow these steps:

1. Select a page draft. You must be in Edit mode to modify the font list; you cannot modify the font list while using Contribute as a Web browser (that is, while you are in Browse mode).

2. Choose Format | Font | Edit Font List. Alternatively, you can click the triangle to the right of the Font field in the toolbar and choose Edit Font List from the pop-up menu. Choose either method and Contribute will display the Edit Font List dialog box shown next. The fonts in the Font List window are the preset fonts and any fonts you've previously added to the list.

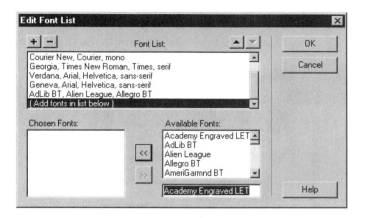

3. In the font list, select a font group to delete. Contribute displays the fonts from that font group in the Chosen Fonts window. You cannot add additional font groups to the Chosen Fonts window; you can only delete one group of fonts at a time.

4. To delete the chosen fonts, click the button that looks like a minus sign (–). The fonts are removed from the font list.

5. Click OK to close the Edit Font List dialog box.

You can also add fonts to the font list. You can add any font that is installed on your computer to the list. To add fonts to the font list, follow these steps:

1. Select a page draft. You can only edit the font list while working in Edit mode.

2. Choose Format | Font | Edit Font List. Alternatively, you can click the triangle to the right of the Font field in the toolbar and choose Edit Font List from the pop-up menu. Contribute opens the Edit Font Dialog box just shown. The Available Fonts window displays the fonts currently installed on your system. If the number of available fonts exceeds the height of the window, a scroll bar appears on the window's right border.

3. Click a font to select it.

4. Double click the selected font, or click the button with two arrows. The font is added to the Chosen Fonts list. Note that you can only add one font at a time.

5. Select additional fonts that you want to add to the list. As you add each font, they appear as part of a group in the Font List window, as shown next.

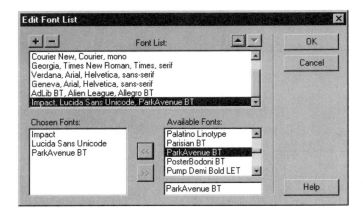

6. Click the plus sign (+) to add the new group to the font list.

7. Click OK to close the Edit Font List dialog box.

When you add a group of fonts to the font list, the first font in the group takes precedence over the succeeding fonts. When you format text using the first font in a group, the user's browser attempts to render that font. If the font is not available on the user's system, the browser attempts to render the second font in the list and so on. For example, if you format text using the Verdana font, Contribute adds the following tag to the underlying HTML:

```
<font face="Verdana, Arial, Helvetica, sans-serif">
```

When the HTML page is displayed in a user's browser, the browser attempts to render the text using the Verdana font, falling back to the succeeding fonts if the user does not have the Verdana font installed. The final fallback, sans-serif, uses the default sans-serif fault from the user's system to display the text.

 *When you add fonts from your system to the list, you run the risk of using a font that will not render properly in a user's browser. In this regard, refrain from using any highly stylized fonts, such as the ones that look like handwriting or graffiti. When you do add a group of fonts to the font list, be sure to add sans or sans-serif as the last font in the group.*

About HTML Styles

When you choose an HTML style from the Contribute menu, the tags in the HTML document are automatically created. There is a tag that tells a Web browser when to begin displaying the style and when to stop displaying it. If you format text using the Heading 1 tag, the resulting HTML code looks like this:

```
<h1>About Us</h1>
```

6

Modifying Font Color and Highlight Color

The default color for text in the pages you edit is determined by the page's properties. The color of a font may also be determined with a Cascading Style Sheet. You can change the text color and the text highlight color by using a menu command or by clicking a button from the toolbar.

To modify text color, follow these steps:

1. Select the page draft that contains the text you want to edit.

2. Select the text whose color you want to change.

3. To change the text color, do one of the following:

   ■ Choose Format | Text Color.

   ■ Click the Text Color button in the text section of the toolbar.

   Choosing either method opens the pop-up color palette shown next. The colors on this palette are Web-safe colors, which means they will look the same in all popular browsers using the Windows or Macintosh operating system.

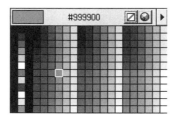

4. Drag your cursor over the color swatches. Your cursor becomes an eyedropper. As you drag over the swatches, the color window in the palette's upper-left window changes to display the color your cursor is currently over.

5. Release the mouse button to select a color. Contribute applies the specified color to the selected text.

TIP   *When you change font color, you can match an existing color on the Web page. When your cursor becomes an eyedropper, drag it over the item on the Web page (an image or photograph) that contains the color to which you want to change the text. Click the mouse button when your cursor is over the desired color and Contribute changes the text color to match.*

Text in a Web page is displayed over the background color of the page or over a background image. You can draw attention to text by applying a highlight color. Applying a highlight color to text is the equivalent of using a highlight marker on printed text in a book. To apply a highlight color to text, follow these steps:

1. Select the page draft that contains the text you want to edit.

2. Select the text to which you want to apply a highlight color.

3. To select the highlight color, do one of the following:

    ■ Choose Format | Highlight Color.

    ■ Click the Highlight Color button in the text section of the toolbar.

    Choosing either method opens the pop-up color palette just shown.

4. Drag your cursor over the color swatches. Your cursor becomes an eyedropper. As you drag over the swatches, the color window in the palette's upper-left window changes to display the color your cursor is currently over.

5. Release the mouse button to select a color. Contribute highlights the selected text with the specified color.

Aligning Text

When you type text in a Web page you are editing, the default alignment is to the left margin of the document or table cell to which you are adding the text. You can choose one of the following alignment options: Left, Center, Right, or Justify. You can change the alignment of text by doing one of the following:

1. Place your cursor inside the text you want to align. Alternatively, you can select several lines or paragraphs of text. If you select a single line within a paragraph, the entire paragraph is reformatted.

2. To align the text, do one of the following:

   ■ Choose Format | Align, then choose one of the options from the submenu.

   ■ Click the desired alignment button in the toolbar.

   Contribute changes the alignment of the selected text.

Creating Lists

6

When you create text for your Web pages in Contribute, you can organize information into lists. This option works similarly to creating lists using your word processing software. You can create the following types of lists for your Web pages:

■ **Numbered list**   Each item in the list is preceded by a number.

■ **Bulleted list**   Each item in the list is preceded by a bullet icon.

■ **Definition list**   Each item in the list is followed by a definition of the item. The definition is indented. A definition list could be used to list company officers, followed by brief descriptions of the officers' duties or contact information.

■ **Sublists**   Each item in the list is preceded by a number or bullet. Items in the sublist are indented and preceded by a number or by a bullet icon.

Creating a Numbered List

You can organize information by creating a numbered list. You can use a numbered list to display instructions that must be carried out in a specific order on a Web page. To create a numbered list, follow these steps:

1. Select the page draft to which you want to add the numbered list.

2. Place your cursor where you want the list to appear.

3. To format the text you type as a numbered list, do one of the following:

   ■ Choose Format | List | Numbered List.

- Click the Numbered List button in the text section of the toolbar, shown previously in Figure 6-2.

After doing either of the preceding, Contribute inserts a 1 followed by a period.

4. Type the text that will appear as the first item in the numbered list.

5. Press ENTER. Contribute adds the next number to the list. Continue adding items to list by pressing ENTER to create a new item.

6. When your list is complete, you can disable numbering by doing one of the following:

- Press ENTER twice.

- Press ENTER, then press the Numbered List button on the toolbar.

You can also create a numbered list from existing text in a Web page you are editing. When you create a numbered list in this manner, Contribute creates a new list, making separate items for each line of selected text. If the selected text is a paragraph or a series of paragraphs, Contribute creates a separate item for each paragraph. To create a numbered list from existing text, follow these steps:

1. Select the text that you want to reformat into a numbered list.

2. To create the numbered list, do one of the following:

- Choose Format | List | Numbered List.

- Click the Numbered List button in the toolbar.

Creating a Bulleted List

Another way to organize information on a Web page is with a bulleted list. You can use a bulleted list to display information about individual products, followed by a brief product description. You can create a bulleted list as you enter information or convert existing text to a bulleted list. To create a bulleted list, follow these steps:

1. Select the page draft to which you want to add the bulleted list.

2. Place your cursor where you want the list inserted.

3. To create the bulleted list, do one of the following:

- Choose Format | List| Bulleted List.

- Click the Bulleted List button in the toolbar.

4. Begin typing the first line of information in your list.

5. Press ENTER, then type the next list item.

6. Repeat steps 4 and 5 as necessary to add other information to the list.

7. When you finish adding items to the list, do one of the following to disable bullets:

   ■ Press ENTER twice.

   ■ Press ENTER, then press the Bulleted List button in the toolbar.

You can also create a bulleted list using existing text in a page draft you are editing. When you create a bulleted list in this manner, Contribute creates a new bullet for each new line. If you select paragraph text, Contribute creates a bullet for each paragraph. To convert existing text to a bulleted list, follow these steps:

1. Select the page draft that contains the text you want to convert to a bulleted list.

2. Select the text that you want to convert to a bullet list.

3. To convert the text to a bullet list, do one of the following:

   ■ Choose Format | List | Bulleted List.

   ■ Click the Bulleted List button in the toolbar.

Creating a Definition List

You can create a definition list to organize information on a Web page. When you create a definition list, each list item is a word or phrase on a single line (or multiple lines if the list item wraps to a new line), and the definition is indented on a new line. You can create a definition list from scratch or by selecting existing text and then converting it to a definition list. To create a definition list, follow these steps:

1. Select the page draft to which you want to add the definition list.

2. Place your cursor at the point in the document where you want to insert the list.

3. To create the definition list, Choose Format | List | Definition List.

4. Type the first item in the list.

5. Press ENTER. Contribute indents the next line of text.

6

6. Type a definition for the item.

7. Press ENTER. Contribute outdents the next line of text.

8. Continue entering items as needed.

9. When you're finished entering information for the list, do one of the following to finish the list:

    ■ Press ENTER twice.

    ■ Press ENTER, then choose Format | List | Definition List.

You can also create a definition list from existing text within a document you are editing. When you select several lines of text and convert them to a definition list, the first line of text is the item, the second line of text is the indented definition, and so on. To convert text to a definition list, follow these steps:

1. Select the page draft that contains the text you want to convert to a definition list.

2. Select several lines of text that you want to convert to a definition list.

3. Choose Format | List | Definition List.

TIP   *If you create a list and want to convert the list to a different type, select the list, choose Format | List, and then from the submenu, choose the type of list you want to convert the existing list to. Alternatively, you can click the desired list button (Numbered or Bulleted) in the toolbar.*

Creating a Sublist

When you need to display Web page data in list format, and items within the list have several options, you can create a sublist that displays additional information for the item. For example, you can nest a bulleted list within a numbered list. When you create a sublist, it is indented below the item from the parent list, as shown in Figure 6-3. To create a sublist for an existing list item, follow these steps:

1. Place your cursor at the end of the current list item for which you want to create a sublist.

2. Press ENTER. Contribute creates a new list item using the current list's style.

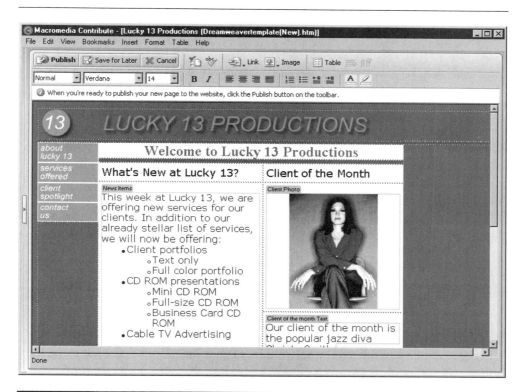

FIGURE 6-3 You can create a sublist for an existing list item.

3. To create the sublist, do one of the following:

- Choose Format | Indent.

- Click the Indent button in the toolbar.

- Press TAB.

After doing either of the preceding, Contribute indents the list and uses the default parent list style for the sublist.

4. Type the information for the first item in the sublist.

5. Press ENTER. Contribute creates an indented line for the next list item.

6. Continue adding items to the sublist.

7. To return to the parent list, do one of the following:

- Choose Format | Outdent.

- Click the Outdent button in the text section of the toolbar.

You can nest additional sublists within a list by placing your cursor to the right of a sublist item and then following steps 5–7 from the preceding instructions.

When you create a sublist, Contribute uses the default formatting style from the parent list. For example, if you create a sublist from bulleted list, the bullets in the sublist are hollow dots. You can change the sublist to a different type by doing the following:

1. Select the items in the sublist.

2. To reformat the sublist, do one of the following:

- Click the desired list button in the toolbar.

- Choose Format | List, then select the desired list type from the submenu.

Changing List Properties

When you create a numbered or bulleted list, Contribute formats the list using the default settings for the list type you choose. You can, however, change these properties to suit your preference or to suit the Web page you are editing. To change the properties of a list in a Web page you are editing, follow these steps:

1. Place your cursor inside the list whose properties you want to change.

2. To reformat the list, do one of the following:

- Choose Format | List | Properties.

- Right-click (Windows), then choose List | Properties from the context menu.

The List Properties dialog box shown next appears.

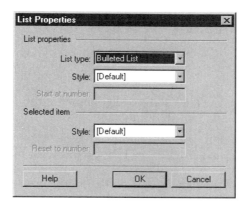

3. In the List Properties section of the dialog box, you can set the following parameters:

- **List type** Select the desired list type from the pop-up menu. You can choose from Numbered, Bulleted, Directory, or Menu. The remaining options vary depending on the type of list you select.

- **Style** This determines the style for numbers or bullets in a numbered or bulleted list. Note that this determines the default style for the entire list unless you choose a different style for individual items in a list.

- **Start at number** Enter the number with which you want a numbered list to begin.

4. Click OK. The List Properties dialog box closes, and your changes are applied to the list.

This option is also useful when you want to change the style for a sublist. For example, if the parent list is a number list, the sublist adopts the style of the parent list. By placing your cursor inside the sublist, you can then choose a different style, such as roman numerals or letters.

NOTE   *If the list style for the page you are editing was defined using a Cascading Style Sheet, you will not be able to edit it.*

You can also modify the style of an individual item in a list by following these steps:

1. Place your cursor within the list item whose style you want to change.

2. To reformat the selected list item, do one of the following:

   ■ Choose Format | List | Properties.

   ■ Right-click, then choose List | Properties from the context menu.

   The List Properties dialog box just shown appears.

3. In the Selected Item section, you can modify the following parameters:

   ■ **Style**   Select a style from the pop-up menu. Note that the list type determines the styles you can choose from.

   ■ **Reset to number**   Enter the value to which you want the list item changed. This option is not available for a bulleted list. If there are additional list items after the selected item, they will be renumbered appropriately.

4. Click OK. The List Properties dialog box closes, and the selected item is updated to reflect your changes.

Spell Checking the Document

There's nothing more embarrassing or unprofessional than a Web page with spelling errors. But spelling errors can happen easily when you're whizzing along, typing frantically to finish page revisions before your deadline. Fortunately, there's a spell checker built into Contribute. You can spell check a page you are revising at any time by following these steps:

1. Click the Spell Check button, or choose Format | Check Spelling.

2. If Contribute finds a suspect word, the Check Spelling dialog box shown next appears. The suspect word is highlighted in the Word Not Found In Dictionary field. In the Suggestions field, Contribute displays a list of words that you can use to replace the suspect word.

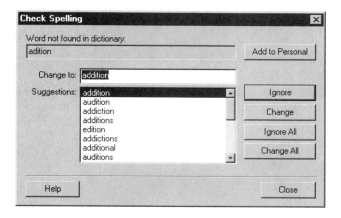

3. Click one of the following buttons to tell Contribute how you want the suspect word handled:

■ **Add to Personal**   Adds the suspect word to your personal dictionary. When Contribute encounters the word again, it will no longer flag it as misspelled.

■ **Ignore**   Ignores the current instance of the suspect word.

■ **Change**   Replaces the suspect word with a word you enter in the Change To field or a word you choose from the Suggestions list.

■ **Ignore All**   Ignores the current instance and all future instances of the suspect word.

■ **Change All**   Replaces the current instance and all future instances of the suspect word with a word you enter in the Change To field or one that you select from the Suggestions list.

After you choose an option, Contribute continues searching the document for misspelled words. After the spell check is complete, Contribute displays an information dialog box telling you the spell check is completed. This dialog box is also displayed even if Contribute finds no spelling errors.

4. Click OK to close the dialog box.

NOTE

If you are editing multiple versions of a Web site that are published in different languages, you can change to a different spelling dictionary by choosing Edit | Preferences and then choosing a different dictionary from the Spelling Dictionary pop-up menu in the General section of the Preferences dialog box. You cannot have more than one dictionary active at the same time. If a page you are editing contains more than one language, spell check the document using one dictionary, then change preferences to the second language in the document and spell check the document again.

Finding and Replacing Text

When editing a page draft, you can search for specific text. You can also search for text and replace it with other text. You can search for a single word or a selection of words. To search for text within a page you are editing, follow these steps:

1. Choose Edit | Find. The Find and Replace dialog box appears, as shown next.

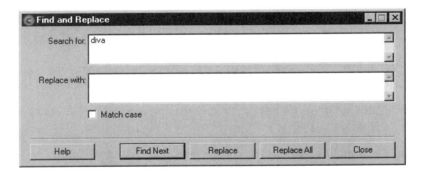

2. Enter a word or phrase in the Search For field. Note that when you enter a phrase, Contribute finds instances of the phrase if the words are next to each other in the document and in the order that you enter them.

3. Click the Match Case check box if you want Contribute to search for the word or phrase only if it matches the case you entered in the Search For field.

4. Click Find Next. Contribute returns the first instance of the word or phrase you entered in the Search For field.

5. Repeat step 4 as necessary to find other instances of the word or phrase in the document.

6. Click Close when you have finished searching the document.

When you search a page draft for words, you can replace the word or words Contribute finds. To find and replace words in a page you are editing, follow these steps:

1. Choose Edit | Find. The Find and Replace dialog box just shown appears.

2. Enter a word or phrase in the Search For field. Note that when you enter a phrase, Contribute finds instances of the phrase if the words are next to each other in the document and in the order that you entered them.

3. Enter a word or phrase in the Replace With field.

4. Click the Match Case check box if you want Contribute to search for the word or phrase only if it matches the case you entered in the Search For field.

5. Click Find Next. Contribute finds the next instance of the specified text in the document.

6. For each instance of your search, click one of the following buttons:

   ■ **Find Next**   Searches for the next instance of the word or phrase

   ■ **Replace**   Replaces the current instance with the replacement text

   Alternatively, you can click Replace All to replace the current and all future instances of your search with the replacement text.

TIP   *You can quickly replace all instances of your search with the replacement text by skipping step 5 and clicking Replace All immediately after entering the replacement text.*

7. After you have finished searching for and replacing text in the page draft, click Close.

CAUTION   *The Contribute Find and Replace dialog box does not provide the option to search for whole words only. This may cause problems if you find and replace a word like "test" with "quiz." If Contribute finds the word you are searching for as part of another word, it will replace it. If you use the Replace All option, Contribute will change the word "testament" to "quizament." To prevent this from happening, leave a space after the word in the Search For field.*

Summary

In this chapter, you learned to use Contribute's text-editing tools to modify text within a Web page or to format new text within a Web page. You learned how to apply preset HTML styles to the text and how to apply styles from a Cascading Style Sheet. You also learned how to spell check the Web page and change text and highlight colors. In the next chapter, you'll learn to create links (also known as hyperlinks) using text or an image as the active element for the link.

Part III

Working with Hyperlinks, Tables, and Frames

Chapter 7

Creating and Editing Hyperlinks

How to...

- Create text links
- Create image links
- Link to an existing page
- Link to a computer file
- Link to an external Web page

When your Web site was created, your site designer created links that viewers use to navigate to different pages within the site and to external Web pages. The links can take the form of text links or images. Your site designer may have created a navigation bar for your site containing text or a series of images that link to other Web pages. The navigation bar is usually positioned below the site header or on the left side of the Web page.

No matter what method of navigation your site designer used, when you edit pages and create new ones, you will inevitably need to create links. You'll create links to new pages, existing pages, or Web site files using text or images. When viewers run their mouse over a link (also known as a *hyperlink*), the familiar pointing hand icon appears, indicating that something will happen when the link is clicked. In this chapter, you'll learn to create text links and image links. You'll see how to modify the links to control whether the linked pages or documents open in the existing browser window or in a new one. You'll also find out how to create links that when clicked open the default e-mail application on the user's computer; and finally, you learn how to edit and test your links.

Creating Text and Image Links

When you create a text link, you can select a word or phrase to be the active area for the link. When you create a text link, it is underlined in most Web browsers; however, your Web designer or site administrator may have linked a Cascading Style Sheet to the pages in your site that causes text links to be displayed without underlines.

You can also use an image as the basis for a link. When users pass their mouse over either a text link or an image link, the familiar pointing hand icon appears, indicating that clicking the link will display another Web page in the user's browser. You can use text or an image as the basis for a link to any of the following:

- A page draft you are editing or a page you have recently published

- A new Web page that Contribute creates when you create a link to a page draft

- An existing Web page at the site you are editing or at an external site

- An individual's e-mail address

- An existing file on your computer

When you create a link, the link is not functional until you publish the page. You can, however, test the link prior to publishing the page to make sure it links to the proper page or file. You'll learn how to link images and text to specific files or pages in the upcoming sections.

Creating a Link to a Draft or Recently Published Page

You can create links to drafts of pages you are currently working on or to recently published pages. Contribute keeps a record of all your page drafts and recently published pages. To create a link to a page draft or recently published page, follow these steps:

1. Select the page draft that will contain the link.

2. To specify the point where the link appears in the document, do one of the following:

- Place your cursor where you want the link to appear.

- Select the desired text in the page draft.

- Select an image.

3. To open the Insert Link dialog box shown in Figure 7-1, do one of the following:

- Click the Link button in the toolbar and choose Drafts And Recent Pages from the pop-up menu.

- Choose Insert | Link | Drafts And Recent Pages.

- Right-click and choose Insert Link from the context menu. When you open the Insert Link dialog box in this manner, you may have to click the Drafts And Recent Pages button when the dialog box opens.

4. If, in step 2, you placed your cursor where you want the link to appear, the Link Text field will appear in the dialog box. Enter a name for the link in this field. The text you enter appears at the point of insertion after you exit the dialog box.

5. From the Select A Page To Link To list, select the desired page draft or recently published page.

6. Click the Advanced button to set the desired options for the link. For more information on advanced options, refer to the section "Using Advanced Link Options" later in this chapter.

7. Click OK. The link is added to your page draft or published page.

NOTE *You can also create a link and a new page at the same time. This option is useful when you're editing a page and you need to link pages you have not yet created. For more information on creating a new page while creating a link, see Chapter 5.*

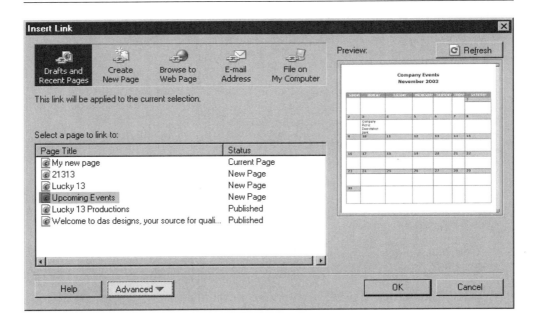

FIGURE 7-1 You can create a link to a page draft or to a recently published page.

Creating a Link to an Existing Page

You can create a link to an existing page within the Web site you are editing or to an external Web site. This is the method you should choose if the page to which you need to link is not a page draft and has not been recently published. To create a link to an existing page, follow these steps:

1. Select the page draft that you want to link to another Web page.

2. To position the link, do one of the following:

   ■ Place your cursor where you want the link to appear.

   ■ Select the desired text in the page draft.

   ■ Select the desired image in the page draft.

3. To open the Insert Link dialog box shown next, do one of the following:

   ■ Click the Link button in the toolbar and choose Browse To Web Page from the pop-up menu.

   ■ Choose Insert | Link | Browse To Web Page.

   ■ Right-click and choose Insert Link from the context menu. When you open the Insert Link dialog box in this manner, you may have to click the Browse To Web Page button when the dialog box opens.

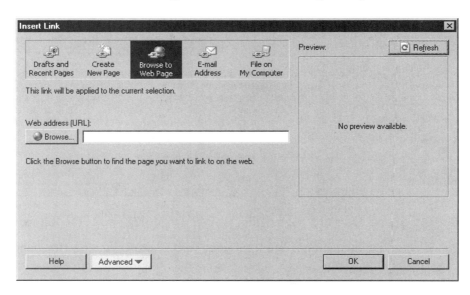

4. If, in step 2, you placed your cursor where you want the link to appear, the Link Text field will appear in the dialog box. Enter a name for the link in this field. The text you enter appears at the point of insertion after you exit the dialog box.

5. Click the Browse button next to the Web Address (URL) field. Alternatively, if you know the Web address (the uniform resource locator, or URL) of the Web page to which you want to link, you can manually enter it in the Web Address (URL) field. If you click the Browse button, the Browse To Link dialog box opens with the home page from your site selected, as shown next. In essence, this dialog box is like a mini–Web browser.

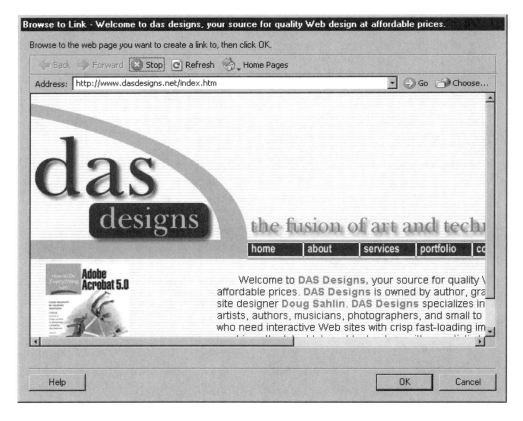

6. You can navigate to a page within your site by doing one of the following:

   ■ Use the navigation menu from your Web site to navigate to the page to which you want to link.

■ Click the Choose button, then choose a file from your Web site's directory.

■ Click the Home Pages button to choose the home page of another site you are editing, then use the site's navigation menu to navigate to the desired page.

■ In the Address window, enter the URL of the home page of a Web site you are not editing, then use that site's navigation menu to select the page to which you want to link.

After you navigate to the desired page, or enter a URL in the Address Window, a preview of the selected page appears.

7. Click OK to close the Browse To Link dialog box. Contribute enters the URL you selected in the Web Address (URL) field.

8. Click the Advanced button to set the desired options for the link. For more information on advanced options, refer to the section "Using Advanced Link Options" later in this chapter.

9. Click OK. The link is added to your page draft.

Creating a Link to a Computer File

You can also create a link to a file on your computer or network. You can create a link to any file that will be recognized by a Web browser, such as a Microsoft Word file, an Adobe Acrobat PDF file, or a JPEG image file. When you create a link in this manner, Contribute copies the file from your computer to your Web site when you publish the page draft. The link will be to the copy of the file Contribute created, not to the file stored on your computer or network. To create a link to a computer file, follow these steps:

1. Select the page draft to which you want to add the link.

2. To position the link, do one of the following:

■ Place your cursor where you want the link to appear.

■ Select the desired text in the page draft.

■ Select the desired image in the page draft.

3. To open the Insert Link dialog box shown in Figure 7-2, do one of the following:

■ Click the Link button in the toolbar and choose File On My Computer from the pop-up menu.

■ Choose Insert | Link | File On My Computer.

■ Right-click and choose Insert Link from the context menu. When you open the Insert Link dialog box in this manner, you may have to click the File On My Computer button when the dialog box opens.

4. If, in step 2, you placed your cursor where you want the link to appear, the Link Text field will appear in the dialog box. Enter a name for the link in this field. The text you enter appears at the point of insertion after you exit the dialog box.

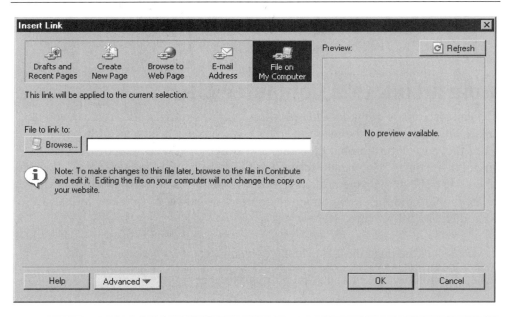

FIGURE 7-2   You can create a link to a file stored on your computer.

5. Click the Browse button in the File To Link To section. Contribute opens the Select File dialog box.

6. Navigate to the file you want to link to the Web page, then click OK to close the dialog box. Contribute inserts the filename in the File To Link To field.

7. Click the Advanced button to set the desired options for the link. For more information on advanced options, refer to the section "Using Advanced Link Options" later in this chapter.

8. Click OK. The link is added to your page draft.

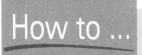

Create and Optimize PDF Documents for the Web

If you use Adobe Acrobat to publish documents in PDF format for your clients and fellow employees, you can also use these documents on your Web site. You can create PDF documents from Microsoft Word documents and other supported file types. You can link a PDF file to a Web page, and the document will be displayed in the user's browser when the link is clicked.

After you create a PDF document by publishing it from a Word document or by using the Acrobat Distiller to create the PDF file, open the file in Adobe Acrobat. Within Adobe Acrobat, you can create navigation to different pages in the document, and you can also create links to other PDF documents or other Web pages. After you finish editing the document in Acrobat, use the Save As command to save the file. When you use the Save As command, Acrobat optimizes the file for Web delivery. When the file is viewed in a Web browser, the file is loaded one page at a time. This allows the viewer to quickly see the first page of the document without having to wait for the entire document to download. For more information on Adobe Acrobat, consider purchasing *How to Do Everything with Adobe Acrobat 5.0* (Berkeley, CA: McGraw-Hill/ Osborne, 2001) by Doug Sahlin.

Creating a Link to an E-mail Address

You can also create a link to an e-mail address. This option makes it possible for viewers of your Web site to send information back to a designated individual's e-mail address. When users click an e-mail link, their default e-mail composition program opens with the e-mail address field already filled in. To create an e-mail link, follow these steps:

1. Select the page draft to which you want to add the e-mail link.

2. To position the link, do one of the following:

   ■ Place your cursor where you want the link to appear.

   ■ Select the desired text in the page draft.

   ■ Select the desired image in the page draft.

3. To open the Insert Link dialog box shown in Figure 7-3, do one of the following:

   ■ Click the Link button in the toolbar and choose E-mail Address from the pop-up menu.

   ■ Choose Insert | Link | E-mail Address.

   ■ Right-click and choose Insert Link from the context menu. When you open the Insert Link dialog box in this manner, you may have to click the E-mail Address button when the dialog box opens.

4. If, in step 2, you placed your cursor where you want the link to appear, the Link Text field will appear in the dialog box. Enter a name for the link in this field. The text you enter appears at the point of insertion after you exit the dialog box.

5. In the E-mail Address field, enter the e-mail address to which you want the user's e-mail sent (for example, joesmith@ourwebsite.com).

6. Click the Advanced button to set the desired options for the link. For more information on advanced options, refer to the next section, "Using Advanced Link Options."

7. Click OK. The link is added to your page draft.

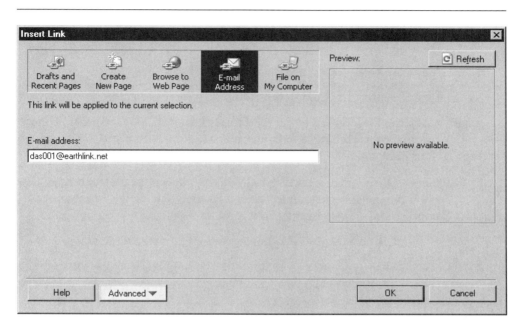

FIGURE 7-3   You can create a link that allows Web site viewers to send e-mail to a specified address.

Using Advanced Link Options

When you create a link, you have three advanced options that you can specify. In the upcoming sections, you'll learn to use these options to do the following:

- Edit URLs

- Specify the target window in which the linked page opens

- Create a link to a specific point in the page

Editing URL Links

If you're familiar with the Hypertext Markup Language (HTML), you can edit the URL of a link. When you browse to a Web page and select it for a link, Contribute writes the entire URL to the Web page, which includes the filename and extension of the Web page. If you're navigating to a site's home page, you usually don't need the filename and extension of the Web page, just the site's domain name. To edit a URL, follow these steps:

1. In a page draft you are editing, select a link.

2. To open the Insert Link dialog box, do one of the following:

   - Click the Link button in the toolbar, and from the pop-up menu, choose the type of page that the link opens. For example, if the link opens a page draft or a page you recently published, choose Drafts And Recent Pages.

   - Choose Insert | Link, and from the submenu, choose the page type the link opens. For example, if the link opens the viewer's e-mail application, choose Insert | Link | E-mail Address.

   - Right-click and choose Link Properties from the context menu.

3. Click the Advanced button to expand the dialog box if it is not already expanded. The expanded Insert Link dialog box is shown in Figure 7-4.

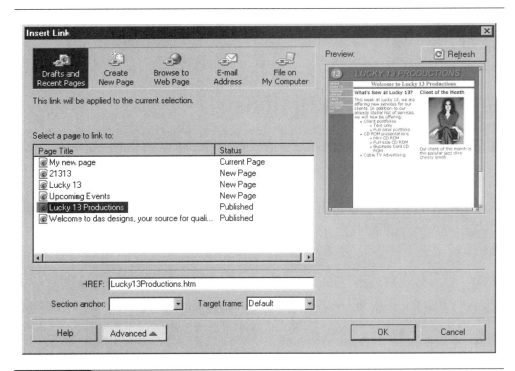

FIGURE 7-4 You can specify advanced link properties.

4. Select the Web address in the HREF field and change it to the desired address.

5. Click OK to exit the Insert Link dialog box.

Specifying Where Linked Pages Open

When you create or edit a link, you can specify where the linked page opens. You can open the linked page in the current window (or in the current frame, if you are working with a frame-based Web page), the entire window (if you are working with a frame-based page and you want the linked page to expand to fill the browser window), or a new browser window. For more information on working with frames, see Chapter 9. To specify where a linked page opens, follow these steps:

1. Create a link as outlined in one of the previous sections. If you're modifying an existing link, select the link in the page draft and then open the Insert Links dialog box by doing one of the following:

    ■ Click the Link button in the toolbar, and from the pop-up menu, choose the type of page that the link opens. For example, if the link opens the viewer's e-mail application, choose E-mail Address.

    ■ Choose Insert | Link, then choose the page type the link opens from the submenu. For example, if the link opens a page draft or a page you recently published, choose Insert | Link | Drafts And Recent Pages.

    ■ Right-click and choose Link Properties from the context menu.

2. Click the Advanced button to expand the Insert Link dialog box.

3. Click the triangle to the right of the Target Frame field and choose one of the following:

    ■ **Default**   Opens the linked page in the current window. If the page draft you are editing contains frames, the linked page opens in the current frame.

    ■ **Entire Window**   Opens the linked page in the current window. If the page draft you are editing contains frames, the linked page expands to fill the browser window, not just the frame that called the linked page.

    ■ **New Window**   Opens the linked page in a new browser window. The page that called the link remains open in another browser window.

4. Click OK to exit the Insert Link dialog box.

7

Creating an Anchor

You can create a section anchor in a page you are editing. A section anchor is like a bookmark. When you create a link to a section anchor, the linked page opens to the section anchor instead of at the top of the page. Creating section anchors is useful when you have a long Web page containing lots of topics. To create a section anchor, follow these steps:

1. In the page draft you are editing, place your cursor at the beginning of the section where you want to place the anchor. This may be the start of a paragraph or section heading.

2. Choose Insert | Section Anchor. The Section Anchor dialog box shown next opens.

3. Enter a name for the anchor in the Section Anchor Name field. The name you enter cannot begin with a number and cannot contain spaces. You can only use an anchor name once on a Web page. Choose a simple name that reflects the section; for example, if you are creating a section anchor for the top of a Web page, enter a name like **top**.

4. Click OK. Contribute inserts the section anchor icon, which looks like a triangular flag on a pole, at the insertion point in your page draft.

If you have modified Preferences and disabled the Show Section Anchors When Editing A Page option, you will not be able to see section anchor icons. You can show section anchors by choosing Edit | Preferences and then enabling this option in the Invisible Elements section of the Preferences dialog box.

Deleting and Modifying Section Anchors

After creating a section anchor, you can later delete it or modify it if necessary. To delete a section anchor, click its icon and then press DELETE. Note, however, that deleting a section anchor will break any links containing that section anchor.

To modify a section anchor, select it, right-click, then choose Anchor Properties from the context menu. Enter a new name for the anchor, then click OK. After you modify the section anchor, you will also have to change any links to the section anchor to reflect the new name; otherwise, the links will be broken.

Linking to a Section Anchor

You can link to a section anchor when creating a new link or when editing an existing link in a page draft. When you link to a section anchor, the link opens to the top of the section where you placed the anchor. To link to a section anchor, follow these steps:

1. Create a link as outlined in the previous sections. Choose to link to a recently published page, a page draft that contains a section anchor, or a Web page that you know contains a section anchor. If you are editing an existing link, do one of the following to open the Insert Link dialog box:

    ■ Click the Link button in the toolbar, and from the pop-up menu, choose the type of page that the link opens.

    ■ Choose Insert | Link, and from the submenu, choose the page type the link opens.

    ■ Right-click and choose Link Properties from the context menu.

> **TIP** *You can link to a section anchor in the current page by selecting the current page in the Page Title section of the Insert Link dialog box.*

2. Click the Advanced button to display the advanced section of the dialog box.

3. Click the triangle to the right of the Section Anchor field. Contribute displays all the section anchors in the page.

4. Click an anchor to select it. Contribute modifies the link, adding the section anchor to the linked page's URL in the HREF field, as shown in Figure 7-5.

5. Click OK to apply the link and close the Insert Link dialog box.

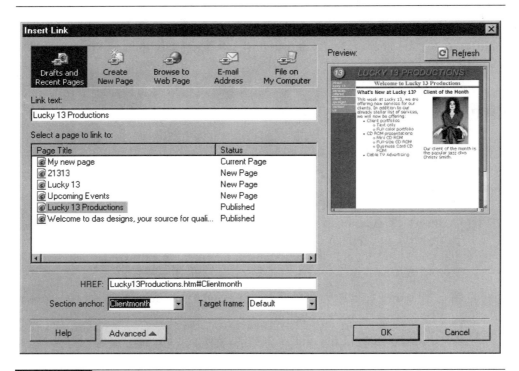

FIGURE 7-5   You can create a link to a section anchor on a Web page.

Editing Links

You can edit a link in any page draft you are working on. When you edit a link, you can perform the following tasks:

- Change the link text.
- Change the link destination.
- Remove a link.

Changing the Link Text and Link Destination

You can change a link's text or the type of page that opens when a link is clicked. You can change the link text to display new information, and you can change the destination when you have tested a link and it does not function properly.

To change a link's text, follow these steps:

1. Select the page draft that contains the link whose text you want to modify.

2. Select the text.

3. Enter new text.

To change a link's destination, follow these steps:

1. Select the page draft that contains the link whose destination needs to be modified.

2. Select the link. If the link is text, click anywhere inside the text; if the link is an image, click the image.

3. Right-click, then choose Link Properties from the context menu. The Insert Link dialog box opens.

4. Click the appropriate button at the top of the dialog box for the modified link's destination. For example, you can change a link from an existing Web page to a page draft you are currently editing; if the correct Insert Link dialog box is already displayed, you can skip this step.

5. If you are modifying the destination of the link to an existing Web page, click the Browse button, then select the Web page. If the modified link will be to a file on your computer, page draft, or e-mail address, enter the e-mail address or choose the file or page draft that the link will open.

6. Click OK to apply the change and close the Insert Link dialog box.

Removing a Link

You can remove a link at any time—if you created it by mistake, for example, or if you no longer need to link to a document or page. To remove a link, follow these steps:

1. Select the page draft that contains the link. If the page has already been published, navigate to the page and then click the Edit Page button.

2. Select the link you want to remove.

3. To remove the link from the page, do one of the next steps.

■ Right-click, then choose Remove Link from the context menu.

■ Choose Format | Remove Link.

After using either method, the image or text no longer links to another file or Web page.

Editing Link Properties

You can also change a link by changing its properties. You can change a link's properties by modifying parameters within the Insert Link dialog box. When you edit a link's properties, you open the Insert Link dialog box, which gives you access to all of the parameters associated with the link. To edit a link's properties, follow these steps:

1. Within the page draft you are editing, select the link whose properties you need to change.

2. To open the Insert Link dialog box shown previously, do one of the following:

   ■ Right-click and choose Link Properties from the context menu.

   ■ Choose Format | Link Properties.

3. Modify any of the existing parameters or add new ones. For example, if you've added section anchors to the linked document, click the Advanced button, then choose the desired section anchor from the Section Anchor pop-up menu.

4. Click OK to apply the changes and close the Insert Link dialog box.

Testing Links

If you've ever navigated to a Web page with broken links, you know how frustrating it can be. You can safeguard against this happening with your pages by testing your links. When you are working on a page draft, you cannot test any of the links, even if you are working online. You can, however, test the links prior to publishing the document by previewing the page in a browser. To test links in your current page draft, follow these steps:

1. Choose File | Preview In Browser. Contribute places a temporary copy of the file in a folder at your server. The copy of the file appears in your system's default browser.

2. One at a time, click every link in the page. When you test the links, make sure the proper pages are loaded into the browser. If you've applied any advanced link options, make sure the linked page opens in the proper window or, if applicable, make sure that the linked page opens at the correct section anchor.

3. Close the browser after you've tested the links.

4. If any links are not functioning properly, follow the steps in the previous sections "Changing the Link Text and Link Destination" or "Editing Link Properties," as necessary.

Summary

In this chapter, you learned to create links—links that open a file, a Web page, an e-mail application, and more. You also learned to specify the link target, to create and link to a section anchor, and to edit links and link properties. In the next chapter, you'll learn how to create and edit tables for your Web pages.

Chapter 8

Creating and Editing Tables

How to...

- ■ Create a table
- ■ Set table properties
- ■ Edit a table
- ■ Modify table appearance
- ■ Sort table data

When your Web site was created, the designer may have used tables to arrange the information displayed on some pages. Tables make it possible to arrange Web page content neatly into columns and rows. For example, each row can be used to display information about an upcoming event. In the first column of the row, the event is listed; in the second column, the data and place are listed; and in the third column, information about the event is displayed. The first row of the table is used to display the headings for each column. A table is also a wonderful tool for displaying thumbnail images of photos.

You can use Contribute to edit tables in existing pages or to add tables to existing pages or new pages that you create. When you edit or create a table, you can control the look of the table by changing the background color of the table, the table rows and columns, or individual cells. You can also change the alignment of data within each cell. In this chapter, you'll learn how to create new tables for your Web pages, how to edit and change the size of a table, and how to resize individual columns and rows. You'll also learn how to sort the data in your tables.

Creating a Table

You can add a table to a Web page whenever you need to display data in an orderly manner. You can quickly create a table with three columns and three rows (the Contribute default), or you can modify the settings to create a custom table. The rows and columns consist of individual cells into which you add information. The default setting of three columns and three rows yields a table with nine cells. You can create a table anywhere within the document. You can also nest a table within another table.

When you create a table, you can add headings. Headings make it easier for people with disabilities to view your table. The text of a heading is boldfaced and centered. When you create the table and define table headings, readers with disabilities can use screen readers to make it easier to read table headings. To create a table, follow these steps:

1. Select the page draft to which you want to add the table.

2. Place your cursor where you want the table to begin.

3. To open the Insert Table dialog box shown in Figure 8-1, do one of the following:

   ■ Click the Insert Table button in the toolbar.

   ■ Choose Insert | Table.

   ■ Choose Table | Insert | Table.

4. Enter a value in the Number Of Rows field or accept the default value of 3.

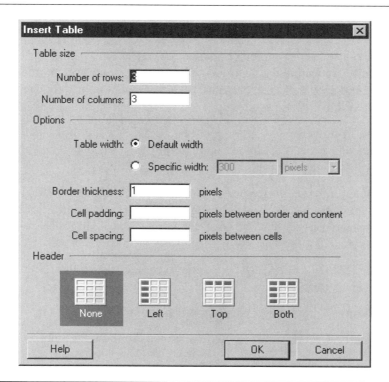

FIGURE 8-1   You can modify the default options when you insert a table.

5. Enter a value in the Number Of Columns field or accept the default value of 3.

6. In the Options section, choose one of the following for Table Width:

   - **Default width** Sizes the table as you add content. Choose this option if you're entering content of varying widths such as images or people's names. When you have a table with multiple rows, each column is sized according to the cell in the column with the widest content.

   - **Specific width** Sizes the table to a specific size. Enter a value in the Specific Width field, and then click the triangle to the right of the text field and choose Pixels or Percentage. When you choose Pixels, the table is sized to the value you enter. When you choose Percentage, the table is sized to the specified percentage of the browser window or the table in which the new table is nested. When you choose the Specific Width option, the table columns are divided equally across the width of the table. You can modify the width of an individual column by selecting it and then changing its width (see "Resizing Column Width Manually" later in this chapter).

7. In the Options section, enter a value in the Border Thickness field. By default, Contribute uses a value of 1 to create a one-pixel border around the table and each cell. You can enter a different value for a thicker border or **0** for a table with no border.

8. In the Options section, enter a value in the Cell Padding field. This is the distance between the content and the border of the cell. The default setting is 1 pixel. Enter **0** for a table with no cell padding.

9. In the Options section, enter a value in the Cell Spacing field. This is the amount of space in pixels between each cell. If you do not enter a value, Contribute uses a value of 3 pixels. Enter **0** if you want a table with no space between cells.

10. In the Header section, click a button to choose one of the following Header options:

    - **None** Creates a table with no header cells.

    - **Left** Creates a table with header cells in the left column.

    - **Top** Creates a table with header cells in the top row.

    - **Both** Creates a table with header cells in the left column and top row.

11. Click OK. Contribute adds the table to your page draft.

Adding Content to a Table

After you add the table to your page draft, you can begin adding content to the table. To add content to a cell, follow these steps:

1. Click the cell to which you want to add content. Your cursor will flash in the selected cell.

2. Add content to the cell. You can add content to the cell by typing, copying and pasting from other documents, or by inserting an image. If you size the cell to a specific width and then enter text that exceeds that width, the text wraps to a new line. Press ENTER to create a new line within a cell. If you insert an image that exceeds the specified width, the cell will expand to accommodate the image. You can resize the image to fit the existing cell width by changing image properties, as discussed in Chapter 10.

3. Press TAB to move to the next cell in the table.

> **TIP** *To see how the table will look to viewers of your Web site, choose File | Preview In Browser.*

Nesting Tables

When you insert a table within a table, this is known as *nesting*. Nesting tables is useful when you need to display tabular content within a table cell that will be formatted differently than the parent table. For example, you can create a table with two columns and one row, which allows you to display text in one column and a table with multiple rows and columns containing different information in the other. To nest a table within a table, follow these steps:

1. Place your cursor within the cell where you want the new table to appear.

2. To nest a new table within the cell, do one of the following:

   ■ Click the Insert Table button in the toolbar.

   ■ Choose Insert | Table.

   ■ Choose Table | Insert | Table.

   The Insert Table dialog box appears.

3. Set the parameters for the nested table, as outlined in the previous section.

4. Click OK. The new table is created and nested in the cell you selected.

Selecting Tables and Table Elements

After you create a table, you can select it or select individual table elements and modify them. For example, you can change the width and height of a table, the width of a column, the height of a row, and much more. You can also modify the content of a selected cell, as well as the background color, the border color, and the alignment of cell content. You can select an entire table or the following table elements:

- One or more rows
- One or more columns
- One or more cells
- A selection of adjacent or nonadjacent cells

Selecting a Table

You can select any table within your document, with the exception of a table that was created by your Web designer and saved as a noneditable region in a Dreamweaver template. After you select a table, you can edit its properties or change its size. To select a table, do one of the following:

- Click the upper-left corner of the table.
- Click the right or bottom border of the table.
- Place your cursor within any table cell, and then choose Table | Select Table.

After you select a table, it is highlighted with a dark border, and handles appear on the right, bottom, and lower-right corner of the table, as shown in Figure 8-2.

Selecting Table Rows or Columns

You can select a single row or column within a table, and then change its properties or resize it. To select one or more rows or columns, follow these steps:

1. Move your cursor toward the row or column you want to select until it becomes a solid arrow.

2. Click the column or row to select it, or click and drag to select adjacent rows or columns. The selected rows or columns are highlighted with a dark border.

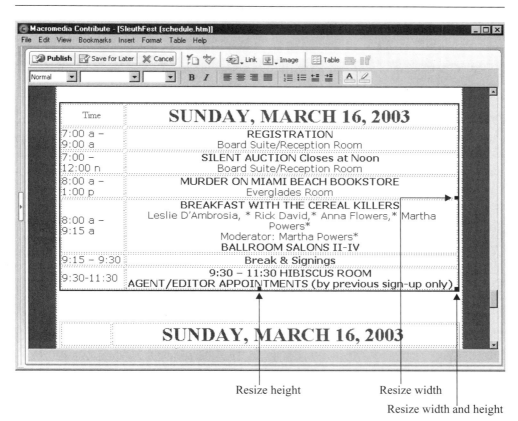

Resize height   Resize width

Resize width and height

FIGURE 8-2 You can select and edit a table in a page draft.

Selecting Table Cells

You can select individual cells whose content you need to modify, or you can select multiple cells. After you select one or more cells, you can edit the properties of the cells, or you can copy or cut the contents of the selected cells.

Selecting a Cell or the Contents of a Cell

To select an individual cell, click inside the cell. To select the contents of a single cell, do one of the following:

- Click and drag inside the cell.

- Click inside the cell, and then choose Edit | Select All.

Selecting Multiple Adjacent Cells

To select multiple adjacent cells, do one of the following:

- Click inside a cell, and then drag to select adjacent cells. You can drag diagonally to select adjacent cells in adjoining columns or rows.

- Click inside a cell and then, while holding down the SHIFT key, click an adjacent cell to add it to the selection.

- Click inside a cell and then, while holding down the SHIFT key, click inside a nonadjacent cell to select all cells within the area.

Selecting Multiple Nonadjacent Cells

To select multiple nonadjacent cells, select a cell and then, while pressing CTRL, click the cells you want to add to the selection.

Resizing Tables and Table Elements

As you add content to a table, you may find it necessary to resize the entire table or one or more columns or rows. When you resize a table, the cells are resized to match, and the cell contents are reflowed accordingly.

Resizing a Table

You can resize the width, height, or both dimensions of a table whenever necessary. To resize a table in a page draft you are editing, follow these steps:

1. Select the table you want to resize using one of the methods outlined previously in the section "Selecting a Table."

2. To resize the selected table, do one of the following:

   - To change the table's width, click and drag the handle on the right side of the table. Release the mouse button when the table is the desired width.

   - To change the table's height, click and drag the handle at the bottom of the table. Release the mouse button when the table is the desired height.

   - To change both the width and height, click and drag the handle at the lower-right corner of the table. To resize the table proportionately, press and hold down the SHIFT key while dragging. Release the mouse button when the table is the desired size. If you are resizing the table proportionately, release the mouse button before releasing the SHIFT key.

Resizing Columns and Rows

You can resize the columns and rows in a table. When you resize a column or row, the cells are changed accordingly. For example, if you have text in a column and you increase the column's width, the text is reflowed to fit the column.

Resizing Column Width Manually

To resize column width manually, follow these steps:

1. Select the column or columns you want to resize.

2. Move your cursor toward the right border of the column. When your cursor becomes two vertical lines with pointing arrows, click and drag. To select contiguous columns, drag left or right. Note that you can only resize contiguous columns.

3. Release the mouse button when the column is the desired size.

Resizing Column Width Numerically in Pixels

To resize column width numerically in pixels, follow these steps:

1. Select the column or columns you want to resize.

2. Click the Insert Table button in the toolbar to open the Table Column Properties section of the Table Properties dialog box shown in Figure 8-3.

3. In the Column Width field, enter the value in pixels to which you want the column resized. Alternatively, click the Fit To Contents radio button to resize the column to fit the existing contents.

4. Click Apply to preview your changes without closing the Table Properties dialog box.

5. Click OK to apply your changes and close the Table Properties dialog box.

Resizing Column Width Numerically by Percentage

You can also change column size to a percentage of the entire table. When you create a table, the columns are divided equally using the unit of measure you specify in the Insert Table dialog box. If you choose Pixels when you create a

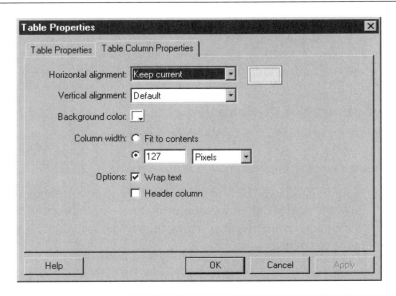

FIGURE 8-3   You can modify the width of a selected column.

table, you can change the unit for an individual column later to Percentage and then specify the percentage of the table to which you want the column sized. You can change one or all columns to a percentage of the table width. To change the unit of measure of a column or columns to a percentage, follow these steps:

1. Select the column or columns that you want to resize. When you resize more than one column, you must select contiguous columns.

2. Click the Insert Table button in the toolbar. The Table Column Properties section of the Table Properties dialog box appears.

3. Click the radio button next to the Column Width text field if it is not already selected.

4. Enter a value for the percentage of the table width you want the column to be.

5. Click the triangle to the right of the unit of measure field and choose Percentage.

6. Click Apply to preview the new column width without closing the Table Properties dialog box.

7. Click OK to apply the changes and close the dialog box.

Resizing Row Height Manually

To resize row height manually, follow these steps:

1. Select the row or rows that you want to resize. If you resize more than one row, the rows must be contiguous. If you attempt to resize non-contiguous rows, you can only resize one of the selected rows.

2. Move your cursor toward the top or bottom border of the row. When your cursor becomes two horizontal lines with pointing arrows, click and drag. If you select more than one row, move your cursor towards the bottommost row.

3. Release the mouse button when the row is the desired height.

Resizing Row Height Numerically

To resize row height numerically, follow these steps:

1. Select the row or rows that you want to resize.

2. Click the Insert Table button in the toolbar to open the Table Row Properties section of the Table Properties dialog box.

3. In the Row Height section, do one of the following:

   ■ Click the Fit To Contents button to size the row height to fit the text or images within the row.

   ■ Click the radio button to the left of the text field, and then enter the number of pixels to which you want the row resized.

4. Click Apply to preview the changes without closing the Table Properties dialog box.

5. Click OK to apply the changes and close the Table Properties dialog box.

Working with Cell Content

After you add content to table cells, you may find it necessary to use the information in another part of the table or in a new table, or you may decide you want to delete some information. You can select multiple cells, and as long as the selection is rectangular, you can copy, cut, and paste the cells into another part of a table, or use the selection to start a new table. You can also delete the contents of a selection. When you copy or cut cells, the cell formatting is preserved.

Copying Cells

To copy one or more cells, follow these steps:

1. Select one or more adjacent cells, or one or more adjacent table rows or columns. Remember that the selection must be rectangular.

2. To copy the selected cells, do one of the following:

   ■ Choose Edit | Copy.

   ■ Right-click, then choose Copy from the context menu.

   Contribute copies the selected cells to the clipboard.

Cutting Cells

To cut one or more cells from a table, follow these steps:

1. Select one or more adjacent cells, or one or more adjacent table rows or columns. Remember that the selection must be rectangular.

2. To cut the selection, do one of the following:

   ■ Choose Edit | Cut.

   ■ Right-click, then choose Cut from the context menu.

   Contribute cuts the selected cells from the table and copies the selection to the clipboard.

Deleting Content from Cells

To delete cell content without removing the cells from the table, follow these steps:

1. Select one or more cells. The selected cells do not need to be adjacent when you want to empty the cells.

2. To remove the content from the selected cells, do one of the following:

   ■ Choose Edit | Clear.

   ■ Press DELETE.

   ■ Press BACKSPACE.

   Contribute removes the cell content but preserves the cells within the table.

CAUTION *If you select an entire row or column of cells, or several rows or columns of cells and perform the previous steps, you will delete the entire row or column of cells along with the cell content.*

Pasting Cells

After you copy or cut a selection of cells to the clipboard, you can paste the cells within the table or in another part of the page draft to begin a new table. To paste copied or cut cells from the clipboard, follow these steps:

1. Within the page draft, do one of the following:

- *Replace the content of adjacent cells that have the same layout as the cells you cut or copied.* Select a rectangular area that contains the same number of cells. For example, if you copied or cut cells that comprise an area two cells wide and three cells high, select a group of adjacent cells that are two wide by three high.

- *Replace the content of a cell and its adjacent neighbors with copied or cut cells that are not entire rows or columns.* Select a cell.

NOTE *If you attempt to paste an area of cells that is not comprised of an entire row or column into an area that does not contain enough cells, Contribute will display a warning to that effect.*

- *Paste one or more rows above an existing row.* Select a cell within the row above which you want to paste the rows.

- *Paste one or more columns to the left of an existing column.* Select a cell within the column to the left of which you want to paste the columns.

- *Create a new table with copied or cut cells.* Place your cursor at the point in the document where you want the new table to appear.

CAUTION *If you attempt to paste copied or cut cells into an existing table cell, you may get an error message saying there are not enough cells to paste the clipboard. If this occurs, you will need to create a new table within the cell to which you want to paste the contents.*

2. To paste the cut or copied cells, do one of the following:

- Choose Edit | Paste.

8

■ Right-click, then choose Paste from the context menu.

Contribute pastes the cells into the area you specified.

Working with Table Elements

After you create a table, you may find it necessary to modify the layout to accommodate the information you want to display in the table. You can modify cells by merging adjacent cells into a single cell or by splitting an existing cell into two or more cells. You can also add rows or columns to a table when you need to add additional information. In the upcoming sections, you'll learn how to modify the layout of a table by working with cells, rows, and columns.

Working with Cells

A table is made up of rows and columns. The table cells appear where the rows and columns intersect. You can modify the layout of the table by splitting a cell into rows or columns or by merging several adjacent cells into a single cell.

Merging Cells

When you merge cells, you must select an entire row or column or a rectangular area of cells. To merge cells, follow these steps:

1. Select the cells that you want to merge.

2. To merge the selected cells into a single cell, do one of the following:

   ■ Choose Table | Merge Cells.

   ■ Right-click, then choose Merge Cells from the context menu.

   Contribute merges the selected cells and content into a single cell.

Splitting a Cell

You can split any cell in a table into multiple rows or columns. When you split a cell that contains text and images, the text and images remain in the parent cell. After splitting the cell, you can select content from the parent cell and then cut and paste or drag and drop it into one of the new cells. To split a cell, follow these steps:

1. Place your cursor inside the cell you want to split. Note that if you select several cells, only the leftmost cell in the selection will be split.

2. To open the Split Cell dialog box shown next, do one of the following:

- Choose Table | Split Cell.

- Right-click, then choose Split Cell from the context menu.

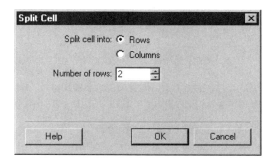

3. In the Split Cell Into section, click either the Rows or Columns radio button, depending on whether you want to split the cell into rows or columns.

4. Enter a value for the number of rows or columns into which you want to split the cell.

5. Click OK. The Split Cell dialog box closes, and Contribute splits the cell.

Working with Rows and Columns

When you work with a new table or edit an existing one, it may be necessary to add or delete rows or columns. You can add rows and columns to make room for additional information, or delete them when they are no longer needed.

Adding a Row

To add a single row to a table, follow these steps:

1. Place your cursor inside a cell that is above or below the point where you want the new row added.

2. To add the row, do one of the following:

    - Click the Add Row button in the toolbar. This inserts a row below the cell you chose as the insertion point.

    - Choose Table | Insert | Insert Row Above. Alternatively, you can right-click and choose Insert Row Above from the context menu.

    - Choose Table | Insert | Insert Row Below. Alternatively, you can right-click and choose Insert Row Below from the context menu.

Adding a Column

To add a single column to a table, follow these steps:

1. Place your cursor inside a cell to the right or left of the point where you want the new column inserted.

2. To insert the new column in the table, do one of the following:

   ■ Click the Insert Column button in the toolbar. This inserts a column to the right of the cell you selected as the insertion point.

   ■ Choose Table | Insert | Insert Column To The Left. Alternatively, you can right-click, then choose Insert Column To The Left from the context menu.

   ■ Choose Table | Insert | Insert Column To The Right. Alternatively, you can right-click, then choose Insert Column To The Right from the context menu.

> **NOTE** *If you place your cursor inside a cell that has been split and then add a row or column, the cell is split into additional rows or columns.*

Adding Multiple Rows or Columns

If you know the amount of information you need to add to a table, you can save some time by inserting multiple rows or columns. To add multiple rows or columns to a table, follow these steps:

1. Place your cursor in a cell that is above or below the point where you want to add rows, or to the left or right of the point where you want to add columns.

2. To open the Insert Rows Or Columns dialog box shown next, do one of the following:

   ■ Choose Table | Insert | Multiple Rows Or Columns.

   ■ Right-click, then choose Insert Multiple Rows Or Columns from the context menu.

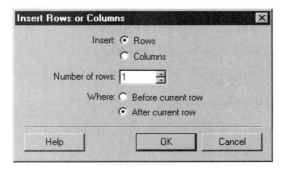

3. Click either the Rows or Columns radio button.

4. Enter a value for the number of rows or columns you want added to the table.

5. In the Where section, choose a placement option.

   ■ If you are inserting rows, choose either Before Current Row or After Current Row.

   ■ If you are inserting columns, choose either Before Current Column or After Current Column.

6. Click OK. The Insert Rows Or Columns dialog box closes, and Contribute adds the specified number of rows or columns to your table.

Deleting Rows or Columns

If you want, you can eliminate one or more rows or columns. To delete rows or columns, follow these steps:

1. Select one or more rows or columns you want to delete.

2. To delete the selected rows or columns, do one of the following:

   ■ Choose either Table | Delete | Row or Table | Delete | Column. Contribute displays the proper command, depending on the selection you make.

   ■ Right-click, then choose either Delete Row or Delete Column from the context menu. Contribute displays the proper command, depending on the selection you make.

   ■ Press DELETE or BACKSPACE.

Contribute deletes the selection from the table.

Modifying a Table's Appearance

When you are editing a table, you have a tremendous amount of latitude concerning the table's appearance, and you can modify any of the following:

- Properties of the table
- Properties of individual cells, columns, or rows
- Format of the table

When you edit a table, it is important to know that there is a hierarchy of elements. When you change the properties of table elements, cells take precedence over rows and columns, and rows and columns take precedence over table formatting. For example, if you change the background color of a cell, the background color of the cell is displayed instead of the background color of rows or columns underneath. If you change the background color of a row or column, the background color of the row or column is displayed instead of the background color of the table.

Editing Table Properties

After you insert a table within a page draft and begin adding content, you may find the table properties need to be modified. For example, you may find the table is not wide enough to display its content properly. You can edit the following properties of a table:

- **Table alignment**   How the table is aligned to the browser window or table within which it is nested
- **Table width**   The width of the table in pixels or as a percentage of the browser window
- **Border thickness**   The thickness of the table and cell borders
- **Cell padding**   The distance between the content of each cell and the cell's border
- **Cell spacing**   The space between each cell
- **Border color**   The color of the table and each cell's border
- **Background color**   The color of the table's background

NOTE   *If you are editing a Web page with tables that were created with a template, you will not be able to modify the table's properties.*

To edit table properties, follow these steps:

1. Select the table whose properties you want to edit.

2. To open the Table Properties dialog box shown in Figure 8-4, do one of the following:

   ■ Click the Insert Table button in the toolbar.

   ■ Right-click, then choose Table Properties from the context menu.

   ■ Choose Table | Table Properties.

TIP   *You can also open the Table Properties dialog box by placing your cursor within a table cell and then choosing Table | Table Properties.*

3. Click the triangle to the right of the Alignment field and choose one of the following options:

   ■ **Default**   Aligns the table to the left side of the browser window or cell within which it is nested. Additional content appears below the table.

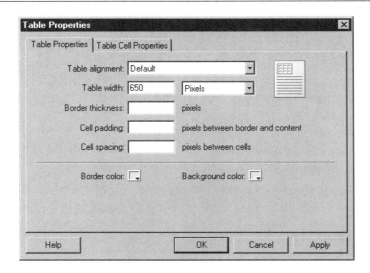

FIGURE 8-4   You can modify the properties of a table at any time.

- ■ **Left**   Aligns the table to the left side of the browser window or cell within which it is nested. Additional content flows to the right side of the table.

- ■ **Center**   Aligns the table to the center of the browser window or cell within which it is nested. Additional content appears below the table.

- ■ **Right**   Aligns the table to the right side of the browser window or cell within which it is nested. Additional content flows to the left of the table.

4. To change the table width, enter a new value in the Table Width field.

5. To change the current unit of measure for the table, choose Pixels or Percentage from the pop-up menu.

NOTE   *You can enter a large value for table width or a percentage greater than 100. If the table width exceeds the viewer's desktop width or the percentage is greater than 100, a scroll bar appears in the user's browser.*

6. To change the border thickness, enter a new value in the Border Thickness field. To remove existing table and cell borders, enter a value of 0.

7. To change the cell padding, enter a new value in the Cell Padding field. To remove cell padding, enter a value of 0.

8. To change the cell spacing, enter a new value in the Cell Spacing field. To remove cell spacing, enter a value of 0.

9. To change the border color, click the Border Color swatch and choose a color from the pop-up color palette.

10. To change the background color of the table, click the Background Color swatch and choose a color from the pop-up palette. When you choose a background color other than the default, choose a color that won't make the text you enter in the table difficult to read. If you don't choose a background color, the background color or background image for the Web page will appear behind the table.

11. Click Apply to preview the changes without closing the Table Properties dialog box. If the table isn't suited to the Web page, repeat any of the previous steps.

12. Click OK to apply the changes and close the Table Properties dialog box.

Editing Row or Column Properties

You can edit the properties of a selected row or column by changing their appearance or specifying how cell contents align within the cells. To modify the properties of a row or column, follow these steps:

1. In your page draft, select the row or column whose properties you want to modify. If desired, you can edit the properties of multiple rows or columns.

2. To open the Table Column Properties or Table Row Properties section of the Table Properties dialog box as shown in Figure 8-5, do one of the following:

   ■ Click the Insert Table button in the toolbar.

   ■ Choose Table | Table Properties, and then click either the Table Column Properties or Table Row Properties tab.

   ■ Right-click, choose Table Properties from the context menu, and then click either the Table Column Properties or Table Row Properties tab.

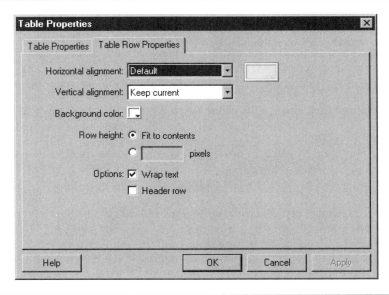

FIGURE 8-5   You can change the properties of an entire row or column.

3. Click the triangle to the right of the Horizontal Alignment field and choose one of the following from the pop-up menu:

- ■ **Default**   Aligns cell content to the left border of all cells in the column or row.

- ■ **Left**   Aligns cell content to the left border of all cells in the column or row.

- ■ **Center**   Aligns cell content to the center of all cells in the column or row.

- ■ **Right**   Aligns cell content to the right border of all cells in the column or row.

4. Click the triangle to the right of the Vertical Alignment field and choose one of the following from the pop-up menu:

- ■ **Default**   Aligns cell content to the top border of all cells in the column or row.

- ■ **Top**   Aligns cell content to the top border of all cells in the column or row.

- ■ **Middle**   Aligns cell content to the middle of all cells in the column or row.

- ■ **Bottom**   Aligns cell content to bottom of all cells in the column or row.

5. To change the background color of each cell in the column or row, click the Background Color swatch and select a color from the pop-up palette.

6. To change the row height or column width, choose one of the options. For more information on resizing columns and rows, refer to the "Resizing Columns and Rows" section presented earlier in this chapter.

7. In the Options section, click the Wrap Text check box if you want text to wrap to the next line when it reaches the border of a cell.

8. In the Options section, click either the Header Row or Header Column check box if you want to format the row or column as a header.

9. Click Apply to preview your changes without closing the Table Properties dialog box.

10. Click OK to close the Table Properties dialog box and apply your changes to the selected column or row.

Editing Cell Properties

You can edit the properties of an individual cell or a selection of cells in a table. You can change the alignment of elements within the cell, the background color of the cell, and the way text is displayed within the cell. To modify cell properties, follow these steps:

1. Select one or more cells whose characteristics you want to modify.

2. To open the Table Cell Properties section of the Table Properties dialog box shown in Figure 8-6, do one of the following:

   ■ Choose Table | Cell Properties.

   ■ Right-click, then choose Cell Properties from the context menu.

3. Click the triangle to the right of the Horizontal Alignment field and choose one of the following from the pop-up menu:

   ■ **Default**   Aligns cell content to the left border of selected cells.

   ■ **Left**   Aligns cell content to the left border of selected cells.

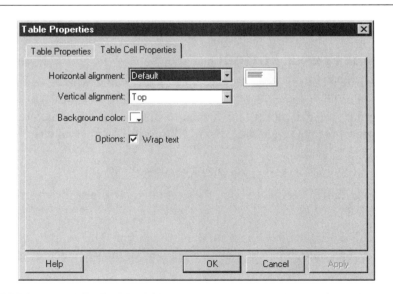

FIGURE 8-6   You can modify the properties of individual cells within a table.

- ■ **Center**   Aligns cell content to the center of selected cells.

- ■ **Right**   Aligns cell content to the right border of selected cells.

4. Click the triangle to the right of the Vertical Alignment field and choose one of the following options:

- ■ **Default**   Aligns cell content to the top of all selected cells.

- ■ **Top**   Aligns cell content to the top border of all selected cells.

- ■ **Middle**   Aligns cell content to the middle of all selected cells

- ■ **Bottom**   Aligns cell content to bottom of all selected cells.

5. To change the background color of selected cells, click the Background Color swatch, and select a color from the pop-up palette.

6. In the Options section, click the Wrap Text check box if you want to enable or disable text wrapping. When this option is selected, text wraps to the next line when you type enough text to exceed the cell's border.

7. Click Apply to preview your changes without closing the Table Properties dialog box.

8. Click OK to close the Table Properties dialog box and apply the changes.

Applying a Preset Format

When you create a table, you can choose one of several Contribute presets to format the table. The presets feature many different table designs. After you choose a format, you can modify the format to suit the table you are creating. To apply a preset format to a table you are editing, follow these steps:

1. Select the table to which you want to add a preset format.

2. Choose Table | Format to open the Format Table dialog box shown in Figure 8-7.

3. Choose one of the designs from the left window. The window on the right side of the dialog box shows you a preview of the selected design.

4. Click Apply to preview the design as it will appear in your table. If the design is acceptable, proceed to step 17; otherwise, select another design. You can modify the selected design by following the next steps.

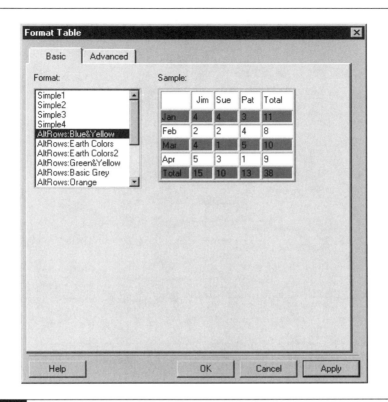

FIGURE 8-7   You can format a table with a preset design.

5. Click the Advanced tab to open the Advanced section of the Format Table dialog box, as shown in Figure 8-8.

6. In the Table Properties section, enter a value for the width of table and cell borders. Enter a value of 0 to create a table with no borders.

7. In the Left Column section, click the triangle to the right of the Text Alignment field and choose one of the following alignment options: None, Left, Center, or Right.

8. In the Left Column section, click the triangle to the right of the Text Style field and choose one of the following options: Regular, Bold, Italic, or Bold Italic.

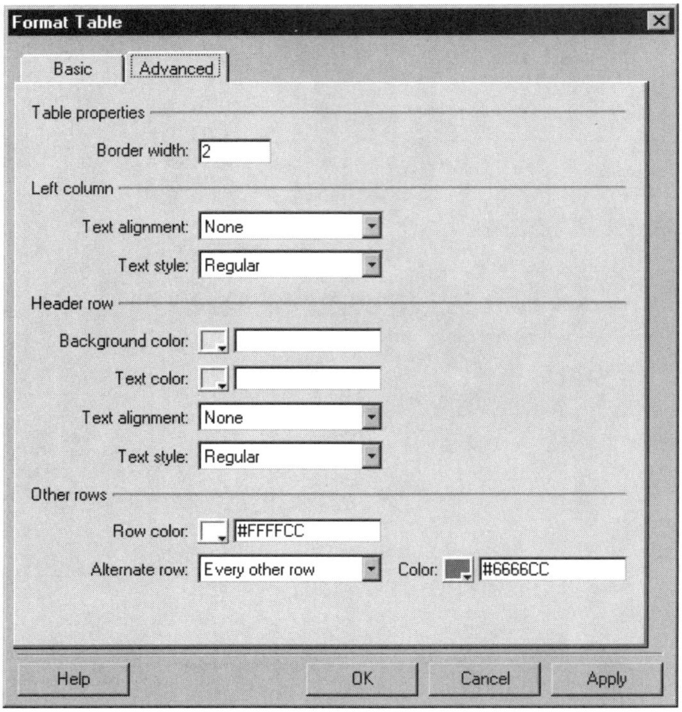

FIGURE 8-8 You can modify the design of preset table formats.

9. In the Header Row section, click the Background Color swatch and select a color from the pop-up palette. After you select a color, the hexadecimal value of the color is displayed to the right of the color swatch.

10. In the Header Row section, click the Text Color swatch and select a color from the pop-up palette. After you select a color, the hexadecimal value of the color is displayed to the right of the color swatch.

11. In the Header Row section, click the triangle to the right of the Text Alignment field and choose one of the following options: None, Left, Center, or Right.

12. In the Header Row section, click the triangle to the right of the Text Style field and choose one of the following options: Regular, Bold, Italic, or Bold Italic.

13. In the Other Rows section, click the Row Color swatch and select a color from the pop-up palette. After you select a color, the hexadecimal value of the color is displayed to the right of the color swatch.

14. In the Other Rows section, click the triangle to the right of the Alternate Rows field, and choose one of the following options: <Do Not Alternate>, Every Other Row, Every Two Rows, Every Three Rows, or Every Four Rows. This option determines whether or not alternating rows in the table display a different background color. You can accept the default alternating row background color or choose your own by following step 15.

15. In the Other Rows section, click the Color swatch to the right of the Alternating Row field and select a color from the pop-up palette. After you select a color, the hexadecimal value of the color is displayed to the right of the color swatch.

16. Click Apply to apply the formatting to your table without closing the Format Table dialog box. If the formatting is acceptable, proceed to step 17; otherwise, modify the options until the design is suitable for the table in the page draft you are editing.

17. Click OK to close the Format Table dialog box and apply the formatting to the selected table.

Sorting Table Data

When you create a table with multiple rows and columns of data, you'll be happy to know you can sort the data by columns. This option is useful if you have to enter data from several sources and the data needs to be displayed in order. You can sort the data alphabetically or numerically, and you can choose which column is used to sort the data. To sort data in a table, follow these steps:

1. Select the table whose data you want to sort.

2. Choose Table | Sort Table. The Sort Table dialog box shown in Figure 8-9 opens.

3. Click the triangle to the right of the Sort By field and choose the column by which you want the data to be sorted.

4. Click the triangle to the right of the Order field and choose either Alphabetically or Numerically.

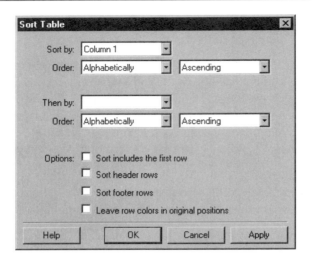

FIGURE 8-9   You can sort the data within a table.

5. Click the triangle to the right of the second Order field and choose either Ascending or Descending.

6. If desired, click the triangle to the right of the Then By field and further refine the sort by choosing a second column by which to sort the data.

7. If you chose a second column by which to sort the data, click the triangle to the right of the Order field and choose either Alphabetically or Numerically.

8. If you chose a second column by which to sort the data, click the triangle to the right of the second Order field and choose either Ascending or Descending.

9. In the Options section, click the appropriate check boxes to include one or more of the following in the table sort:

■ **Sort includes the first row**   Includes data from the first row in the sort. Do not select this option if the first row of your table contains column headings.

■ **Sort header rows**   Includes data from header rows in the sort. Do not include this option if the header rows contain row headings.

- ■ **Sort footer rows**   Includes data from footer rows in the sort.

- ■ **Leave row colors in original positions**   Does not change the color of rows even though sorting the table may move data to a different row.

10. Click Apply to preview the sort before exiting the Sort Table dialog box. If the table data did not sort as you expected, change one or more of the preceding options and click Apply to preview the sort again. When the data is sorted to your satisfaction, proceed to step 11.

11. Click OK to close the Sort Table dialog box and sort the data.

Summary

In this chapter, you discovered how to create and edit tables within a Web page. You learned how to change table, row, column, and cell properties; how to merge and split cells; and how to add and delete rows and columns. You also learned how to cut, copy, and paste cells, as well as modify the way data is arranged in cells. In the next chapter, you'll learn how to work with Web pages that were created using frames.

8

Chapter 9

Working with Frames

How to…

- Edit frame-based pages
- Specify frame targets
- Publish frame-based pages

If the Web site you are editing was designed with frames, each Web page is broken down into windows, or, as some designers refer to them, regions. Each window contains a different HTML document. Each document does something different; for example, the document in one window may be the site's navigation menu, while the document in another window contains the site's header, and the document in another contains text and images.

Some designers think frames are the greatest thing since sliced bread; others avoid them like the plague. Frame-based pages do simplify site navigation; however, they can cause problems with search engines. They also cause problems for viewers with browsers that don't support frame-based pages. If the site you are editing is designed with frame-based pages, your site designer has probably provided alternate pages for viewers using browsers that don't support frame-based pages.

If your site uses frames, it was probably designed in a program such as Macromedia Dreamweaver MX or Microsoft FrontPage. You can edit frame-based pages with Contribute. Editing frame-based pages can be a bit confusing, because in Contribute you don't see the big picture; you see only the frame you are editing. This chapter provides a brief overview of frame-based Web pages. It explains how to edit and publish frame-based pages and shows you a workaround to compensate for not being able to see page drafts within a frameset.

Understanding Frames

If your Web site was designed with frames, it means your site designer divided the site into regions, or windows. Each window displays different content. The content of some windows remains static. For example, the window that contains the site navigation menu usually does not change. Your site many also have a window at the top of the page that contains your company's logo and other information. This window is likely to remain unchanged as well.

Frame-based sites generally have a main window whose content changes when a new menu selection is made. If the main window contains a lot of text and images, a scroll bar appears on the right side of the window. A scroll bar may also appear at the bottom of the window if the frame page is wider than the viewer's available desktop space. When viewers scroll down the page, the content in the navigation menu window stays put. This is one of the advantages of a frame-based design: the page viewer can access the navigation menu from any point on the page. Figure 9-1 shows a typical frame-based design.

The main page is called a *frameset*, a separate file that defines the overall layout of the frame-based pages. The layout information for the pages includes the number of frames, the size and placement of each frame, and the URL (the Web site address) of the page that initially appears in each frame.

Each frame organizes content for the page. Each frame within the page is a container or window for content. The frameset determines the initial content that loads when a visitor first enters the site. However, the flexible nature of frame-based pages makes it possible for the site designer to load any page into a frame.

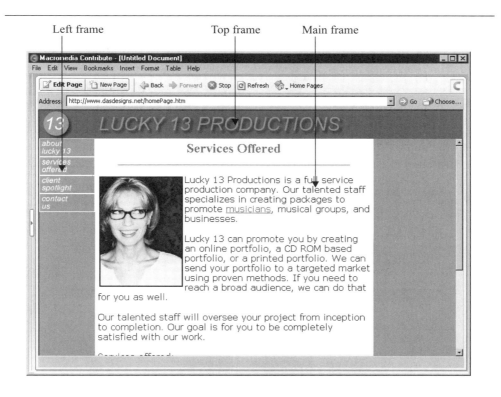

FIGURE 9-1   Each page of a frame-based Web site is divided into windows.

Each file that loads into a frame is a separate file. If the site you are editing has three frames, such as the page shown in Figure 9-1, there are really four files involved: the frameset file, and a separate file for the content of each frame. Each individual file can be displayed as a Web page; however, it is the frameset that creates the structure in which each page is displayed. It may help to think of a frameset as an unfurnished house. Each room of the house is a frame, while the furniture is the content of each frame.

When you edit frame-based pages with Contribute, it's important to note that any page can be loaded in a frame, even a page from another Web site. You will be able to edit only frame content from pages that are within a site to which you have made a connection.

Editing Frames

When you navigate to a frame-based Web page to which you have made a connection, you can use Contribute to edit the content in any frame. After you select a frame to edit, you can modify any of the content that your user group has permission to edit. To edit a frame-based Web page, follow these steps:

1. Navigate to the frame-based page that contains content you want to edit.

2. Click the Edit Page button. Contribute opens the Select A Frame To Edit dialog box shown next. Within the dialog box, you'll find a list of page titles for the individual pages in the frameset, including the URLs for each page.

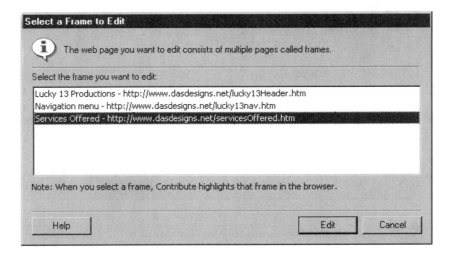

3. Select the title of the page you want to edit. Contribute displays a border around the selected frame.

4. Click OK. The selected page is displayed in the Contribute workspace without the other frame pages.

5. Make the necessary edits to the page, as outlined in previous chapters.

6. Publish the page. You can also save the page as a draft and edit it later.

When you edit a frame-based page, Contribute creates a draft of the page, which is displayed in the Contribute workspace without the frameset. Therefore, you won't be able to see what your edits look like within the frameset. This may be a bit confusing to some. While there is no perfect solution to this, you can use another browser to view the frame-based page as it currently appears on your Web site. By switching between Contribute and another browser displaying the current version of the page you are editing, you'll have an idea what the edited page will look like when you publish it, because the current version of the page you're editing will be displayed within its frameset. Figure 9-2 shows the main frame from Figure 9-1 as it would appear while being edited in Contribute.

9

Specifying Content Targets

When you edit a Web site with frame-based pages, you can edit the content within an individual frame or replace the content within a frame by creating a link in one frame that opens a linked page in another frame. If, for example, your Web site designer has created a navigation window using text links in one frame, you can add a new text link to the menu that replaces the content of the main window with the content from the page that the link calls.

When you create a link in one framed page that opens a page in another frame, you must specify the frame target in which the linked page appears when a user clicks the link. If you do not specify a target, by default the linked page will open in its parent frame.

When the frame-based pages you are editing were designed, each frame in the frameset should have been given a unique name. This enables you to select a specific frame as a target.

To create a link in a frame-based Web page, follow these steps:

1. Navigate to the frame-based Web page that you want to edit.

2. Click the Edit Page button. Contribute displays the Select A Frame To Edit dialog box.

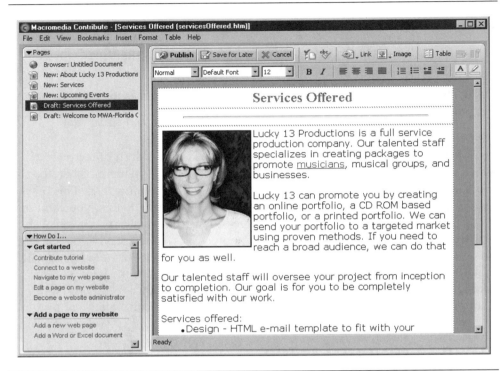

FIGURE 9-2   When you edit a frame-based page, it is displayed without the frameset.

3. Select the title of the page you want to edit. Contribute displays a red border around the page.

4. Click OK. Contribute creates a draft of the page.

5. Select the text or image that will be the basis for the link. Alternatively, place your cursor where you want the link to appear in the document.

6. Open the Insert Link dialog box by doing one of the following:

   ■ Click the Link button, and then from the pop-up menu, select the type of page to which you want to link.

   ■ Choose Insert | Link, and then from the submenu, choose the type of page to which you want to link.

7. Select the page you want displayed when the link is clicked.

8. Finish filling in the dialog box for the type of page to which you are linking. For more information on using the Insert Link dialog box, refer to Chapter 7.

9. Click the Advanced button if the Advanced section of the Insert Link dialog box is not already open.

10. Click the triangle to the right of the Target Frame field shown in Figure 9-3, and choose one of the following options:

    ■ **Default**   Opens the linked page in the same frame as the current page.

    ■ **Entire Window**   Opens the linked page in the entire browser window, replacing the frameset in which the current page appears.

    ■ **New Window**   Opens the linked page in a new browser window. The frameset in which the page that called the link is displayed in the old browser window.

    The names of each frame in the frameset also appear on the Target Frame pop-up menu. (In Figure 9-3, these are topFrame, leftFrame, and mainFrame.) Click the name of the frame in which you want the linked page to appear.

11. Click OK. The Insert Link dialog box closes. The link is added to your page draft.

12. Click Publish. Contribute publishes the page to your Web server. Alternatively, you can click Save For Later, and Contribute will save the page draft for future editing.

Did you know?

About Frames and Search Engines

If your Web site depends on search engines to drive traffic to your site, there is an important fact you need to know about frame-based pages. A search engine sends a crawler to your site to search the pages for keywords and other content that is added to the search engine's index. The search engine uses this information to direct users to your site when they enter keywords or phrases into the search engine's Search field. Unfortunately, crawlers only read the parent frames, which may cause your Web site to be indexed incorrectly. If your site is designed with frames, make sure that your designer has included the <no frames> tag so that your site can be viewed by people using browsers that don't support frames. If your designer has included this tag, search engine crawlers will be able to properly access site content and correctly index your site.

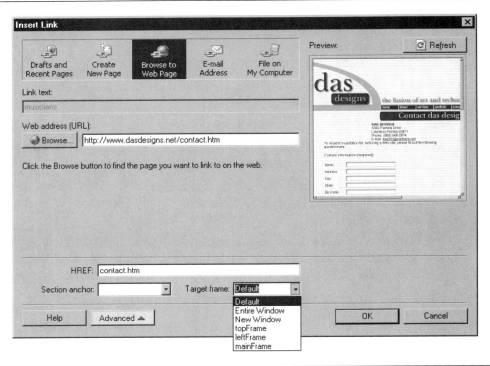

FIGURE 9-3   You can specify a target for the linked page.

Saving and Publishing Web Pages with Frames

When you edit a frame-based Web page, you only work on a page within the frameset. The frameset itself is not affected by your edits. After you edit a page from within a frameset, you publish the edited page, not the frameset.

Publishing edited pages is covered in Chapter 13. Prior to publishing an edited frame-based Web page, you can do any one of the following:

■ *Click the Cancel button in the toolbar or choose File | Cancel.* When you choose this command, any edits you've applied to the page draft are cancelled. After you click the Cancel button, the page you were editing will appear in the browser without the parent frameset. Click the Back button to view the page within the frameset.

■ *Click the Save For Later button in the toolbar or choose File | Save For Later.* When you choose this command, Contribute saves a draft of the page and the associated files to your computer for future editing. When you edit the page draft, you will not see the page within the frameset.

■ *Choose File | E-mail Review.* When you choose this command, you can send an invitation to other colleagues to review the page.

NOTE *When you send a frame-based page for e-mail review, Contribute creates a temporary file on your Web server for the page you are editing, and the link in the reviewer's e-mail will be to the temporary file, which will not be displayed in the parent frameset. This may give the reviewer a false impression of how the page will look when loaded into the parent frameset. You may want to include a note to that effect to avoid confusion.*

To publish the frame-based Web page, click Publish. Contribute publishes the edited page to your server.

9

Summary

In this chapter, you learned to work with frame-based Web pages. You saw how frame-based pages are created and how to edit them. You learned how to create a link from a frame-based page and to specify where the linked page opens. In Chapter 13, you'll learn to publish edited pages to your Web server. In the next part of this book, you'll learn to work with images in your Web pages and publish edited pages and images to your Web server.

Part IV

Working with Images and Publishing Web Pages

Chapter 10

Modifying Document Images

How to...

- Add images to a Web page
- Add horizontal rules to a Web page
- Change image properties
- Resize images
- Align images
- Reposition images
- Add Flash movies to a Web page

When the Web site you edit with Contribute was created, your Web designer probably used images on several pages. You can use Contribute to add, delete, or replace images in the pages you edit. You can also use Contribute to change the properties of an image, such as its size and alignment, and to reposition an image within a document. In addition to images, you can insert interactive animations into your pages in the form of Flash movies and add horizontal rules to separate graphic elements from text elements.

In this chapter, you'll learn to work with the images in the pages you edit with Contribute. You'll learn to add new images to Web pages you edit and to replace existing images. You'll also learn to modify the properties of images in your page drafts, as well as resize and reposition them.

Working with Images for Web Pages

Images are the hallmark of any compelling Web site. You can add an image to a page you are editing. Your site administrator may have limited the size of images you can add to your Web site. If so, this was done to guard against pages that load slowly into the user's browser. If your site administrator did not limit the size of images, you are advised not to exceed the Contribute default limit of 64K (64 kilobytes).

Even though your site administrator may have limited the size of an image you can add to a Web page, there is no limitation on the number of images you can add to a page. However, it is strongly advisable not to go overboard when adding images to a page. When you add several images to a page, the file size increases to a point where the file will load slowly, especially if your pages are viewed with a dial-up modem. If you need to display several images at your Web site and they are all related to a specific topic, create a new page that is linked to the original page.

When you add an image to a Web page, the file size is displayed in the Select Image dialog box directly below the image preview. A 64K image takes about 18 seconds to download when a page is viewed with a dial-up modem. If you add one 64K image to your page and factor in the other items such as text, menu navigation items, and other images your Web designer added to the original design, you begin to see how import it is to be judicious with your use of images. Pay attention to the file sizes of the images as you add them to a page. Keep a tally on a sheet of paper. When you factor in the other elements on your page, it's probably best to limit yourself to a total of 50K worth of images. When you exceed that mark, create a linked page.

Another thing you need to pay careful attention to is where the image is inserted. If you insert an image that is wider than a table cell, the table expands to accommodate the image. If your site designer arranged everything in a table, adding a wide image can destroy the design. You may end up with visual anomalies like blank spaces between menu buttons. If this happens, you'll have to resize the image so that it is smaller than the width of the cell in order for your site to display correctly.

Inserting Images into Web Pages

You can add an image to a page draft you edit with Contribute at any time, and you can add images with any of the following extensions: .jpg, .jpeg, .jpe, .jfif .gif, and .png. If you have images in other file formats that you want to add to pages you are editing, you will need to use an image-editing program such as Macromedia Fireworks to convert the image into one of these Web-friendly formats.

You can use one of the following methods to add an image to a Web page:

- Choose Insert | Image.

- Click the Image button on the toolbar.

- Drag an image from another application into the page draft you are editing.

- Copy an image from another application, then paste it into the page you are editing.

Inserting Images with the Insert Menu or Image Button

You can insert an image into a page draft you are editing from any folder on your computer. When you publish the file, Contribute automatically uploads the file to your Web server. To add an image from your computer to a page draft using the Insert menu or the Image button, follow these steps:

1. Place your cursor at the point where you want the image to appear in your page draft.

2. Choose Insert | Image or click the Image button on the toolbar.

3. Choose From My Computer from the pop-up menu to open the Select Image dialog box shown in Figure 10-1. Choosing this option means that when you publish the page, Contribute automatically uploads the file to the Images directory at your Web site.

4. Navigate to the folder where the image can by found and select the desired image. After you select the image, a thumbnail of the image is displayed in the preview window, as shown in Figure 10-1. Below the preview window, Contribute also displays the image size and the projected download time for a viewer with a 56 Kbps dial-up modem connection.

5. Click Select. Contribute inserts the image into the page draft.

When you insert an image from your computer into a Web page, you can modify the image properties within Contribute, but you will not be able to edit the image in an external image-editing program until you publish the page.

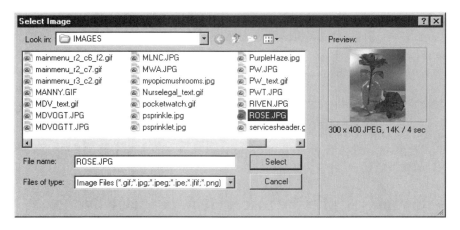

FIGURE 10-1   When you insert a figure, Contribute displays a preview of the image, listing the file size and download time.

When you insert an image from your computer by choosing Insert | Image or by clicking the Image button and the image is larger than what is allowed by your site administrator, the warning dialog box shown next appears.

Inserting Images from Your Web Site

In addition to being able to insert images that are stored on your computer, you can also add images that are already stored in a folder at your Web server. If you are editing multiple Web sites with Contribute, you can select an image from any Web page to which you have made a connection. To add an image to a page draft from your Web site, follow these steps:

1. Place your cursor at the point where you want the image to appear in your page draft.

2. Choose Insert | Image or click the Image button on the toolbar.

3. Choose From Website from the pop-up menu. The Choose Image On Website dialog box appears. If you are editing more than one Web site with Contribute, a folder icon for each Web site appears. The site's URL appears to the right of the folder. If you have disabled a connection to a Web site, Contribute does not display the information for that Web site.

4. Click the folder of the Web site that contains the image you want to insert, then navigate to the folder in which the image is stored.

5. Click the desired image to select it. Contribute displays a thumbnail preview of the image in the Preview window. The URL for the image is displayed as well.

6. Click OK to insert the image. Contribute adds the image to the page draft you are editing.

After you insert an image from your Web site to a page draft, you can modify the image properties within Contribute, or you can edit the image in an image-editing program.

Inserting Images by Dragging and Dropping

You can also insert images by dragging them from another application into the page draft you are editing. A word of caution is in order here. When you insert images in this manner, Contribute does not detect the image's file size and will not prevent you from inserting an image that is larger than the limit specified by your site administrator. In this regard, it is always advisable to insert files that are stored in a folder on your computer. However, if you are sure the image file size is reasonable (no more than 50K), you can insert the image into a page draft by doing the following:

1. Minimize Contribute, then resize the application so that you can also view the application from which you will drag the image.

2. Switch to the other application and select the image.

3. Drag the image into Contribute and release your mouse button where you want the image to appear. Contribute inserts the image into the page draft you are editing.

Note that when you drag an image from an application and drop it into Contribute, the image no longer appears in the original document. To preserve the image in the original document, copy the image to the clipboard and then paste it into Contribute as outlined in the next section. Alternatively, if the application from which you are dragging the image supports this feature, you can press CTRL to create a copy of the original image rather than moving it from one application to Contribute.

 You cannot drag and drop images from certain applications into Contribute. For example, Corel Photo-Paint and Macromedia Fireworks MX do not support dragging and dropping images into a page draft you are editing in Contribute.

After you drag and drop an image to a page draft, you can modify the image properties within Contribute, but you will not be able to edit the image in an external image-editing program until you publish the page to your Web site.

Inserting Images by Copying and Pasting Them into a Web Page

You can also copy images from an application and then paste them directly into a page draft you are editing. When you copy and paste an image, the original document is unaffected. To copy and paste an image into a page draft, follow these steps:

1. In the application that contains the image you want to insert into your page draft, select the image.

2. Use the application's Copy command to copy the image to the clipboard. Alternatively, you can press CTRL-C.

3. In Contribute, place your cursor at the point in your page draft where you want the image to appear.

4. Choose Edit | Paste. The image appears in your page draft. Alternatively, you can press CTRL-V.

CAUTION *You will not be able to copy and paste from certain applications into Contribute. For example, you cannot copy an image from Macromedia Fireworks MX or Corel Photo-Paint and then paste it into Contribute.*

Deleting Images

If you add an image to a page draft you are editing, you can delete it anytime you are editing the page. For example, you can delete an image if it is no longer needed or if you decide that the page looks better without the image. To delete an image, follow these steps:

1. Select the image that you want to delete.

2. To delete the image from the page draft, do one of the following:

   ■ Choose Edit | Cut.

   ■ Press DELETE.

   ■ Press BACKSPACE.

Adding a Horizontal Rule to a Web Page

You can add a horizontal rule to a page draft you are editing. A horizontal rule is a graphic element that you can use whenever you need to differentiate content on a page. For example, you can place a horizontal rule under an image to separate it from other content on the page or to create a visual divide between text elements. Figure 10-2 shows a Web page with horizontal rules.

To insert a horizontal rule, follow these steps:

1. In the page draft you are editing, place your cursor where you want the horizontal rule to appear.

2. Choose Insert | Horizontal Rule. Contribute adds the horizontal rule to the page draft.

After you add a horizontal rule to a page, you can edit its properties. You can change the width, height, and shading properties of the horizontal rule. To edit the properties of a horizontal rule, follow these steps:

1. Select the horizontal rule whose properties you want to change.

2. To open the Horizontal Rule Properties dialog box shown next, do one of the following:

   ■ Right-click and choose Properties from the context menu.

   ■ Choose Format | Horizontal Rule Properties.

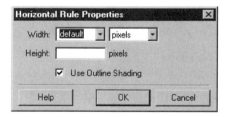

3. To change the width of the horizontal rule, click the triangle to the right of the Width field and enter a value. The value you enter will depend on the unit of measure specified. The default value is pixels.

 *If the horizontal rule is within a table cell of specified width, do not enter a value larger than the width of the table cell, or the table will stretch to accommodate the wider rule and may adversely affect the positioning of other elements in the table.*

4. To change the horizontal rule's unit of measure, click the triangle to the right of the second Width field and choose one of the following:

■ **Pixels** The default unit of measure. Choose this unit of measure if the horizontal rule is displayed within a table cell of set width. For example, if the table column is 300 pixels, you can enter any value smaller than that to change the appearance of the horizontal rule.

■ **Percentage** Choose this option to size the horizontal rule to a percentage of the Web page or table in which it is displayed. If you choose this option, enter a value between 1 and 100. You can enter a value greater than 100, but this is not advisable because if the horizontal rule is displayed in a table, the rule will stretch the table cell in which it is displayed. If the rule is not displayed in a table, entering a value larger than 100 will extend the horizontal rule beyond the boundary of the Web page, causing a scroll bar to appear at the bottom of the viewer's browser.

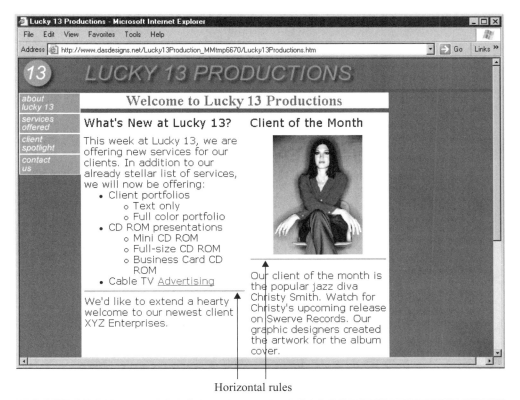

Horizontal rules

FIGURE 10-2 You can use a horizontal rule to visually separate elements on your Web pages.

5. Enter a value in the Height field to increase the height of the horizontal rule.

6. Choose the Use Outline Shading option, and the rule will display as a shaded outline. If you deselect this default option, the horizontal rule will display as a solid line.

7. Click OK to apply the changes and close the dialog box. Alternatively, click Cancel to void your changes.

Modifying Image Properties

You can modify the properties of any image in a Web page you are editing. For example, you can change the dimensions of an image, change its alignment to the Web page or table cell in which it is displayed, or change the size of the area between the image and surrounding elements. Modifying the size of an image and its alignment are covered in the next two sections. Here you'll learn to modify other image properties. To modify an image's properties, follow these steps:

1. Select the page draft that contains the image whose properties you need to modify.

2. Open the Image Properties dialog box shown in Figure 10-3 by doing one of the following:

   ■ Select the image, then choose Format | Image Properties.

   ■ Select the image, right-click, then choose Image Properties from the context menu.

   ■ Double-click the image.

3. To replace the existing image with another one, click the Browse button and choose either Image On My Computer or Images On Website from the pop-up menu. Follow the prompts to insert an image, as outlined previously in the section "Inserting Images into Web Pages."

4. To modify the size of the image, enter new values in the Width or Height fields. Resizing an image is covered in detail later, in the section "Resizing Images."

5. Enter a value in the Horizontal Padding field. This value is in pixels and determines the amount of empty space to the right and left of an image. For example, if you enter a value of 2, two pixels of empty space appear to the right and to the left of the image.

6. Enter a value in the Vertical Padding field. This value is in pixels and determines the amount of empty space above and below an image. For example, if you enter a value of 4, four pixels of empty space appear above and below the image.

7. Click the triangle to the right of the Alignment field and choose an option from the pop-up menu. Aligning images will be covered in detail later, in the section "Aligning Images."

8. Enter a value in the Border field. This value is in pixels and creates a border around the image.

9. Enter a description of the image in the Description (ALT Text) field. Alt text gives people who are visually impaired a description of the image. Viewers who have their browsers set to text only also use Alt text to get a description of the image. Certain browsers display Alt text as a tooltip when viewers hold their mouse pointer over the image.

10. Click OK to close the Image Properties dialog box. Contribute applies the changes to the image.

Resizing Images

You can resize any image in a Web page either manually or numerically. When you resize an image, you can resize it proportionately so it is not distorted.

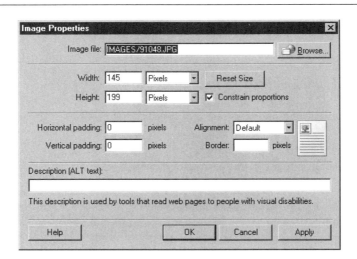

FIGURE 10-3   You can modify an image by changing its properties.

When you resize an image in Contribute, you are not changing the physical size of the image, you are merely instructing the Web browser to display it as if it were a smaller image. In other words, if you insert an image with the dimensions of 640×480 pixels and resize it within Contribute to 160×120 pixels, the image is still 640×480 pixels, and the file size is the same. When the Web page loads into the browser, the image is displayed with the dimensions you specified when you resized the image in Contribute; however, the image at the Web server is still 640×480 pixels and will take longer to load than an image that is actually 160×120 pixels. In this regard, you are advised to use this Contribute feature sparingly. If you have to resize several images within a page you are editing, you are better off resizing the images in an image-editing program such as Macromedia Fireworks MX, Jasc Paint Shop Pro, or Corel Photo-Paint. Editing images with image-editing software is covered in Chapters 11 and 12.

You can increase the size of an image using Contribute. However, this will lead to image degradation because Contribute increases the size of the individual pixels that make up the image. Figure 10-4 shows the results of increasing the size of

FIGURE 10-4   Increasing the size of an image results in image degradation.

a small image within a Web page. The original image is shown on the left, the resized image on the right. If you need a larger version of an image in a page draft you are editing, contact your site administrator or the designer who created your Web site.

If you need to make some minor adjustments to an image in order to fit it within the page you are editing, you can do so by dragging the handles that appear around the image or by changing the image's properties.

Resizing an Image Manually

You can manually resize an image by selecting the image and then dragging one of the handles such as one of those shown in Figure 10-5. You can change the width of the image by dragging the handle on the right side of the image, change the height by dragging the handle on the bottom of the image, or change both dimensions by dragging the handle in the corner.

> **TIP** *To resize the image proportionately, hold down the* SHIFT *key while dragging the corner handle.*

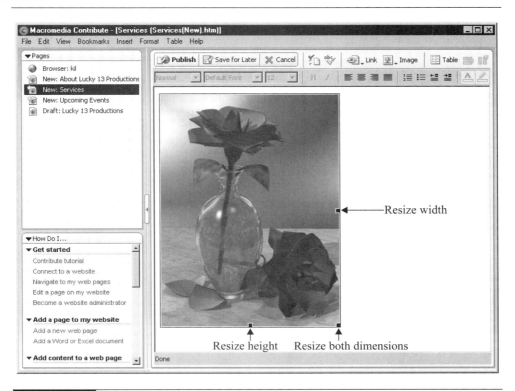

FIGURE 10-5   You can resize an image manually by dragging one of these handles.

Resizing an Image Numerically

If you know the exact dimensions to which you want to resize an image, you can change the image to those dimensions by modifying the image's properties. You can resize the width, height, or both by entering values in the Image Properties dialog box. To resize an image numerically, follow these steps:

1. Open the Image Properties dialog box by doing one of the following:

   - Select the image, then choose Format | Image Properties.

   - Select the image, right-click, then choose Image Properties from the context menu.

   - Double-click the image.

2. To change the size of the image, do one of the following:

   - To resize the image proportionately, enter a value in either the Width or Height field. Contribute will supply the other dimension, as shown in Figure 10-6, so that the image is resized proportionately.

   - To resize only the width, uncheck the Constrain Proportions check box and enter a new value in the Width field.

   - To resize only the height, uncheck the Constrain Proportions check box and enter a new value in the Height field.

   - To resize both dimensions disproportionately, uncheck the Constrain Proportions check box and enter new values in the Width and Height fields.

3. Click Apply to preview the results without closing the Image Properties dialog box. If the results are acceptable, proceed to step 4. Alternatively, enter new dimensions and click Apply to preview the image with the new dimensions.

NOTE   *To revert to the image's original size, click the Reset Size button.*

4. Click OK to apply the changes. Contribute resizes the image.

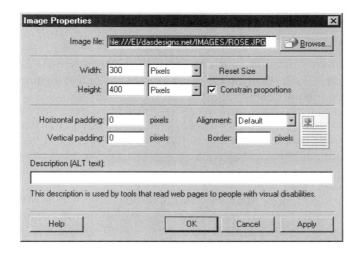

FIGURE 10-6   You can resize an image by changing its width, height, or both.

Aligning Images

When you insert an image into a Web page or table cell, the image is aligned to the upper-left corner, and text flows beneath it. You can change the default image alignment to the left, right, top, or bottom. The image alignment you choose also determines how text flows around the image. To change the default image alignment, follow these steps:

1. Open the Image Properties dialog box shown previously by doing one of the following:

   ■ Select the image, then choose Format | Image Properties.

   ■ Select the image, right-click, then choose Image Properties from the context menu.

   ■ Double-click the image.

2. Click the triangle to the right of the Alignment field, and choose one of the following:

   ■ **Default**   Aligns the image to the upper-left corner of the Web page or table cell. Text flows beneath the image.

- **Left**   Aligns the image to the upper-left corner of the Web page or table cell. Text flows to the right of the image, beginning at the upper-right corner of the image.

- **Right**   Aligns the image to the upper-right corner of the Web page or table cell. Text flows from the left of the image, beginning at the upper-left corner of the image.

- **Middle**   Aligns the image to the upper-left corner of the Web page or table cell. The first line of text flows to the right of the image, starting at the middle of the image. Succeeding lines of text flow beneath the image.

- **Top**   Aligns the image to the upper-left corner of the Web page or table cell. The first line of text flows to the right of the image, starting at the top of the image. Succeeding lines of text flow beneath the image.

3. Click Apply to preview the changes without closing the Image Properties dialog box. If the image is aligned as desired, proceed to step 4. Alternatively, choose another alignment option and click Apply to preview the new alignment.

4. Click OK to apply the changes and close the Image Properties dialog box.

Repositioning Images

You can reposition an image within a page draft you are editing. You can move an image to a different position in the document or to a different table cell.
To reposition an image, do one of the following:

- Select the image, then drag and drop it to a new location within the document.

- Select the image, then choose Edit | Cut. Move your cursor to the location where you want the image moved to, then choose Edit | Paste.

Adding Flash Movies to a Web Page

When the Web site you are editing with Contribute was designed, Flash movies may have been used on one or more pages. Flash movies add visual appeal to a Web page by giving viewers something interesting to view. Flash movies can be simple text animations or full-fledged applications such as quizzes or forms requiring user input. Flash movies are published in the SWF (Small Web File) format.

Inserting a Flash Movie into a Page Draft

You can insert a Flash movie into a Web page you are editing. When you insert a Flash movie into a Web page, there are a few things you should keep in mind, such as the fact that a Flash movie has dimensions just like an image. If you insert the Flash movie into a table cell that is smaller than the movie, the table cell will expand to accommodate the dimensions of the Flash movie. This may cause problems in other parts of the page design. For example, if the table in which you are inserting the movie is nested within a table that contains the site navigation menu, when the table expands after you insert the Flash movie, the navigation buttons may jump out of alignment. When you insert a Flash movie, the dialog box doesn't give you an indication of the movie's dimensions. Therefore, if you're not sure whether the movie will fit, contact the creator of the Flash movie to ask for the dimensions.

To insert a Flash movie in a page draft you are editing, follow these steps:

1. Place your cursor at the point where you want the Flash movie to appear.

2. Choose Insert | Flash Movie. The Open dialog box appears.

3. Navigate to the folder where the Flash movie is located.

4. Select the Flash movie, then click Open. Contribute inserts the movie into your page draft, as shown in Figure 10-7.

Setting Flash Movie Properties

After you insert a Flash movie into a page draft, you can modify the movie's properties. You can specify when the movie starts playing and whether or not the movie plays continuously. To modify the properties of a Flash movie, follow these steps:

1. Select the page draft that contains the Flash movie whose properties you want to modify.

2. Open the Flash Movie Properties dialog box shown next by doing one of the following:

   ■ Select the Flash movie, then choose Format | Flash Movie Properties.

- Select the Flash movie, right-click, then choose Flash Movie Properties from the context menu.

- Double-click the Flash movie object.

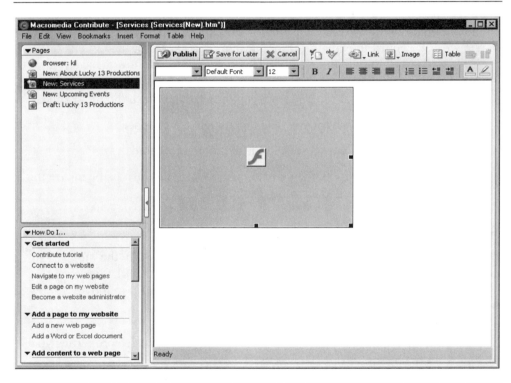

FIGURE 10-7 You can add Flash movies to your Web pages.

3. Select Start Playing The Movie When The Page Loads, and the Flash movie will begin playing as soon as it loads into the page in which it is embedded. This is the default option. Deselect this option if you know that the designer of the Flash movie included a button to begin playing the movie.

4. Select Loop The Movie Continuously, and the movie will play repeatedly after it loads into the page. Deselect this option if you want the movie to play only once.

5. Click OK. Contribute applies your changes to the HTML code that embeds the Flash movie within the page draft you are editing.

You will not be able to preview the Flash movie within Contribute. To preview the Flash movie as it will appear when your page is published, choose File | Preview In Browser.

CAUTION *After you insert a Flash movie into a Web page, you may be tempted to use the handles to resize the movie. If you manually resize a Flash movie, it will be displayed at that size in a viewer's browser. This may lead to distortion, especially if there are images in a Flash movie. If a Flash movie needs to be resized, contact your site administrator or the creator of the movie.*

10

Summary

In this chapter, you learned to work with images. You learned how to add images to your Web pages and how to change an image's size, alignment, and positioning. You also learned how to modify an image by adding a border around it and adding horizontal and/or vertical padding to leave some empty space around the image. Finally, you learned how to add Flash movies to your Web pages. In the next chapter, you'll learn to edit images using an external image editor.

Chapter 11

Editing Images in an External Image-Editing Program

How to...

- ■ Specify an external image editor
- ■ Launch an external image editor
- ■ Resize an image
- ■ Crop an image
- ■ Color correct an image
- ■ Sharpen an image
- ■ Change an image's resolution
- ■ Export an image

As you learned in the Chapter 10, you can modify images in your Web pages by modifying the image's properties. This is fine when you need to make minor changes to an image such as to fit it within a table cell; however, when you need to make major changes to an image's size, this is not feasible. If, for example, you insert an 800×600 image with a file size of 46K (kilobytes) into a table cell and then modify the image's properties so that it is displayed at a size of 200×150 pixels, the physical size and file size remain the same. When you publish the page with the resized image, Contribute uploads the 800×600 pixel image to your Web server. When visitors to the site view the page, they'll have to wait for the 46K file to download before they can view the image. It takes approximately 10 seconds to download a file of this size on a 56K dialup connection. When you add this to the other elements in your page, you can see it may be quite a lengthy wait for the page to fully load.

The better alternative is to resize the image in an image-editing program. If you have image-editing software at your disposal, you can do much more than just resize an image. You can crop images to remove unwanted portions, change image resolution, color correct images, and more. You can launch the external image editor from within Contribute, and when you're done editing the image, your changes are reflected in the page draft you are editing. You can also edit an image prior to inserting it in a page. In this chapter, you'll learn how to specify which program is used to edit your images from within Contribute; how to resize, crop, and color correct an image; and how to change image resolution.

Choosing an Image-Editing Program

There are a wide variety of image-editing programs on the market. In fact, you may already have an image-editing program installed on your machine. If you don't have image-editing software on your machine, look for a program that can do the following:

- Import and export the following file formats: BMP, JPG, JPEG, GIF, and PNG.

- Crop an image.

- Adjust the brightness and contrast of an image.

- Resize an image.

- Adjust the saturation of an image.

- Automatically color correct an image.

- Sharpen an image.

- Export an image with a resolution of 72 pixels per inch.

There are several programs on the market that can achieve these goals. If all you need to do is edit images for page drafts you are editing, invest in a program that is easy to use and supports the previously listed features. Image editing can be a lot of fun. If you're going to be doing a lot of image editing for Web pages, and perhaps for printed publications for your company, you may want to consider investing in a program that supports image filters. Filters can be used to add interesting effects like lens flares, image borders, and more.

Your local office supply store can guide you in choosing the right software for your needs. The following list in by no means all-inclusive, but it lists some of the popular applications for editing images.

- **Adobe Photoshop**   Considered to be the Cadillac of image-editing programs. Photoshop has a fairly steep learning curve and is one of the more expensive applications.

- **Corel Photo-Paint**   A full-featured program that supports plug-in filters. The program also allows you to use sophisticated image-editing tools such as masks.

11

■ **Jasc Paint Shop Pro**   An image-editing program with a lot to offer, especially considering its price. You can perform all of the tasks mentioned at the start of this chapter, as well as add custom touches with paint tools. Paint Shop Pro has an export optimizer you can use to achieve the best quality image at the smallest possible file size.

■ **Ulead PhotoImpact**   Another impressive offering considering its price. You can use the software to crop, resize, and optimize images, and more.

■ **Macromedia Fireworks MX**   A program specifically designed to optimize images for the Web. You'll learn how to use some of its powerful features in Chapter 12.

Specifying an External Image Editor

When you install Contribute, the install utility searches your hard drive and creates an association to the default program your system associates with each file type. For example, if you have Microsoft Word installed on your computer, it is usually the program associated with the .doc filename extension. If you wish, you can associate more than one program with a file type; this option is useful when you install new image-editing software and you want to associate an image file type with your new software. To associate an image-editing program with an image file type, follow these steps:

1. Choose Edit | Preferences. The Preferences dialog box opens.

2. Click the File Editors category. The Preferences dialog box is reconfigured, as shown next.

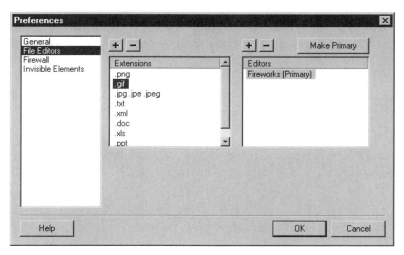

3. Click the desired image file type in the Extensions pane. You can specify an image-editing program for the following file types: PNG, GIF, JPG, JPEG, JPE, and JFIF.

4. Click the plus sign (+) above the Editors pane. The Select External Editor dialog box appears, as shown next.

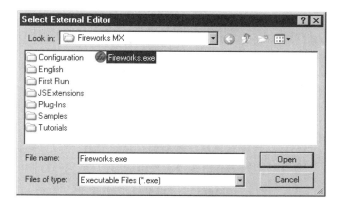

5. Navigate to the filename of the image editor you want associated with the file type. The filename will have the .exe extension, which means that the file is an executable file. For example, the filename that launches Fireworks MX is Fireworks.exe.

6. Click Open. In the Preferences dialog box, Contribute adds the editor to the Editors list for the file type. If you want the added program to be the primary editor for the file type, follow the instructions in step 7.

7. In the Preferences dialog box, while the application name is still selected, click the Make Primary button to make the program the primary editor for the file type. When you make a program the primary editor, you can launch the program from within Contribute to edit an image of the associated file type.

NOTE *You can change the primary editor for a file type at any time (for example, when you install additional software that supports a file type currently edited by another program).*

8. Click OK to close the Preferences dialog box. Alternatively, choose another image file type in the Extensions pane to associate with an external image-editing program.

Launching an External Image Editor

After you specify an external image editor, you can use it to edit an image that is displayed in a Web page you have already published or to edit an image that you select from a folder on your Web site.

Editing Images Displayed in Web Pages

You can edit images that are displayed in Web pages that have been previously published. You cannot edit images saved in page drafts that have not been previously uploaded to your Web site. To edit an image in a Web page using your primary image-editing program, follow these steps:

1. Navigate to the Web page that contains the image you want to edit, and then click the Edit Page button.

2. Select the image you want to edit.

3. To launch the external image-editing program associated with the image file type, do one of the following:

    ■ Choose File | Edit Image.

    ■ Right-click, and then choose Edit Image from the context menu.

    After choosing one of the above, Contribute launches the external image editor.

4. Edit the image as needed. Figure 11-1 shows an image being edited in Corel Photo-Paint.

5. Save the File in the external image editor, and then close the application. Note that if you are editing an image in Fireworks MX, you can save your changes from within the program and exit with the click of a button. Editing images in Fireworks MX is covered in Chapter 12.

6. When you return to Contribute, you'll see the Editing Draft In Another Application window, as shown in Figure 11-2.

7. To preview your changes using your system's default Web browser, choose File | Preview In Browser.

8. After you preview the image, close your browser.

FIGURE 11-1   You can launch your primary image editor for an associated file type from within Contribute.

9. If the changes are satisfactory, click the Publish button to publish the edited image and Web page to your Web site. Alternatively, click the Launch link to open the image in the primary image editor for the associated file type and perform additional edits. After you publish the page, Contribute opens the page in the browser.

Editing Images Stored in Web Site Folders

When you edit images in folders at your Web site, the images will also be changed in any Web pages in which they are present. However, if you change the size of an image displayed in a Web page, the HTML code for the page will not change, and the image will be displayed at its former dimensions, which results in distortion.

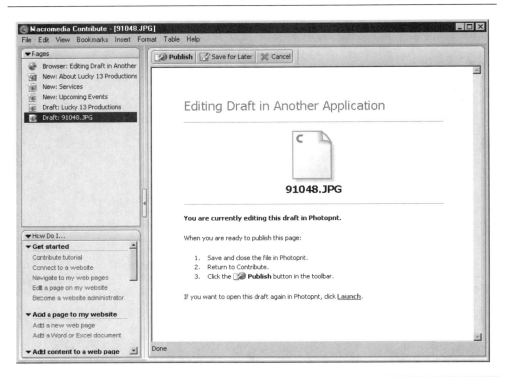

FIGURE 11-2   When you are editing a draft in an external editor, Contribute displays this window in lieu of the page.

If you are editing an image that is already displayed in a Web page, you should consider editing it using the instructions in the preceding section. However, if you are editing images stored at your Web site that will be used in pages you have yet to create, this is the only means to achieving this end. To edit an image stored at your Web site, follow these steps:

1. While using Contribute in Browse mode, click the Choose button. Contribute displays the Choose File From Website dialog box.

2. Navigate to the folder in which the image is stored and select it. Contribute displays a thumbnail preview of the image, as shown next.

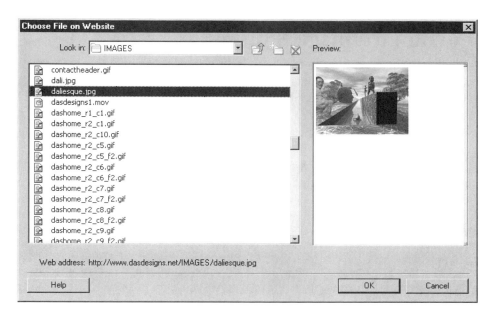

3. Click OK. Contribute displays the image in the browser.

4. Click the Edit button. Contribute launches the external image editor associated with the image file type.

5. Edit the image as needed.

6. Save your work and close the image-editing program.

7. Click the Publish button. Contribute uploads the edited image to your Web server.

Editing Image Files Stored on Your Computer

You cannot edit image files stored on your computer from within Contribute. However, you can edit images by opening them from within an image-editing program installed on your computer. It's advisable not to edit an original image file, however. If you're editing images on your computer that you intend to use in Web pages you have yet to create, select the original image and copy it to a folder that you use specifically for images and other assets associated with your Web site.

11

Introduction to Image Editing

When you use image-editing software to modify images in your Web pages, you have the ability to change the image to suit the page draft you are editing. If you're creating new pages based on templates created by your Web designer, you can edit images to fit within table cells. You can also enhance images that are not clear or that are too dark. In the upcoming sections, you'll learn to do some basic image-editing tasks. The upcoming sections will use Jasc Paint Shop Pro as a model because this software is a popular choice for businesses in need of an easy-to-learn, inexpensive image editor. The sections that follow assume that Paint Shop Pro is the primary editor for image file types.

Resizing an Image

One of the more common image-editing tasks is resizing an image. The actual command you use to resize an image differs depending on the type of software you use to edit your images. For example, some programs such as Fireworks MX refer to the entire document as a "canvas," and in such programs the command to resize an image is within the Canvas menu. Corel Photo-Paint uses the Resample command to resize an image or change its resolution, while Paint Shop Pro uses the Resize command for this purpose. To resize an image with Paint Shop Pro, follow these steps:

1. Select the image and launch Paint Shop Pro from within Contribute using one of the methods outlined previously in the section "Launching an External Image Editor." Alternatively, while in Paint Shop Pro, you can open an image from a folder on your computer.

2. In Paint Shop Pro, choose Image | Resize to open the Resize dialog box shown in Figure 11-3.

3. To resize the image to exact dimensions, select the Pixel Size radio button and then enter a value in either the Width or Height field. Paint Shop Pro supplies the value for the other field to resize the image proportionately.

4. To resize the image by percentage, select the Percentage Of Original radio button and then enter a value in either the Width or Height field. This value is a percentage of the original image. Paint Shop Pro supplies the identical percentage for the other field so that the image is resized proportionately.

5. Save the image and exit Paint Shop Pro.

6. Publish the image to your Web site. Alternatively, if you did not launch Paint Shop Pro from within Contribute in step 5, you can save the image to the appropriate folder for future use.

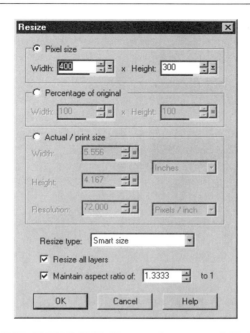

FIGURE 11-3   You can resize an image to a given pixel size or to a percentage of the original image.

 *When you resize an image, you can enter values larger than the original image, but this is not advisable because it results in image distortion.*

Cropping an Image

When you crop an image, you remove unwanted portions of the image. For example, if someone sends you an image, intended for a Web page, of a person surrounded by a vast expanse of white wall, you can crop the image to remove the white area and show only the person. Cropping is the digital equivalent of taking a pair of scissors and cutting away unwanted areas of a photograph or picture before adding it to a photo album or scrapbook. To crop an image in Paint Shop Pro, follow these steps:

1. Select the image and launch Paint Shop Pro from within Contribute using one of the methods outlined previously in the section "Launching an External Image Editor." Alternatively, while in Paint Shop Pro, you can open an image from a folder on your computer.

2. Select the Crop tool shown in Figure 11-4.

Crop tool

Crop area

FIGURE 11-4   You can remove unwanted areas of an image with the Crop tool.

3. Click on the image and drag diagonally to define the cropping area. The *cropping area* is the area of the image that will remain after you complete the cropping operation. As you drag your cursor across the image, a bounding box appears, showing you the current size of the cropping area.

4. Release the mouse button when the cropping area is the desired size and the bounding box contains the contents you want to preserve.

5. You can modify the cropping area by doing one of the following:

   ■ Change the height of the cropping area by moving your cursor toward the top or bottom of the bounding box. When your cursor becomes a vertical line with two arrowheads, click and drag up or down. Release the mouse button when the bounding box is the desired height.

■ Change the width of the cropping area by moving your cursor toward either side of the bounding box. When your cursor becomes a horizontal line with two arrowheads, click and drag right or left. Release the mouse button when the bounding box is the desired width.

■ Change the width and height of the cropping area by moving your cursor toward a corner of the bounding box. When your cursor becomes a diagonal line with two arrowheads, click and drag diagonally. Release the mouse button when the bounding box is the desired size.

■ Move the bounding box to a different area of the image by moving your cursor toward the center of the bounding box. When your cursor becomes a vertical and horizontal line with four arrowheads, click and drag the bounding box to a different location. Release the mouse button when the bounding box is in the desired location.

6. Double-click anywhere inside the bounding box to crop the image.

Color Correcting an Image

If you have an image that is too light, too dark, or lacks contrast, you can correct these faults to some degree using image-editing software. You can also modify images by changing the hue (color), saturation (amount of color), or lightness of an image.

Changing the Brightness and Contrast of an Image

When you receive an image that needs to be displayed in a Web page, and the image lacks visual punch, you can give the image more visual appeal by modifying its brightness or contrast. This is not a cure-all for an image that is very dark or very light, but you can touch up an image that is slightly off kilter and achieve good results when you display it in a Web page. To adjust an image's brightness and contrast in Paint Shop Pro, follow these steps:

1. Select the image and launch Paint Shop Pro from within Contribute using one of the methods outlined previously in the section "Launching an External Image Editor." Alternatively, while in Paint Shop Pro, you can select an image from a folder on your computer.

2. Choose Colors | Adjust | Brightness/Contrast. The Brightness/Contrast dialog box appears, as shown in Figure 11-5.

3. To adjust the brightness of the image, do one of the following:

■ Enter a value in the Brightness text field. Enter a positive value to brighten the image or a negative value to darken it.

11

■ Click the up-pointing triangle to the right of the Brightness text field to brighten the image or the down-pointing triangle to darken it. Each click increases or decreases the value by one.

■ Click the large down-pointing triangle to the far right of the Brightness text field and drag right to make the image brighter or left to darken it.

4. To adjust the contrast of the image, do one of the following:

■ Enter a value in the % Contrast text field. This value is a percentage. Enter a positive value to increase the contrast of an image or a negative value to decrease the contrast.

■ Click the up-pointing triangle to the right of the % Contrast text field to increase the image contrast or the down-pointing triangle to decrease the contrast.

■ Click the large down-pointing triangle to the far right of the % Contrast text field and drag right to increase the image contrast or left to decrease the contrast.

As you change the values, the image in the right window of the Contrast/Brightness dialog box updates to show how the image will appear with the new settings.

5. Click OK to close the dialog box. Paint Shop Pro applies your changes to the image.

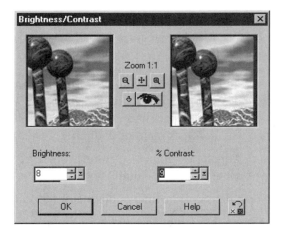

FIGURE 11-5   You can touch up an image by modifying its brightness or contrast.

Changing the Hue, Saturation, and Lightness of an Image

You can also improve the looks of a washed-out image by changing its hue, saturation, or lightness. Most image-editing programs group all three operations within a single dialog box. When you modify the hue of an image, you modify the image colors. When you modify the saturation of an image, you modify the amount of color. You can modify a separate color range within the image (for example, red, green, or blue), or you can modify all colors within the image by a given amount. When you increase the saturation of an image, you make the image more vibrant by adding additional color to it. You can increase the lightness of an image to compensate for a dark image or decrease the lightness to darken a washed-out image. To modify an image's hue, saturation, or lightness in Paint Shop Pro, follow these steps:

1. Select the image and launch Paint Shop Pro from within Contribute using one of the methods outlined previously in the section "Launching an External Image Editor." Alternatively, while in Paint Shop Pro, you can select an image from a folder on your computer.

2. Choose Colors | Adjust | Hue/Saturation/Lightness. The Hue/Saturation/Lightness dialog box shown in Figure 11-6 appears.

3. Click the triangle to the right of the Edit field and choose one of the following from the pop-up menu:

   ■ **Master**   Applies the settings to all colors in the image.

   ■ **Reds**   Applies the settings to red hues in the image. Choose this option to modify red hues in an image saved with the RGB (Red, Green, Blue) color model. The RGB color model mixes reds, greens, and blues to derive image colors. Most of the images in your Web pages use the RGB color model.

   ■ **Yellows**   Applies the settings to yellow hues in the image. Choose this option to modify red hues in an image saved using the CMYK (Cyan, Magenta, Yellow, blacK) color model. The CMYK color model mixes cyan, magenta, yellow, and black to derive image colors. It is rare that you'll run into an image using this color model when working with images for your Web pages.

   ■ **Greens**   Applies the settings to green hues in the image. Choose this option to modify green hues in an image saved with the RGB color model.

   ■ **Cyans**   Applies the settings to cyan hues in the image. Choose this option to modify bluish hues in an image saved using the CMYK color model.

11

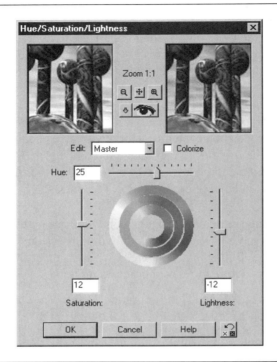

FIGURE 11-6   You can change the hue, saturation, and lightness of an image.

■ **Blues**   Applies the settings to blue hues in the image. Choose this option to modify blue hues in an image saved using the RGB color model.

■ **Magentas**   Applies the settings to magenta hues in an image. Choose this option to modify reddish hues in an image saved using the CMYK color model.

4. Click the Colorize check box, and the settings you choose will colorize an image, giving the image an artistic poster-like feel.

5. To change the hue of an image, do one of the following:

■ Enter a value in the Hue field. Enter a positive value to increase the amount of hue in the image or a negative value to decrease the amount of a hue. The hues affected are determined by the option you choose in the Edit field.

- Drag the hue slider to the right to increase the hue or to the left to decrease the hue. Again, the hues affected are determined by the option you choose in the Edit field.

6. To change the saturation of colors in an image, do one of the following:

   - Enter a value in the Saturation field. Enter a positive value to increase the saturation of image colors or a negative value to decrease the saturation.

   - Drag the Saturation slider up to increase the saturation of image colors or down to decrease the saturation.

7. To darken or lighten the image, do one of the following:

   - Enter a value in the Lightness field. Enter a positive value to lighten the image or a negative value to darken it.

   - Drag the Lightness slider up to lighten the image or down to darken it.

   As you modify the hue, saturation, and lightness settings, the image in the preview window changes to reflect the current settings.

8. Click OK to close the dialog box. Paint Shop Pro applies the changes to your image.

Sharpening an Image

If someone sends you an image to display on a Web page and the image is a bit fuzzy, you can sharpen the image so it looks better in the published Web page. Most image-editing programs have a command called Sharpen. When you sharpen an image, the edges of objects are enhanced and the image appears to be clearer. To sharpen an image in Paint Shop Pro, follow these steps:

1. Select the image and launch Paint Shop Pro from within Contribute using one of the methods outlined previously in the section "Launching an External Image Editor." Alternatively, while in Paint Shop Pro, you can select an image from a folder on your computer.

2. Choose Effects | Sharpen | Sharpen. You can apply the command as many times as necessary.

If the image needs a lot of sharpening, you can choose Effects | Sharpen | Sharpen More to apply a higher level of sharpening to the image.

11

Changing the Resolution of an Image

If you are adding an image to a Web page that has been acquired from a scanner, you're probably working with an image that has a resolution of 200 pixels per inch (ppi) or greater. A resolution of 200 ppi is correct if you're going to print the image, but it's more than you need for displaying an image on a Web page.

An image with a high resolution also has a large file size. If you insert an image with a high resolution in a Web page you are editing, the published page will take longer to download than it would with an image that has the proper resolution for the Web.

The resolution of a computer monitor is 72 pixels per inch, which is the correct resolution for images you edit for your Web pages. Many programs give you the option of changing image resolution, while others set image resolution when the image is exported. Paint Shop Pro sets image resolution to 72 pixels per inch on export, while with Corel Photo-Paint, you use the Resample command to change image resolution.

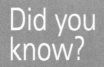

How Do You Choose the Right Resolution?

When you choose a resolution for an image, you match it as closely as possible to the intended display device (such as a PDA screen or computer monitor) or the intended output device (your printer, or the printer that will be used to print the document for which you are editing the image).

When you modify the resolution for display as wallpaper on a computer monitor, or for display on a Web page, it's a no-brainer: choose 72 ppi or, at most, 96 ppi. You simply don't need any more pixels per inch than that. If you're choosing the resolution for an image that will be part of a printed document, consult your printer manual for the maximum print resolution, or contact the staff at the service center; ask them what resolution is correct for their printer and choose that resolution. When you change an image's resolution, be sure to choose the image-editing program's resample option as well. When the resolution is changed, the image is resampled (resized) to the correct size for the resolution you select. For example, if you have an image that is 300×300 pixels and the resolution is 300 ppi, when you change the resolution to 100 ppi, the image is resampled to 100×100 pixels. Remember, you can always choose a lower resolution for an image and achieve good results, but when you choose a higher resolution, you're instructing the image-editing software to add pixels where there once were none, and the result is a distorted image.

Exporting an Image

When you edit images from within Contribute, you save the image with the applied edits and then return to the page draft you are editing. When you return to the page draft, the image you edited is updated to reflect your changes. However, there may be times when you are editing images prior to inserting them into new or existing Web pages. Each image-editing program has a different method for exporting images for an intended destination. When you export an image, the image is compressed to a file size that is considered optimal for the image's intended destination. Some programs give you a considerable amount of control over the export process, enabling you to view the original image and the compressed image side by side. Fireworks MX has an export wizard that enables you to specify a file size that is used to determine the amount of compression applied to the image. In Paint Shop Pro, you can export an image for a specific format. The ideal format for displaying images of people in your Web pages is JPG. (JPG is derived from JPEG, an acronym for the Joint Photographic Experts Group.) To export an image as a JPG file from Paint Shop Pro, follow these steps:

1. Choose File | Export | JPEG Optimizer. The JPEG Optimizer dialog box opens, as shown in Figure 11-7.

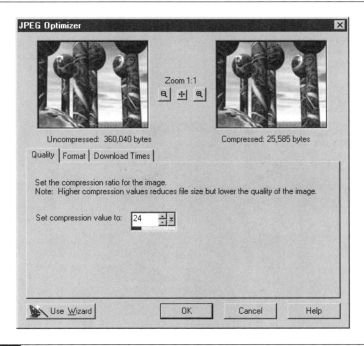

11

FIGURE 11-7   You can optimize the image for the Web using the JPEG Optimizer.

The quickest and easiest way to export an image is to use the JPEG Wizard.

2. Click the Use Wizard button. The Quality dialog box shown next appears.

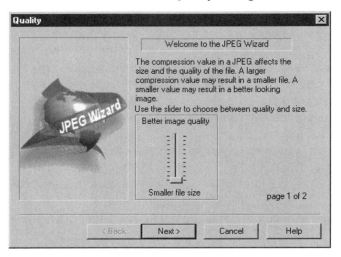

3. Accept the default smaller file size setting or drag the slider up to export a higher quality image. You may want to consider using the default setting. If the image isn't to your liking, you can come back to this dialog box later and change the setting to export a better looking image.

4. Click Next. The JPEG Wizard dialog box shown next appears. This dialog box shows you how your image will look after it is exported. It also shows you the projected file size.

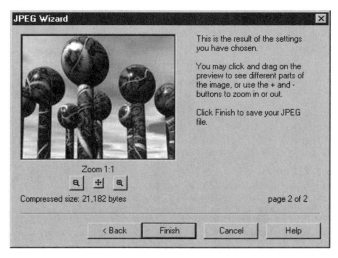

5. If the image file size and quality are acceptable, click Finish to export the image; otherwise, click Back to change the setting.

Summary

In this chapter, you were given an introduction to image editing. You learned how to edit an image in an external image editor from within Contribute and how to perform some rudimentary image-editing tasks. The subject of editing images warrants a book of its own. If you're interested in learning more about image editing, check out the selection of books at www.osborne.com. In the next chapter, you'll learn how to harness some of the power of Fireworks MX to perform sophisticated image-editing tasks. You'll also learn how to create an image gallery.

11

Chapter 12

Advanced Image Editing with Macromedia Fireworks MX

How to...

- Optimize for the Web
- Apply special effects
- Scan images
- Use digital images
- Preview images
- Export images

In previous chapters, you've learned to work with images for the Web pages you edit with Contribute. You also learned the importance of resizing an image in an image-editing program as opposed to resizing the image in Contribute. There are several programs you can use to edit the images displayed in your Web pages, but few that are made especially for Web graphics. Macromedia Fireworks MX is one program that is tailored for Web page graphics. In fact, you can use Macromedia Fireworks MX to create navigation menus and other items for your Web pages.

Macromedia Fireworks MX is an ideal solution for working with images for your Web pages. You can use the software to prepare images prior to inserting them in Web pages, or use the software to edit existing images in your Web pages. With the software, you can crop, resize, and color-correct images and much more. Macromedia Fireworks MX features powerful tools for optimizing images for delivery over the Internet. In addition, you can use the built-in "Live Effects" to add drop shadows to text, add beveled borders to images, and more. In this chapter, you'll learn to use Macromedia Fireworks MX to edit images and optimize them for the Web. You'll learn to use the round-trip editing feature to edit an image while working in Contribute. You'll also learn to work with scanned images, as well as images from digital cameras.

Understanding Image Formats

When you begin to explore image editing, you'll see that there is a vast array of image formats. Many image formats are proprietary to a particular image-editing program, for example, Corel's CPT format. Other formats were originally proprietary to software, but became so popular that other image-editing programs now recognize them. A perfect example is the Adobe PSD image format. When you work with images for a Web site, you only need concern yourself with a few formats. In the sections that follow, you'll learn which image formats to use for Web site images.

Working with the GIF Format

When you're working with an image with large areas of solid color and text, such as your company's logo or an illustration with large areas of solid color, the best format to work with is the GIF format. Images saved using the GIF format have a 256-color palette. GIF images can have areas of transparent color as well. When you optimize a GIF image in Macromedia Fireworks MX, you can choose the color palette with which to export the image. Your best bet is to use one of the Web-safe options. The Web-safe color palette comprises 216 colors that look the same whether viewed on a Windows-based computer or on a Macintosh. Figure 12-1 shows an image in Fireworks MX that was exported as a GIF file.

You can use the GIF format to export photos of people and landscapes. However, when you work with photographs, you're working with millions of colors. As mentioned previously, the GIF format is capable of handling only 256 colors. If you use the GIF format to export a photo that exceeds the 256-color limitation, missing colors are dithered from the Web-safe color palette. When a missing color is dithered, two or more colors from the Web-safe palette are mixed to create a

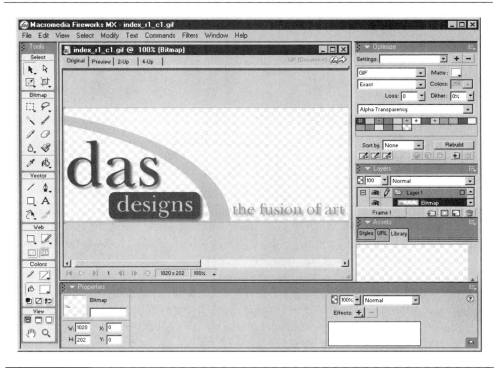

FIGURE 12-1   When you have an image with large areas of solid color, GIF is the ideal export format.

reasonable facsimile of the missing color. When a photo with millions of colors is exported using the GIF format, the exported image is limited to a 256-color palette, which causes the file size to become unnecessarily large. If you export the same photo using the JPEG format, the end result is a better quality image and a smaller file size. When you optimize photographs for a Web page you are editing, you'll achieve better results using the JPEG format.

Working with the JPEG Format

Images such as photographs of people, places, or buildings consist of a wide variety of colors. When you consider the different hues and variations that occur when the colors of an image are displayed in vibrant sunlight and shade, you end up with a palette of millions of colors. With images like these, your best bet is to use the JPEG format for export. Images exported using the JPEG format are compressed in order to keep the file size as small as possible. When an image is compressed, however, certain color information is lost. For example, if an image has two shades of red that are close in hue, one of the hues may be dropped (or lost) when the image is exported in JPEG format. JPEG is referred to as a *lossy* format for this reason. When you heavily compress an image, you'll notice some blurring of fine details. You may also notice some visual anomalies that look like star bursts around text objects. You can determine how much color information is lost when you optimize the image. Figure 12-2 shows two JPEG images. The image on the right was highly compressed when the file was exported.

Working with the PNG Format

When you use Fireworks MX to create documents that comprise images and text, and then save the document, your only choice is the PNG format. When you open the PNG file in Fireworks MX, all of the objects in your document are still fully editable. You can also export a document in the PNG format for use in a Web page. The PNG format supports image transparency; however, not all Web browsers support transparency with the PNG format. You can export an image from Fireworks MX using the following PNG formats: PNG 8 (256 colors), PNG 24 (24-bit, millions of colors), or PNG 32 (32-bit, millions of colors).

NOTE *If you use the Fireworks Save or Save As commands, the image is saved using the native Fireworks PNG format. When you save a document as a PNG file, Fireworks preserves layers and any effects you've applied to the image. When you open the file in Fireworks, you can edit any of these items. Using the Fireworks Save or Save As commands results in a larger PNG file than exporting the image as a PNG file.*

FIGURE 12-2   You can control image quality and file size when you use the JPEG format to export an image.

12

Round-trip Editing from Contribute

If you have Macromedia Fireworks MX installed on your system and specify it as your primary editor for image files in Contribute, the process of editing images is streamlined. When you choose to edit an image from a page draft, Fireworks MX launches, just like any other image editor you choose as the primary editor for a file type. After Fireworks MX launches, you edit the image, and then you click a button to save the image and return to Contribute.

NOTE   *For more information on specifying Macromedia Fireworks MX as your primary image editor, refer to Chapter 11.*

To edit an image from Contribute in Fireworks MX:

1. Select the image and launch Fireworks MX from within Contribute using one of the methods outlined in Chapter 11. When Fireworks MX launches, a dialog box appears asking you if you want to use an existing Fireworks MX document as the source for your edits. Click No, unless you have a copy of a Fireworks MX PNG file of the image before it was exported to its current format. The image you are editing appears in the Fireworks MX workspace, as shown in Figure 12-3.

 If you have the original PNG file, you can update it at the same time that you modify the image from your Web page by clicking Yes and then navigating to the original PNG file. After you edit the image and click the Done button, the original PNG file is updated to reflect your changes as well as the image in the page draft you are editing within Contribute.

2. Perform the necessary edits.

3. Click the Done button. Fireworks MX saves the image, the application is minimized, and you are returned to Contribute.

4. Click the Publish button to publish the edited image to your Web site.

FIGURE 12-3   After you edit an image in Fireworks MX, click the Done button to save your changes.

 *After you click the Done button, the Fireworks MX application is still active. If your computer has limited memory, exit the application to regain resources used by the Fireworks MX application.*

Optimizing for the Web

When you use Fireworks MX to optimize an image for the Web, you can compare the original version of an image to a compressed version of the image. By comparing the two versions of the image side by side, you can see the effects your current compression settings will have on the image when it is exported. For example, if you add an image to a Web page that someone from Human Resources sent and notice that the file size is a bit hefty, you can optimize the image in Fireworks MX to achieve the smallest possible file size while still maintaining acceptable image quality. In upcoming sections, you'll learn to optimize GIF images and JPEG images.

Optimizing a GIF Image

The designer of your Web site has probably already optimized most of its GIF images. However, there may be occasions when someone in your organization sends you a GIF image to add to a Web page. After adding the image to the page and publishing it, you may be able to achieve a smaller file size by optimizing the image in Fireworks MX. To optimize a GIF image displayed in a Web page, follow these steps:

1. Select the image and launch Fireworks MX from within Contribute using one of the methods outlined in Chapter 11. When Fireworks MX launches, a dialog box appears asking you if you want to use an existing Fireworks MX document as the source for your edits. Click No, unless you have a copy of a Fireworks MX PNG file of the image before it was exported to its current format.

2. Click the 2-Up tab. Fireworks MX displays two versions of your image: the original and optimized.

3. Choose Window | Optimize. The Optimize panel opens.

4. In the Optimize panel, click the triangle to the right of the Settings window and choose GIF WebSnap 128. This optimizes the image using 128 colors from the Web-safe palette.

5. Compare the two versions of the image. Pay careful attention to the image quality of the optimized image. Also note the file size and download times

12

of the original image and compare them to the file size and download times of the optimized image. You'll find these values at the bottom of the document window, as shown in Figure 12-4.

6. To achieve a smaller file size, click the triangle to the right of the Colors field and choose a value from the pop-up menu. If you've already determined that the image quality and file size is acceptable with 128 colors, choose 64.

7. Repeat steps 5 and 6 until you notice image degradation and then choose the next highest number of colors. For example, if you select 16 colors and the image quality is no longer acceptable, repeat step 6 and choose 32 colors from the pop-up menu.

8. After you optimize the image, click the Done button. Fireworks MX saves the image, and you're returned to Contribute.

9. Click the Publish button. Contribute publishes the optimized file to your Web server.

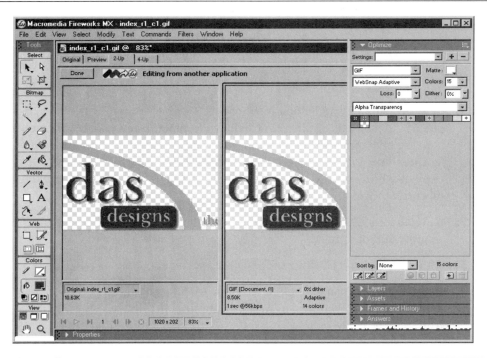

FIGURE 12-4   You can optimize GIF images to achieve a smaller file size.

Optimizing a JPEG Image

When you optimize a JPEG image, you adjust the compression settings to achieve the smallest possible file size while still maintaining acceptable image quality. You can optimize an image in a Web page you are currently editing, or from an image file on your computer that you are editing for future use. To optimize a JPEG image, follow these steps:

1. Select the image and launch Fireworks MX from within Contribute using one of the methods outlined in Chapter 11. When Fireworks MX launches, a dialog box appears asking you if you want to use an existing Fireworks MX document as the source for your edits. Click No, unless you have a copy of a Fireworks MX PNG file of the image before it was exported to its current format. Fireworks MX displays the image in the workspace, as shown previously in Figure 12-3.

2. Click the 2-Up tab. Fireworks MX displays two versions of the image.

3. Choose Window | Optimize. The Optimize panel opens, as shown in Figure 12-5.

4. In the Optimize panel, click the triangle to the right of the Quality field and drag the slider down to apply more compression to the image. Or, you can enter a value in the Quality field. As you apply further compression, compare the quality of the original image to the compressed one. Also, compare the file size and download time at the bottom of each window.

5. When you've achieved the optimal compression rate for the image, click Done. Fireworks MX minimizes, and you're returned to Contribute.

6. Click the Publish button. The optimized image is published to your Web site.

12

Working with Text

When you edit an image in Fireworks MX, you can add text, titles, and other information to images by using the Text tool. To add text to an image, follow these steps:

1. Select the image and launch Fireworks MX from within Contribute using one of the methods outlined in Chapter 11. When Fireworks MX launches, a dialog box appears asking you if you want to use an existing Fireworks

FIGURE 12-5 You can optimize a JPEG image to achieve a smaller file size.

MX document as the source for your edits. Click No, unless you have a copy of a Fireworks MX PNG file of the image before it was exported to its current format. Fireworks MX displays the image in the workspace as shown previously in Figure 12-3.

2. Select the Text tool, which looks like a capital A.

3. Choose Window | Properties to open the Property inspector shown in Figure 12-6.

4. Click the triangle to the right of the Font field and choose a font type from the pop-up menu.

5. Click the triangle to the right of the Size field and drag the slider to specify the font size.

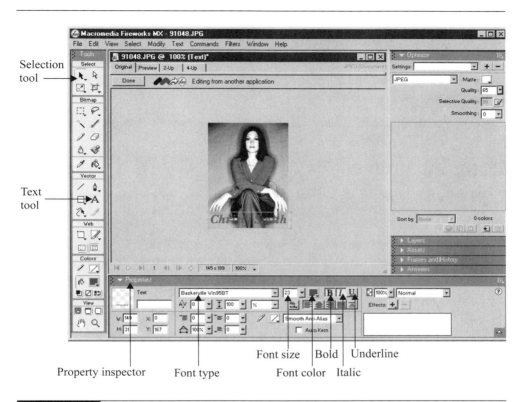

Selection tool

Text tool

Property inspector   Font type   Font size   Bold   Underline

Font color   Italic

FIGURE 12-6   You can use Fireworks MX to add text to your images.

12

6. To specify the font color, click the color swatch to the right of the Size field and click a color swatch from the pop-up palette.

7. Click the desired style buttons. You can use any or all of the following styles: Bold, Italic, or Underline.

8. Click inside the image where you want the text to appear.

9. Enter the text you want to display on the image.

10. To move the text to a different position, select the Selection tool, then click and drag the text to the desired location.

11. Optimize the image as outlined in the previous section. If the image is a JPEG image, pay special attention to the text because visual anomalies may appear beside the text if you compress the image too much.

12. Click the Done button. Fireworks MX saves your changes and you are returned to Contribute.

13. Click the Publish button to publish the image to your Web site.

Resizing an Image

If you use Fireworks MX as your primary image editor, you can quickly resize an image. You can resize an image proportionately by following these steps:

1. Select the image and launch Fireworks MX from within Contribute using one of the methods outlined in Chapter 11. When Fireworks MX launches, a dialog box appears asking you if you want to use an existing Fireworks MX document as the source for your edits. Click No, unless you have a copy of a Fireworks MX PNG file of the image before it was exported to its current format.

2. Choose Canvas | Image Resize. Fireworks MX opens the Image Size dialog box, as shown in Figure 12-7.

3. Enter a value in either the Width or Height field. Fireworks MX changes the other value to resize the image proportionately.

4. Click OK. The image is resized.

5. Click the Done button. Fireworks MX saves your changes and Contribute becomes the active application.

6. Click the Publish button. Contribute publishes the resized image to your Web server.

You can also change the height or width of an image without affecting the other dimension by deselecting the Constrain Proportions check box shown in Figure 12-7.

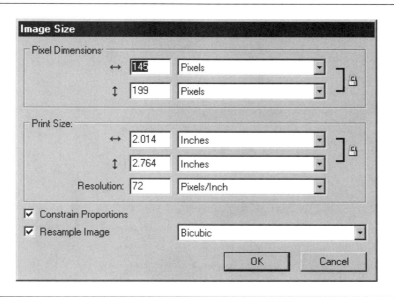

FIGURE 12-7   You can use Fireworks MX to resize images.

Applying Live Effects

Fireworks MX has a powerful feature called Live Effects. You can apply one of these effects to an image you are editing, and then edit several other parameters of the image. If after editing the image you decide that the Live Effect needs to be modified, you can do so quickly without having to undo the edits you applied after adding the Live Effect. You use Live Effects to modify an image. For example, you can color correct an image, sharpen an image, add a beveled border to an image, and more by selecting the image, clicking the Add Effects button, which looks like a plus sign (+) in the Property inspector, and then selecting an effect from the menu shown in Figure 12-8.

The subject of Live Effects could easily fill an entire book chapter. In the upcoming sections, you'll learn to use some of the more popular effects.

12

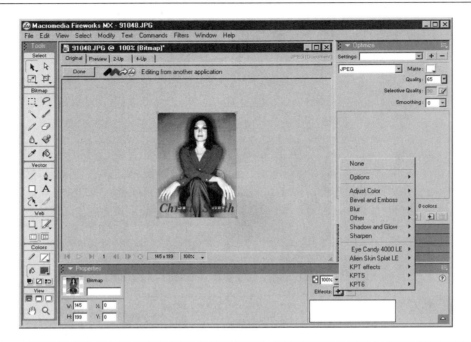

FIGURE 12-8   You can modify an image by adding any effect from this menu.

Color Correcting an Image

When you color correct an image in Fireworks MX, you can adjust the hue/
saturation and lightness of an image, change the brightness and contrast, or have
Fireworks MX automate the process. You'll find each of these effects and more
in the Adjust Color submenu of the Effects menu.

Adjusting Image Brightness and Contrast

You can use this effect to darken a washed-out image or lighten an image that is
too dark. To adjust an image's brightness and contrast, follow these steps:

1. Select the image and launch Fireworks MX from within Contribute using
    one of the methods outlined in Chapter 11. When Fireworks MX launches,
    a dialog box appears asking you if you want to use an existing Fireworks
    MX document as the source for your edits. Click No, unless you have a
    copy of a Fireworks MX PNG file of the image before it was exported to
    its current format.

2.   Choose Window | Properties. The Property inspector opens.

3.   Click the Effects button. From the Effects menu, choose Adjust Color |
     Brightness/Contrast. The Brightness/Contrast dialog box appears, as
     shown next.

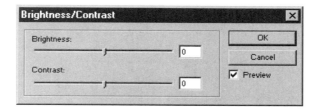

4.   Drag the Brightness slider to the right to lighten the image, to the left to
     darken it.

5.   Drag the Contrast slider to the right to add more contrast to the image, to
     the left to decrease the level of contrast. As you drag the sliders, the image
     updates to reflect your changes.

6.   Click OK. Fireworks MX applies your edits to the image.

7.   Click the Done button. Fireworks MX saves your changes and Contribute
     becomes the active application.

8.   Click the Publish button. Contribute publishes the edited image to your
     Web server.

Adjusting Image Hue, Saturation, and Lightness

You can compensate for a washed-out image or achieve special effects by changing
the hue, saturation, or lightness of an image. When you change the hue of an image
in Fireworks MX, you modify each color in the image, as opposed to modifying
only the reds, greens, or blues. When you change the saturation, you either increase
the amount of color or remove color from the image. To modify the hue, saturation
and lightness of an image, follow these steps:

1.   Select the image and launch Fireworks MX from within Contribute using
     one of the methods outlined in Chapter 11. When Fireworks MX launches,
     a dialog box appears asking you if you want to use an existing Fireworks
     MX document as the source for your edits. Click No, unless you have a
     copy of a Fireworks MX PNG file of the image before it was exported to
     its current format.

12

2. Choose Window | Properties. The Property inspector opens.

3. Click the Effects button, which looks like a plus sign, and then choose Adjust Color | Hue/Saturation. The Hue/Saturation dialog box shown next appears.

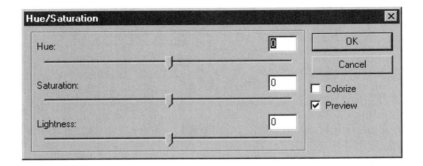

4. Drag the Hue slider to the right or left to modify the image color.

5. Drag the Saturation slider to the right to increase color saturation, to the left to desaturate the color. If you drag the slider all the way to the left, you remove all color and the image becomes shades of gray and looks like a black and white photograph.

6. Drag the Lightness slider to the right to lighten the image, to the left to darken it. As you drag the individual sliders, Fireworks MX updates the image to reflect the current settings.

7. Click the Colorize button to colorize the image. This option can be used to add a color tint to black and white photos.

8. Click OK. Fireworks MX applies your edits to the image.

9. Click the Done button. Fireworks MX saves your changes and Contribute becomes the active application.

10. Click the Publish button. Contribute publishes the edited image to your Web site.

You can have Fireworks MX automatically adjust the color levels of an image by choosing Window | Properties and then choosing Adjust Color | Auto Levels from the Effects menu.

Sharpening an Image

If an image is a little blurry, you can sharpen it. When you sharpen an image, the edges are enhanced so that the image appears to be in sharp focus. To sharpen an image from a page draft you are editing, follow these steps:

1. Select the image and launch Fireworks MX from within Contribute using one of the methods outlined in Chapter 11. When Fireworks MX launches, a dialog box appears asking you if you want to use an existing Fireworks MX document as the source for your edits. Click No, unless you have a copy of a Fireworks MX PNG file of the image before it was exported to its current format.

2. Choose Window | Properties. The Property inspector opens.

3. Click the Effects button and from the Effects menu choose Sharpen | Sharpen. You can apply this command as many times as needed to achieve the desired result.

TIP *You can increase the amount of sharpening by choosing Sharpen | Sharpen More.*

4. Click the Done button. Fireworks MX saves your changes and Contribute becomes the active application.

5. Click the Publish button. Contribute publishes the edited image to your Web site.

12

Creating a Beveled Border

You can add a bit of visual appeal to an image by adding a beveled border to it. When you bevel an image, it appears as though it is in a three-dimensional frame. To bevel an image in a Web page, follow these steps:

1. Select the image and launch Fireworks MX from within Contribute using one of the methods outlined in Chapter 11. When Fireworks MX launches, a dialog box appears asking you if you want to use an existing Fireworks MX document as the source for your edits. Click No, unless you have a copy of a Fireworks MX PNG file of the image before it was exported to its current format.

2. Choose Window | Properties. The Property inspector opens.

3. Click the Effects button and choose Bevel And Emboss | Inner Bevel. The Inner Bevel dialog box appears, as shown next.

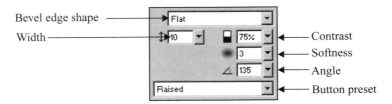

4. Click the triangle to the right of the Shape field and choose a shape for the bevel. Choose an option that suits the image you are editing. When you choose an option, Fireworks MX updates the image to reflect your current choice.

5. Click the triangle to the right of the Width field and drag the slider to set the bevel width.

6. Click the triangle to the right of the Contrast field and drag the slider to select a setting. Increasing the contrast gives you a more pronounced bevel; decreasing it creates a more subtle bevel.

7. Click the triangle to the right of the Softness field and drag the slider to select a setting. Increasing this value softens the bevel edge; decreasing it creates a sharper edge.

8. Click the triangle to the right of the Angle field and drag the circular dial to specify a setting. This value determines the angle of the light source that is shining on the bevel.

9. Click the triangle to the right of the Button Preset field and choose an option. This setting is a matter of personal taste. When you choose a setting, Fireworks MX updates the image to reflect your current choice.

10. Click the Done button. Fireworks MX saves your changes, and Contribute becomes the active application.

11. Click the Publish button. Contribute publishes the edited image to your Web server.

TIP   *You can apply multiple effects to images you edit in Fireworks MX.*

Applying a Drop Shadow to Text

You've probably seen the drop shadow applied to text numerous times. Illustrators and Web designers often use the effect to make it appear as though text is floating above the images behind it. When you add text to an image as outlined previously in this section, you can also apply a drop shadow to it. To add the drop shadow effect to text, follow these steps:

1. Select the text to which you want to apply the effect.

2. Choose Window | Properties. The Property inspector opens.

3. Click the Effects button, and then choose Shadow And Glow | Drop Shadow. The Drop Shadow dialog box shown next opens.

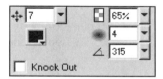

4. Click the triangle to the right of the Distance field and drag the slider to select a setting. This value represents the distance in pixels that the shadow appears from the text.

5. Click the color swatch and choose a color from the pop-up palette. Choose a color that contrasts well with the background. The default black shadow color works well in most instances, except when the text is displayed over dark colors.

6. Click the triangle to the right of the Contrast field and drag the slider to select a value. Select a high value to make the shadow more prominent. As you vary the settings in the Drop Shadow dialog box, Fireworks MX updates the shadow to reflect the current settings.

7. Click the triangle to the right of the Softness field and drag the slider to specify a setting. This value determines how the shadow is blended with the text. Select a high value for a subtle shadow effect, a low value for a stark, hard-edged shadow that appears to be cast from a bright light source.

8. Click the triangle to the right of the Angle field and then drag the circular dial to select a setting. This value determines the angle from which the light source is casting the shadow.

12

Editing a Live Effect

When you apply an effect to an image you are editing in Fireworks MX, you can edit the effect while still editing the image. If you are working on a Fireworks MX document that was saved using the native PNG format, you can edit an effect whenever you open an image. To edit an effect, follow these steps:

1. Select the object to which you have applied the effect. If you are editing a single image and have not added text or other objects, this step is not necessary.

2. Choose Window | Properties. The Property inspector opens.

3. If you have more than one effect applied to the image, select the effect that you want to edit.

4. Click the Edit And Arrange Effects icon, which looks like a blue circle with a lowercase *i* in the center. This opens the dialog box for the effect you have selected.

5. Edit the effect and then click anywhere within the workspace to close the dialog box and apply the new settings.

Deleting a Live Effect

If after editing an image and applying an effect to it, you decide the image looks better without the effect, you can delete it. To delete an effect you have applied to an image, follow these steps:

1. Select the object to which you have applied the effect. If you are editing a single image and have not added text or other objects, this step is not necessary.

2. Choose Window | Properties. The Property inspector opens.

3. If you have more than one effect applied to the image, select the effect that you want to delete.

4. Click the Delete Effect button, which looks like a minus sign (–).

Working with Digital Cameras

If you have a digital camera attached to your computer, you can use it to capture images for your Web pages. Many digital cameras feature a USB cable, which enables you to take a picture and edit it within Fireworks MX. To create a picture while working in Fireworks MX, follow these steps:

1. Launch Fireworks MX.

2. Choose File | Scan | Twain Select. After choosing this command, the Select Source dialog box opens. Within this dialog box you'll find a list of devices attached to your system that are capable of capturing images.

3. Select the proper source for your digital camera.

4. Choose File | Scan | Twain Acquire. Fireworks MX opens the dialog box for your digital camera. Figure 12-9 shows the dialog box for a Logitech camera.

FIGURE 12-9   You can capture an image from your digital camera and edit it in Fireworks MX.

12

5. Follow the prompts within the dialog box to take a picture.

6. Edit the picture as needed.

7. Optimize the image as outlined previously. Your best option is to optimize the image as a JPEG file.

8. Choose File | Export. The Export dialog box opens.

9. Enter a name in the Filename field.

10. Navigate to the folder in which you want to save the image.

11. Click Save.

 You can also save the image using the native Fireworks MX PNG format. For more information on saving images in the PNG format, refer to the Fireworks MX user manual.

If your digital camera uses Flash memory, follow the manufacturer's instructions to transfer the images from the camera to your computer. You can then insert the images into a Web page you are editing, or you can launch Fireworks MX to edit and optimize the image prior to adding it to your Web page.

Scanning Images for Use on a Web Page

If you have a scanner attached to you computer, you can use it to capture images for your Web pages. If you use the scanner manufacturer's software, you may have the option to specify the output resolution. If so, make sure you choose a resolution of 72 dpi, or the closest setting to this value provided by your scanning software.

You can also scan an image from within Fireworks MX and edit the image within Fireworks MX before exporting it. To scan an image from within Fireworks MX, follow these steps:

1. Choose File | Scan | Twain Select. The Select Source dialog box opens.

2. Select your scanner from the list.

3. Choose File | Scan | Twain Select. Fireworks MX launches the dialog box for capturing images from your scanner. Figure 12-10 shows the dialog box for capturing images from an HP ScanJet 5370C.

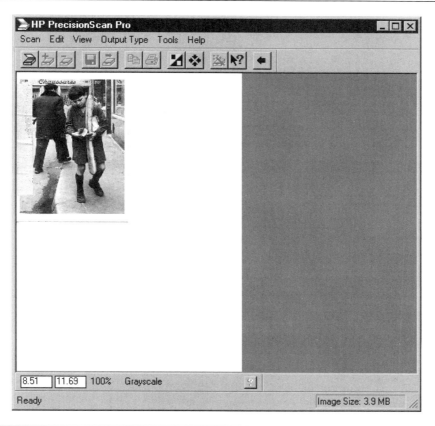

FIGURE 12-10   You can scan an image and edit it in Fireworks MX.

12

4. Follow the prompts to capture the image. After you successfully scan the image, it appears in the Fireworks MX workspace.

5. Edit the image as needed.

6. Choose Modify | Canvas | Image Size. The Image Size dialog box shown next appears. If the value in the Resolution field is 72, proceed to step 9; otherwise, follow the next step.

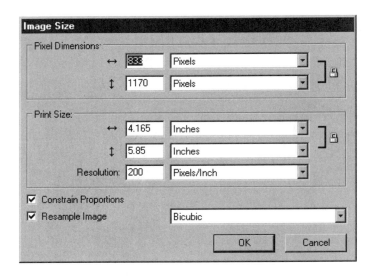

7. Click the Resample Image check box to deselect the option.

8. Enter a value of 72 in the Resolution field and then click OK to close the dialog box and apply the new resolution.

9. Optimize the image as outlined previously.

10. Choose File | Export. The Export dialog box appears.

11. Enter a name for the image in the File name field.

12. Navigate to the folder in which you want to save the image.

13. Click Save. Fireworks exports the image.

 *When you save an image, or for that matter, any other file that will become part of a Web page, do not use any spaces in the filename. If you must use two words in the filename, capitalize the second word to differentiate it from the first, or enter an underscore (_) between words.*

Creating an Image Gallery

If you have several images that you want to display on a page, you can create an image gallery. When you create an image gallery, you can use an image-editing program such as Fireworks MX to create smaller versions of the images, which are also known as thumbnails. If you use Fireworks MX to resize your images, you can create all the thumbnails at once using Fireworks MX Batch Process command.

After editing the images, you create a table with enough cells and rows to display the images. After adding the images to the cells, you create a link from the image in the table cell to the full-sized image.

Preparing your Assets

When you use Fireworks MX Batch Process command, you can select images from any folder on your computer. However, it helps to be a bit organized. In this regard, it's a good idea to move all the images for your gallery to one folder. After organizing the images, you can create the thumbnails by following these steps:

1. Launch Fireworks MX.

2. Choose File | Batch Process. The Batch Process dialog box opens.

3. Click the triangle to the right of the Look In field and navigate to the folder where your images are stored.

4. Select the images that will appear in your image gallery and then click the Add button, as shown next. Fireworks adds the images to the list of files to process.

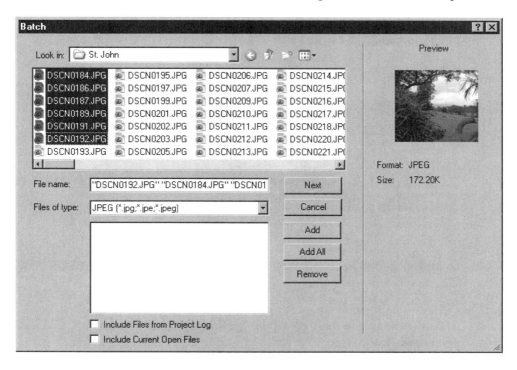

5. Click the Next button. The Batch Process dialog box is reconfigured to display two windows. In the Batch Options window are the commands you can apply to the selected images.

6. From the Batch Options window, select Scale and then click the Add button. The Scale command is added to the batch process.

7. Click the triangle to the right of the Scale field and choose Scale To Size from the pop-up menu.

8. Click the triangle to the right of the Width field and choose a value from the pop-up menu. A value of 150 is good for thumbnail images (or you can enter a different value).

9. Click the triangle to the right of the Height field and choose Variable from the pop-up menu, as shown next. When you choose this option, Fireworks MX resizes the height of each image proportionately to the width.

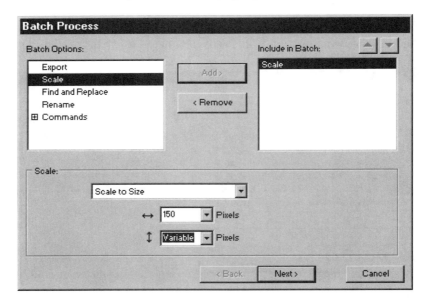

10. In the Batch Options window, click Rename and then click the Add button. When you rename the thumbnail images, the thumbnail images are saved with different filenames, therefore the original files are unaffected.

11. Click the triangle to the right of the Rename field and choose Suffix. When you choose this option, Fireworks MX appends the end of the filename with the suffix you specify.

12. Enter **t** in the blank field to the right of the Suffix field. You can enter any character you want; *t* for thumbnail is a logical choice.

13. Click the Next button. The Batch Process dialog box is reconfigured, as shown next.

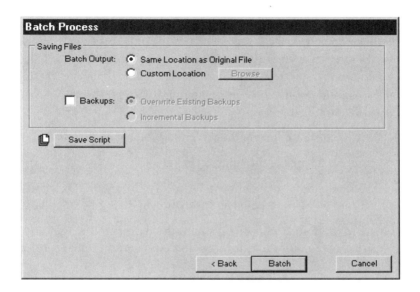

14. Click the Same Location as Original File radio button.

15. Click the Batch button. Fireworks MX processes the files.

After the images are resized, you're ready to begin your work in Contribute.

Creating the Image Gallery

After preparing the thumbnail images, you're ready to create the image gallery. You can add the image gallery to an existing page, or create a new page. To create the image gallery, follow these steps:

1. Launch Contribute.

2. Select the page draft where you want the image gallery to appear. Or, create a new page.

3. Place your cursor where you want the thumbnail images to appear.

4. Click the Table button. Or, choose Insert | Table. The Insert Table dialog box appears.

5. Enter the number of rows and columns needed to display the thumbnail images for your gallery. For example, if you have nine images to display, enter a value of **3** for rows and **3** for columns.

NOTE   *If you want to display titles for each image in your gallery, add one row for each row of thumbnails.*

6. Specify the other options for your table. For more information on tables, refer to Chapter 8.

7. Click OK. Contribute inserts the table into your page draft.

8. Place your cursor inside the first cell.

9. Click the Image button and choose From My Computer. Or, choose Insert | Image | From My Computer. The Insert Image dialog box appears.

10. Navigate to the folder where you stored the thumbnail images and select the desired image. For more information on inserting images, refer to Chapter 10.

11. Click Select. Contribute inserts the image in the table cell.

12. Repeat steps 8 through 12 to add the rest of the thumbnail images to the table.

To finish creating the image gallery table, add any titles you want to appear below the image. Remember, you can always add a row below a row of images if you decide to display a title for each image.

Creating the Links

To finish the image gallery, you link each thumbnail image to a full-sized version of the image. The linked image opens in a new window, which keeps your thumbnail gallery open in another browser window. To create the image links, follow these steps:

1. Select the first thumbnail image in the gallery.

2. Click the Link button and choose File On My Computer. Or, choose Insert | Link | File On My Computer. The Inset Link dialog box appears.

3. Click the Browse button. The Select File dialog box appears.

4. Navigate to the folder where the full-sized image is stored and then select the file. Remember to choose the corresponding file for the thumbnail image. If you followed the instructions on how to batch process the images in Fireworks MX, this file will have the same filename, but no prefix.

5. Click Select.

6. Click the Advanced button if the Advanced section is hidden.

7. Click the triangle to the right of the Target Frame field, and from the pop-up menu, choose New Window.

8. Click OK. Contribute links the full-sized version of the image to the thumbnail.

9. Repeat these steps until all the thumbnails are linked to their full-sized counterparts. Remember to choose New Window as the Target Frame option for each link.

10. Click the Publish button. Contribute publishes the image gallery to your Web server, along with the thumbnail and full-size images.

Summary

In this chapter, you learned some advanced image-editing techniques that are available with Fireworks MX. You learned how to do round-trip editing from Contribute to Fireworks MX. You learned to optimize images for the smallest possible file size. You also learned to apply special effects to the images you edit. You learned to work with digital images as well as scanned images. The chapter ended with a tutorial showing you how to create an image gallery. In the next chapter, you'll learn to become a site administrator.

Chapter 13

Publishing Web Pages

How to...

- Preview edited pages
- Send pages for review
- Publish pages
- Roll back to a previous page version

After you finish working on a Web page, you have several options. Before publishing the page, you can preview the page in your default Web browser to make sure everything is formatted properly and page links are working properly. If you're working within a team, you can e-mail the page to colleagues for review. If you decide not to publish the page after previewing the page in a browser or receiving feedback from colleagues, you can cancel your edits.

If all is in order with your edited or new Web page, you can publish the page. When you publish a page that already exists on your Web site, Contribute replaces the version on the Web server with your edited page. If the page you are publishing is a new page, Contribute adds it to the files on your site.

If, after publishing a page, you realize the older version of the page looked better, you'll be happy to know you won't have to re-create the older version. You can unpublish a page by rolling back to a prior version of the page.

In this chapter, you'll learn how to preview your work in your default system browser and how to set up an e-mail review of a page draft with other members of your organization. To complete the process of editing a Web page, you'll learn how to publish the page to your Web server. You'll also learn how to roll back to a previous version of an existing page on your Web site.

Previewing the Edited Page

As you create a new Web page or edit an existing one, it's a good idea to preview your work from time to time, as outlined in Chapter 4. When your page is complete and ready to publish, it's a good idea to give the page one more review to make sure everything looks proper in the browser and that all your links open the proper pages in the proper target windows.

To preview a page prior to publishing, do one of the following:

- Choose File | Preview In Browser.
- Press F12 on your computer keyboard.

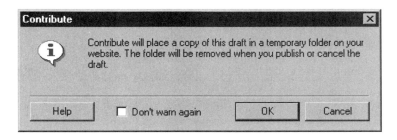

FIGURE 13-1 Contribute creates a copy of pages you preview.

Contribute then displays a dialog box, as shown in Figure 13-1, informing you that a draft of the file will be placed in a temporary folder and that the file will be deleted when the page draft is published or canceled. Click OK to preview the file. Alternatively, click Cancel to abort the file preview.

TIP *To prevent the warning dialog box in Figure 13-1 from appearing every time you preview a page, click the Don't Warn Again check box.*

When the file opens in your default browser, pay careful attention to the overall layout of the page. The following list highlights some issues to consider:

- Is the text aligned properly?

- Is the browser rendering the proper font style?

- If your page uses tables, are the contents of each cell aligned properly?

- If the page uses tables, have you inserted an image or nested a table within a table that causes visual gaps between buttons and other graphic items your designer included in the original design?

- If your page uses tables, are the borders displaying as desired?

- If your page uses tables, are the cells spaced the desired distance apart?

- Are the images in your page aligned as desired?

- Do the links open the proper pages when clicked?

- Do linked pages open in the desired targets?

13

- Does the page print properly? Note that if you insert a table, or for that matter any element, wider than 740 pixels, the page will be too wide to print.

- Have you spell checked the document?

- Have you proofread the text to ensure you don't have any grammatical errors?

 *If you know which browser the majority of your Web site's viewing audience uses, install that browser as your default browser. When you press* F12 *to preview the page you are editing, you'll see exactly what your viewing audience sees when they view the published page.*

If the page looks good in your default browser, you're ready to publish the file to your Web server. Alternatively, you can send the page to colleagues for review.

Using Contribute's E-mail Review Feature

If you work in a major organization, your edited pages may need to be approved prior to publishing them to your Web server. You can easily do this with Contribute using the e-mail review feature. When you institute an e-mail review, you are not sending a page draft, you are sending the URL to a folder on your Web site where Contribute creates a copy of the page draft you send for review. Other members of your organization can then view your work using their system's default Web browser.

About the Reviewing Process

A Web site says volumes about the company or organization that creates and maintains it. A Web site is an organization's window to the world. In this regard, it's best to publish Web pages that are error free and appealing to Web visitors. When you send a page draft for review, other members of your Web publishing team and your superiors can review your work for accuracy, ensuring that only aesthetically pleasing, error-free Web pages are published.

When you request an e-mail review, the following happens:

1. Contribute creates a copy of your page draft and places it in a temporary folder at your Web server.

2. Contribute launches your default e-mail application with the subject and message fields filled in.

3. After you fill in the Address fields with the e-mail addresses of the people you want to review the page and click Send, your default e-mail application sends the message to your reviewers.

4. When your e-mail message is received, recipients can click a link in the message to view the temporary copy of the page draft.

5. Your designated reviewer can view your work and send comments by replying to your original e-mail message.

6. After reading the reviewer's comments, you can make any necessary edits.

7. After making the necessary edits, you are ready to publish the page.

Sending the Page for Review

Whether you are required to send the page for review or you just want others to review your work for aesthetics and accuracy, you send the request to review the page and make it available online. Other members of your team will not be able to edit your work, because the page is unpublished as far as Contribute is concerned. The original page draft remains on your computer. To institute an e-mail review, follow these steps:

1. Open the page draft that you want to make available for review.

2. Choose File | E-mail Review. Contribute displays the information dialog box shown in Figure 13-2, telling you the file will be placed in a temporary folder on your Web server and will be deleted when you publish or cancel the page draft.

13

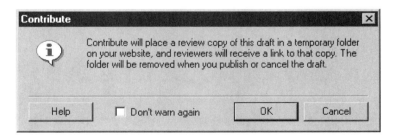

FIGURE 13-2   Contribute creates a temporary copy of a page you send out for e-mail review.

If you don't want to see the dialog box in Figure 13-2 every time you send a page out for review, click the Don't Warn Again check box.

3. Click OK to close the dialog box and open your default e-mail application. Alternatively, you can click Cancel to abort the e-mail review.

4. Enter the e-mail addresses of the team members that you want to review your pages. Contribute has already filled in the message section of the page and provided the link to the temporary file, as shown in Figure 13-3. Enter any additional information in the message section of the e-mail that you deem necessary.

5. Send the e-mail. Note that the method used to send the message varies depending on the default e-mail application you use. Most applications have a Send or Send/Receive button.

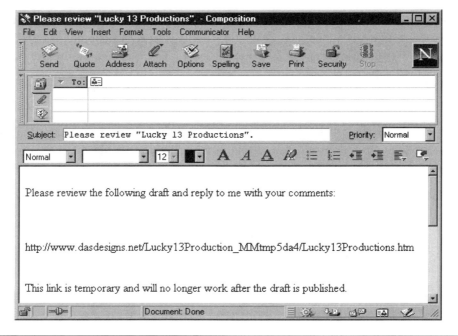

FIGURE 13-3 When you send a page out for review, Contribute launches your default e-mail application.

6. After you send the request to your reviewers, click the Save For Later button on the Contribute toolbar to save the current copy of your draft for editing upon receipt of your reviewer's feedback.

After you receive feedback from your reviewers, click the page draft title in the Pages panel and apply the necessary edits. After editing the page, you are ready to publish the page to your Web server. When you publish the page, Contribute removes the review copy of your draft from the Web server.

> **NOTE** *If, after reviewing comments from your reviewers, you decide to cancel the page and void your edits, Contribute removes the review copy from your Web server.*

Publishing Web Pages

After you use Contribute to edit an existing page or create a new page, review the page in your default browser, and receive approval from your reviewers, you are ready to publish the page to your Web server. When you publish an edited page, Contribute replaces the current copy of the page at your Web server with your edited version. When you publish a new page, Contribute puts it online for the world to see. You can publish the following types of documents to your Web server:

- Edited versions of existing Web pages

- New pages that have not previously been published to your Web server

- Edited versions of existing pages as new pages

Publishing Edited Versions of Existing Pages

When you decide to publish an edited version of an existing page, Contribute replaces the Web page at your server with your edited page. If you have created links in the edited page that link to new pages you have created, Contribute uploads the new pages at the same time as the edited page. When Contribute uploads new pages linked to the page draft you are publishing, you are prompted to give a filename for the new page. The automatic publishing of new pages that are linked

13

to an existing page is a wonderful Contribute feature that ensures that you have no broken links at your site.

To publish an edited version of an existing page, follow these steps:

1. Select the page draft that you want to publish.

2. Click the Publish button. If you have not created new pages that are linked to your page draft, Contribute publishes the page; otherwise, the Publish New Linked Pages dialog box shown next appears. The first linked page is selected and highlighted.

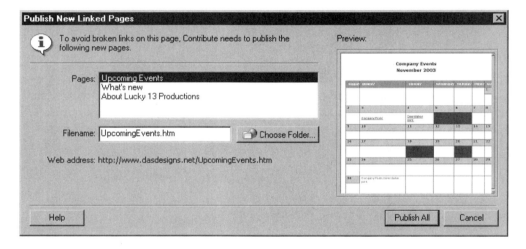

3. To change the filename of a linked page, click its title to select it and enter a new name in the Filename field. Remember not to include any spaces in the filename. If you must differentiate between two words in a filename, capitalize the first letter of one of the words, or separate the words with an underscore (_).

4. After changing filenames of linked new pages, click Publish All. As Contribute publishes the pages to your server, a dialog box appears, informing you of the current status of the upload, including which files are being loaded and other actions that occur. After Contribute successfully uploads the pages to your Web server, the congratulatory message shown in Figure 13-4 appears.

5. Click OK to close the dialog box.

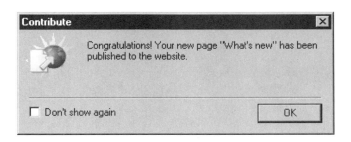

FIGURE 13-4   After you successfully publish a Web page, Contribute displays this dialog box.

TIP   *The dialog box shown in Figure 13-4 is a nice touch when you first use Contribute; however, after you have successfully published several pages, you might begin to find it intrusive. You can prevent the dialog box from appearing again by clicking the Don't Show Again check box.*

Publishing a New Web Page

When you and your reviewers decide that a new Web page is ready to be viewed on the World Wide Web, you publish it to your Web server. When you publish a new Web page, Contribute prompts you for a filename for the new page and for filenames for any new pages to which it may link. To publish a new Web page, follow these steps:

1. Select the page draft you want to publish by clicking its title in the Pages panel. Contribute displays the page draft in the workspace.

2. Click the Publish button. The Publish New Page dialog box shown in Figure 13-5 appears.

3. If desired, enter a new filename for the page in the Filename field. A filename is what appears at the end of the page's URL. When you enter a filename, it's best not to have spaces in the filename. Certain browsers have a difficult time loading pages with spaces. Choose a short name that reflects the page's content. Remember, some of your viewers may end up manually entering the URL for the page in their browsers.

13

If you enter a new filename, you do not have to add an extension. When you enter the desired filename, Contribute automatically appends it with the extension .htm.

4. Click the Choose Folder button to the right of the filename if you want to save the file in a different folder at your Web site than the default folder where Web pages are saved.

5. If you click the Choose Folder button, the Choose Folder dialog box appears. Navigate to the folder in which you want to store the file.

6. Double-click a folder's name to select it. The folder's name is added to the Select button at the bottom of the dialog box.

7. Click the Select [ ] button to close the Choose Folder dialog box. If you selected a different folder, Contribute adds the path to the folder to the page's URL and displays it at the bottom of the Publish New Page dialog box, as shown in Figure 13-5.

8. Click the Publish button to publish the page. Alternatively, click Cancel to void the upload. After you click the Publish button, Contribute uploads the new page to your Web server and displays a dialog box showing you the progress of the upload. After the new page is uploaded, Contribute displays a dialog box telling you the page has been successfully published.

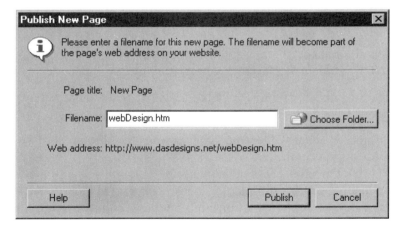

FIGURE 13-5 When you publish a new page, you can specify the filename and folder in which the file is saved.

If the new page you are publishing is linked to other pages, the Next button will appear in step 8 of the preceding instructions instead of the Publish button. If the Next button appears when you publish a new page, follow these steps to publish the linked pages with the new page:

1. Click the Next button. The Publish New Linked Pages dialog box shown in Figure 13-6 appears. Each page draft that is linked to the page you are publishing is listed in the Pages panel.

2. Click the title of a linked page to select it.

3. If desired, enter a new filename for the page in the Filename field.

4. If desired, click the Choose Folder button to upload the file to a different folder at your Web site. If you choose this option, follow steps 5–7 of the preceding set of instructions to upload the file to a different folder.

5. Click the Publish All button. Contribute publishes the new page and any linked pages to your Web server. As the pages are being uploaded, Contribute displays a dialog box informing you which files are being uploaded and which operations are being performed. When the upload is complete, Contribute displays a dialog box telling you the new pages have been published.

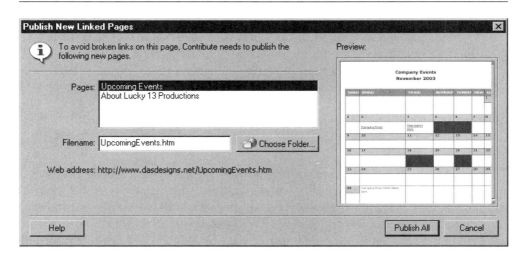

FIGURE 13-6   You can publish page drafts that are linked to a new page you are publishing.

 *If you click the Cancel button in the Publish Linked Pages dialog box, none of the pages will be published, not even the original page draft to which the unpublished pages are linked.*

   6. Click OK to close the dialog box.

   Even though you are prompted to create a link for a new page, it is still possible to create and edit a page without creating a link to it. However, if you publish an unlinked page, visitors to your Web site will not be able to find it unless they know the complete URL to the page and enter it in the Address window of their browsers. When you publish a new page that is not linked, Contribute displays the warning dialog box shown next. If, after reading the warning, you still want to publish the page without a link, Click Yes. If not, click No and select a page draft to which you want the page linked, or edit an existing page on your Web site and create a link to the new page.

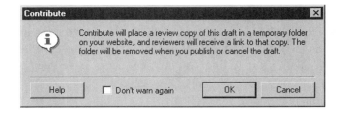

   If you publish an unlinked page, you can still create a link to it after you publish it. After you publish the page, simply select a page draft and create a link to the newly published page, or edit an existing page on your site and create a link to the newly published page. For more information on creating links, see Chapter 7.

Publishing an Existing Page from Your Web Site as a New Page

If you're editing an existing page from your Web site and you decide to publish it as a new page, you can do so easily with Contribute. This feature is useful when your site administrator decides that the changes made to the existing page warrant publishing the file as a new page on your Web site.

   Due to the fact that Contribute creates a page draft when you begin editing and does not replace the original page until you've clicked the Publish button, it is possible to add the page draft to the site as a new page without affecting the page you originally began editing. This feature is similar to the Save As command in other software that you use.

Publishing a Page Using FTP

Before the advent of WYSIWYG HTML editors, Web designers used ftp programs to upload their pages. In fact, some designers from the old school may still use ftp software. When a page is uploaded using ftp software, the user must remember to upload all of the images and other items linked with a page. If this is not done, the page will not display properly when loaded into a user's browser. With WYSIWYG HTML editors like Dreamweaver, the designer is prompted as to whether or not to upload all associated files with a page. When you publish a page with Contribute, the software automatically uploads all associated files, assuring you that your pages will display properly when the Web site you are editing is visited.

To publish an existing page draft as a new page, follow these steps:

1. Select the page draft that you want to publish.

2. Choose File | Publish As New Page. Contribute displays the warning dialog box just shown, telling you that the page is not linked.

3. Click Yes to close the dialog box and display the Publish As New Page dialog box shown next.

13

Publish As New Page   ☒

   (i) Please enter a filename for this new page. The filename will become part of the page's web address on your website.

Page title: | Meet the author

Filename: | Upcomingevents.htm   📁 Choose Folder...

Web address: http://www.mdianevogt.com/Upcomingevents.htm

| Help | | Publish | Cancel |

4. If desired, enter a new title for the page in the Page Title field. Remember, the page title is what displays at the top of a viewer's browser and is not a part of the URL to the newly published page.

5. Enter a new filename for the page in the Filename field. If you do not enter a new filename, Contribute will display a warning dialog box telling you that the existing filename already exists, a feature that makes it impossible to overwrite the existing page. If this dialog box appears, click OK, and then enter a new filename.

6. To store the new Web page in a different folder, click the Choose Folder button to the right of the Filename field.

7. If you click the Choose Folder button, the Choose Folder dialog box appears. Navigate to the folder on your Web site where you want to store the file.

8. Double-click the desired folder's name to select it. The folder's name is added to the Select button at the bottom of the dialog box.

9. Click the Select [ ] button to close the Choose Folder dialog box. If you selected a different folder, Contribute adds the path to the folder to the page's URL and displays it at the bottom of the Publish As New Page dialog box.

10. Click the Publish button to publish the page. Alternatively, the Next button may appear if you have other unpublished pages linked to the page draft you are publishing as a new page. Click the Next button to open the Publish New Linked Pages dialog box, and publish the new linked pages as outlined in the steps 3–5 of the earlier section "Publishing Edited Versions of Existing Pages."

Reverting to a Prior Version of a Page

There may be times that you'll need to revert to a previously published version of a page. For example, if you edit a Web page to display information about a product launch, and the release date of the new product is going to be delayed, you can quickly roll back to a previous version of the page you just published. This is due to the fact that whenever you edit an existing page and publish it, Contribute creates a copy of the original page, provided your site administrator has not disabled this feature.

The default number of rollbacks is three, although your site administrator may have specified a larger or smaller number of rollbacks. When you have more than one version of a page to roll back to, you can select any of the rollback versions, and all of the text from that version of the page will be recovered. However, you may not be able to recover all of the assets associated with the page. For example, if you edit a page and replace an image using the same filename as the previous image, Contribute replaces the image on your server when the page is published. If you edit pages that may require you to roll back to previous iterations of the page, consider giving images and other associated assets, such as Word documents, different names rather than replacing them. If you do this, and you later need to roll back to an earlier version of a page, the assets from the previous iteration of the page will be available at your server, as well as the page itself.

You can roll back to a previous version of a Web page at any time by following these steps:

1. Navigate to a Web page at your site that needs to be rolled back to an earlier version.

2. Choose File | Roll Back To Previous Version. Contribute displays the Getting Version Information dialog box. As Contribute retrieves the information, a bar at the bottom of the dialog box displays the progress of the operation. This may take some time if the rollback versions have a lot of linked assets or if you have several iterations of the page to which you can roll back. After Contribute retrieves the information, the Roll Back Page dialog box shown in Figure 13-7 appears.

NOTE   *Rollbacks will not be available if your site administrator disabled the Rollback feature.*

13

3. Select the version of the page to which you want to roll back. In the Preview window, Contribute displays the version of the page you selected.

4. Click the Roll Back button. Contribute rolls back to the selected page. Viewers will see this version of the page when they visit your Web site.

NOTE   *When you roll back to a previous version of a page, Contribute makes a copy of the page you are replacing and adds it to the rollback list.*

FIGURE 13-7   You can roll back to previous versions of a Web page.

Summary

In this chapter, you learned how to publish edited and new Web pages, how to publish existing pages as new pages, and how to publish new pages that are linked to the page draft you are publishing. You also learned how to roll back to previous versions of a published page. In the next chapter, you'll learn you'll learn to become a site administrator.

Part V

Administering Web Sites

Chapter 14

Working As Site Administrator

How to...

- Become site administrator
- Define user permissions
- Specify site settings

Contribute makes it possible for an individual to control which elements of a Contribute site can be edited and by whom. This individual is the site administrator. Contribute does not require a site administrator. However, assigning a site administrator for a large Web site that is maintained by several employees will ensure that the edited Web pages maintain the look and feel of the original design.

A site administrator is responsible for setting permissions for user groups. The site administrator determines who has access to the pages and what items in the pages can and cannot be edited. The site administrator can also specify which site folders users have access to, as well as whether files can be deleted or not. Site administrators can also set the maximum size for images that are added to Web pages.

In this chapter, you'll learn to set up a Contribute site and become an administrator for the site. You'll also learn to define site permissions, specify site index pages, and remove site administration. If a Web site designer created the site you are administering, you'll also function as the liaison between your Web editing team and the designer.

Setting Up the Site

If you've been assigned the responsibility of being the site administrator for a site that has just been designed, you'll have to set up the site. When you set up a site, you create a connection to the site, become the site administrator, set up permissions for each user group you create, and then send the connection information to your team members that will be editing your Web site pages. To set up a Contribute Web site, follow these steps:

1. Install Contribute on your computer (see Appendix A).

2. Create a connection to the Web sites your team will edit with Contribute. For more information on creating a connection, refer to Chapter 3.

3. Create user groups for the members of your Web page editing team. You can set up as many user groups as needed and assign different permissions to different user groups. For example, you may have one user group that does nothing but update text content, while another user group is responsible for updating the graphic elements in your Web site. For more information on creating user groups, refer to Chapter 15.

4. Specify sitewide settings. You can modify permissions for each user group. For more information on specifying user group permissions, refer to Chapter 15.

5. Send site connection keys to each member of your Web editing team. For more information on sending connection keys, refer to Chapter 16.

6. Check with each member of your team to ensure that they've been able to successfully connect to the Web site. If any of your team experiences difficulties connecting to the Web site, refer to Chapter 16.

Become Your Site's Administrator

When you create a connection to a Web site, you have the option to become the site administrator. You can, however, set up the site without assigning an administrator, and then assign this duty to another member of your team. After you become a site administrator, you can create user groups and define sitewide settings.

Becoming Administrator for a New Contribute Site

You can become the administrator for your Web site while creating the connection. When you become site administrator, you are prompted for a username and password. After submitting this information, you can specify sitewide settings immediately or perform administrative tasks at a later date. To become a site administrator while creating a connection, follow these steps:

1. Create a connection to your Web site, as outlined in Chapter 3.

2. When the dialog box shown next appears, click the "Yes, I want to be the administrator" radio button. Click Next.

14

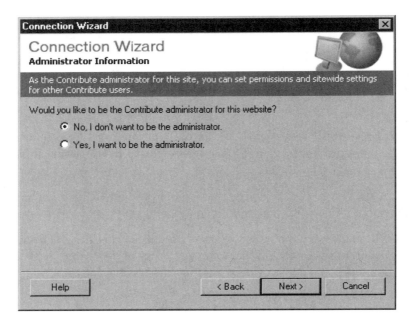

3. Enter a password. The password enables you to administer the Web site at any time.

4. Confirm the password.

5. Click Next. The Administer Web Site dialog box appears, as shown in Figure 14-1.

6. Define settings for your site and then click OK.

After defining settings for a new Web site connection, you have to complete the Connection Wizard, as outlined in Chapter 3.

You can administer the Web site at any time. You'll learn to specify sitewide settings and administrator settings in upcoming sections of this chapter. You'll learn to specify user group settings, create user groups, and create connections in Chapter 15.

Becoming Administrator for an Existing Contribute Site

If a Web site to which you've made a connection does not have a site administrator, you can become the site administrator. After becoming a Web site administrator, you specify settings for the site and user groups, and become the liaison between

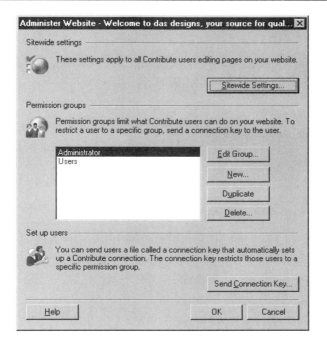

FIGURE 14-1   After becoming a site administrator, you can specify sitewide settings and user group settings.

user groups and your site designer. To become the administrator for a Web site to which you have made a connection, follow these steps:

1. Choose Edit | Administer Websites. If you have made connections to multiple Web sites, they are listed on this menu.

2. Choose the Web site you want to administer. Contribute displays the dialog box shown next.

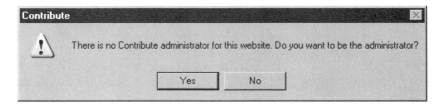

3. Click the Yes button. Contribute displays the Administrator Password dialog box shown next.

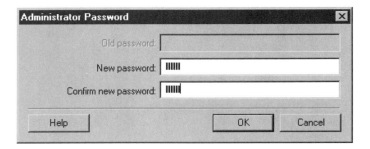

4. Enter a password in the New Password field.

5. Verify the password in the Confirm Password field.

6. Click OK. Contribute uploads the information to your Web server and then displays the Administer Website dialog box.

Defining Sitewide Settings

After you become the administrator for your Web site, you can specify sitewide settings that apply to all members of your team that have a connection

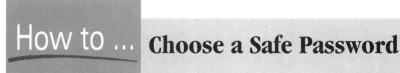

Choose a Safe Password

When you choose a password, and security is an issue, do not choose a password someone else might guess. For example, your employee number or birthdate will be easy for someone to uncover. Choose a password that is a combination of letters, numbers, and characters. Make sure you have at least eight characters in your password. If you have a lot of passwords to remember, store your passwords in a safe place, such as a locked file cabinet. If you store your passwords on a PDA that is password protected, remember to store the password for your PDA in a safe place. Change your password any time you feel security has been compromised.

to the site. When you administer the Web site, you can specify the following sitewide settings:

- Web site administrator information.

- The number of previous versions of a page that are saved at the Web server. This determines the number of previous iterations of a page to which your team can roll back.

- The filenames of index pages.

- Alternate addresses for your Web site.

Changing Site Administrator Information

When you become administrator of a Web site, your e-mail address is often the only link between you and other members of your team. You can change the site administrator e-mail address and password when you edit sitewide settings.

Changing the Site Administrator E-Mail Address

You can assign the task of site administrator to another member of your team by changing the site administrator e-mail address. After you do this, contact the members of your Web editing team and inform them of the new site administrator's e-mail address. To change the site administrator e-mail address, follow these steps:

1. Choose Edit | Administer Websites and select the name of the Web site you want to administer. If the selected site has a site administrator, the Administrator Password dialog box appears.

2. Enter your password and then click OK or press ENTER. The Administer Website dialog box appears.

3. Click the Sitewide Settings button. The Sitewide Settings dialog box for the Web site appears, as shown in Figure 14-2.

4. Enter the new site administrator e-mail address in the Administrator Contact E-mail field.

5. Click OK. Contribute uploads the changes to your Web server.

14

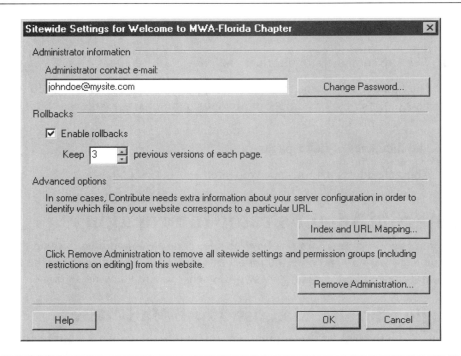

FIGURE 14-2   You can change the site administrator contact information.

Changing the Site Administrator Password

You can change the site administrator password if you feel security has been breached; you can also change the site administrator password when changing site administrators. To change the site administrator password, follow these steps:

1. Choose Edit | Administer Websites and select the name of the Web site you want to administer. If the selected site has a site administrator, the Administrator Password dialog box appears.

2. Enter your password and then click OK or press ENTER. The Administer Website dialog box appears.

3. Click the Sitewide Settings button. The Sitewide Settings dialog box for the Web site appears, as shown in Figure 14-2.

4. Click the Change Password button. The Change Administrator Password dialog box appears, as shown next.

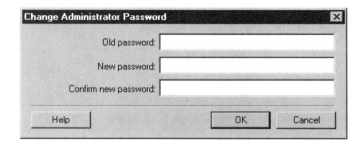

5. Enter your current password in the Old Password field.

6. Enter the new site administrator password in the New Password field.

7. Confirm the new password in the Confirm New Password field.

8. Click OK to close the Change Administrator Password dialog box.

9. Click OK to close the Sitewide Settings dialog box. Contribute uploads the changes to your Web server.

Defining the Number of Rollback Pages

As site administrator, you can determine whether or not your Web editing team has the ability to roll back to a previous version of a page. If you enable this feature, members of your Web editing team will be able to replace the current version of a Web page with a previously published version of the page. This feature is useful if the current version of a page contains errors, or if the published page contains information about a product or event that has been postponed. Rollbacks are enabled by default. Rollback versions of pages published with Contribute are stored in a folder on your Web server. You can have up to 99 rollbacks available. To specify the number of rollback pages, follow these steps:

1. Choose Edit | Administer Websites and select the name of the Web site you want to administer from the submenu. If the selected site has a site

14

administrator, the Administrator Password dialog box appears. If the site does not have an administrator, you can become the administrator by following the steps outlined in the "Becoming Administrator for an Existing Contribute Site" section earlier in this chapter.

2. Enter your password and click OK. The Administer Website dialog box appears.

3. Click the Sitewide Settings button. The Sitewide Settings dialog box appears.

4. In the Rollbacks section, select the Enable Rollbacks option. This option is selected by default. If you deselect this option, whenever a new page is published to your site, Contribute will not make a copy of the previous version available.

5. Enter a value for "Keep [ ] previous versions of each page." Or, you can click the arrow buttons to specify the number of rollback pages. Contribute can maintain up to 99 previous versions of each page.

6. Click OK to close the Sitewide Settings dialog box.

7. Click OK to close the Administer Websites dialog box. Contribute saves the settings to your Web server.

Setting Advanced Sitewide Settings

Contribute is configured so that you and your Web editing team can connect to the most popular types of index pages. An index page is the page that is displayed when users type the name of your Web site in their browser windows. For example, when a user types http://www.yoursite.com, the default index page is loaded. Contribute has a list of the most commonly used default index pages. If your site is set up with a different index page, you can modify this by changing advanced sitewide settings.

If the default index page at your Web site can be accessed through several Web addresses (URLs), your site uses DNS (Domain Name Services) aliases. A DNS alias directs viewers to the default home page of your site. You can configure Contribute to recognize these alias URLs by changing advanced sitewide settings.

Adding Index Page Filenames

Your Web server is configured to search for a default index page when users enter only the Web address (URL) for your site in their browsers. Most Web servers are set up to search for a page with the filename of index.htm, index.html, default.htm, or default.html. Contribute is also set up to recognize one of these filenames as the default index page for your site.

In addition, Contribute is also set up to recognize the most popular file type extensions. Contribute will recognize your default index page if it has a filename of *index* or *default*, and any of the following extensions: .htm, .html, .shtm, .shtml, .asp, .aspx, .ascx, .cfm, .cfml, .php, .php3, .php4, .phtml, .jsp, or .inc. If your default Web page uses a filename and extension previously listed, you do not have to add any index filenames to Contribute's list. However, if your site uses a different filename, for example, home.asp, you must add this name to the filename list in order for Contribute to recognize it as the default page for your Web site. To add a filename to the list, follow these steps:

1. Choose Edit | Administer Websites and select the name of the Web site you want to administer from the submenu. If the selected site has a site administrator, the Administrator Password dialog box appears.

2. Enter your password and click OK. The Administer Website dialog box appears.

3. Click the Sitewide Settings button. The Sitewide Settings dialog box appears.

4. In the Advanced Options section, click the Index And URL Mapping button. The Index And URL Mapping dialog box shown next appears.

14

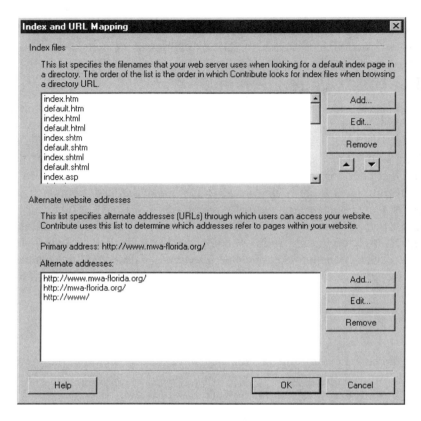

5. In the Index Files section, click the Add button. The Add Or Edit Index Filename dialog box appears.

6. Enter the filename you want to add to the list.

7. Click OK. Contribute adds the new filename to the bottom of the list.

8. To arrange the order in which Contribute recognizes a filename, select the filename whose order you need to rearrange, and then click either the Up or Down button to move the name up or down the list.

9. Click OK to close the Index And URL Mapping dialog box.

10. Click OK to close the Sitewide Settings dialog box.

11. Click OK to close the Administer Website dialog box. Contribute uploads the changes to your Web server.

TIP   *You can also remove an index filename from the list if the filename is not used by your Web site. To remove a filename, open the Index And URL Mapping dialog box as outlined in the previous steps, select the filename you want to delete, and then click the Remove button.*

Defining Alternate URLs

Your Web site may be set up so that different Web addresses point to the same page. The alternate URLs are known as aliases. Even though visitors see the same page when using an alternate URL, Contribute recognizes DNS aliases as different Web sites.

Another possibility is for your Web site to be set up as a virtual server. If your site is a virtual server, several URLs may point towards the same IP, but different pages are served up depending on the Web address entered by the user.

If your Web site can be reached by multiple Web addresses, or if it is set up as a virtual server, you'll need to specify the alternate URLs for your Web site. If you're not sure of the alternate URLs that will point to your Web site, contact your Web designer. To add alternate URLs, follow these steps:

1. Choose Edit | Administer Websites and select the name of the Web site you want to administer from the submenu. If the selected site has a site administrator, the Administrator Password dialog box appears.

2. Enter your password and click OK. The Administer Website dialog box appears.

3. Click the Sitewide Settings button. The Sitewide Settings dialog box appears.

4. In the Advanced Options section, click the Index And URL Mapping button. The Index And URL Mapping dialog box appears.

5. In the Alternate Website Addresses section, click the Add button. The Add Or Edit Alternate Addresses dialog box appears. The main URL for the site is displayed in the Alternate Website Address (URL) field.

6. Edit the site's URL, or enter a new URL.

7. Click OK. The alternate URL is added to the list.

8. Add additional alternate URLs by repeating steps 5–8.

14

9. Click OK to exit the Index And URL Mapping dialog box.

10. Click OK to exit the Sitewide Settings dialog box.

11. Click OK to exit the Administer Websites dialog box. Contribute uploads the new site settings to your server.

You can remove alternate URLs no longer in use by following the previous steps to open the Index And URL Mapping dialog box. Select the alternate URL you want to remove from the list and then click Remove.

Removing Site Administration

You can remove all restrictions on editing a site by removing site administration. If you remove site administration, the shared settings for the site are changed and user groups will no longer be valid. You should only remove site administration as a last resort when you want to start with a clean sheet and redefine user groups and site permissions. To remove site administration from a Web site, follow these steps:

1. Choose Edit | Administer Websites and select the name of the Web site you want to administer from the submenu.

2. Enter your password and click OK. The Administer Website dialog box appears.

3. Click the Sitewide Settings button. The Sitewide Settings dialog box appears.

4. In the Advanced Options section, click Remove Administration. Contribute displays a dialog box telling you that the action cannot be undone.

5. Click Yes. Contribute displays a second dialog box telling you the action cannot be undone.

6. Click Yes. Contribute displays a dialog box telling you that all administration settings have been removed from the site.

After you remove administration settings from a site and navigate to a site page, Contribute will display a warning dialog box at the top of the browser telling you that you can no longer edit the page because the user group you belonged to is no longer valid. You can reestablish the connection by following these steps:

1. Choose Edit | My Connections. The My Connections dialog box appears.

2. Select the Web site from which you just removed administrator settings.

3. Click the Edit button. The Connection Wizard dialog box appears. Contribute has filled in the fields with the information you entered when you made the connection.

4. Follow the prompts in the Connection Wizard. When you click Next after the Connection Information section of the Connection Wizard, Contribute displays this warning dialog box:

5. Click OK. The warning dialog closes and Contribute displays the Administrator Information section of the Connection Wizard.

6. Click the "Yes, I want to be the administrator" radio button. Click the Next button.

7. Enter a password and then verify it.

8. Click the Next button. Contribute displays the Connection Summary dialog box.

9. Click the Done button to close the Connection Wizard. Contribute displays a dialog box asking if you'd like to change administrator settings for the Web site.

10. Click Yes to change the administrator settings. Contribute prompts you for your administrator password before opening the Administrate Website dialog box. Or, you can click No and administer the Web site at a later date.

Summary

In this chapter, you learned to become the administrator of a Contribute Web site. You learned to edit sitewide settings, define the number of rollback pages, and set advanced sitewide settings. You also learned to remove all administration from a Web site when you need to start from scratch and redefine all site settings. In the next chapter, you'll learn to create user groups and define permissions for user groups.

Chapter 15

Defining Site Permissions

How to...

- Create a user group
- Administer user group permissions
- Set editing permissions
- Specify formatting and new Web page permissions
- Limit new image file size

As site administrator, you are responsible for overseeing your Web site. You are responsible for maintaining the look and feel of the site when members of your team use Contribute to edit it. The site designer used his or her knowledge of HTML, graphic design, and other tools to create a unique Web site to portray your organization's message to the world via the Internet. Contribute makes it possible for members of your team to easily update the Web site.

Contribute provides your Web editing team with all the necessary tools to keep your organization's Web site up-to-date. However, giving users carte blanche access to every facet of your Web site can be a recipe for disaster. For example, with unlimited editing power, your Human Resources page may end up filled with large images that make it impossible for the page to download quickly. Fortunately, as site administrator, Contribute gives you the power to restrict the amount of editing that can be performed on Web pages. You do this by creating user groups and then assigning different permissions for each user group.

In this chapter, you'll learn to create user groups and control the amount of editing members of each user group can perform. You'll learn to restrict folder and file access for a user group, determine which documents a user group can edit, and control the formatting of Web page text. You'll also learn to restrict the type of Web pages a user group can create, as well as limit the size of images that are added to Web pages.

Settings and Permissions Administrators Can Control

Contribute enables you to restrict the items that can be edited by members of a user group. When you administer a Web site, you can define sitewide permissions, as outlined in Chapter 14. You can also set permissions for individual user groups.

When you edit permissions for a user group, you open a dialog box that is divided into the following sections:

- **General**   Modify the group description and set the home page for the user group.

- **Folder/File Access**   Restrict the folders to which members of a user group have access. You can also determine whether members of a user group can delete files from your Web server.

- **Editing**   Restrict the amount of editing members of a user group can perform on pages not created with templates.

- **Styles and Fonts**   Restrict the fonts and styles that members of a user group can apply to Web page text.

- **New Pages**   Control the look of new Web pages created by a user group by specifying which type of page or template can be used as the basis for a new Web page.

- **New Images**   Restrict the file size of new images that members of a user group can add to Web pages.

When you administer a Web site, you can create as many user groups as you need. You can create one user group for colleagues responsible for editing text, another user group responsible for editing graphic elements in the sites you administer, and so on.

Working with User Groups

If you administer a small Web site and have only a few members on your Web editing team, you may find it acceptable to work with the Contribute default of one user group. However, if you are responsible for a Web site with hundreds of pages, you'll find it easier to manage the editing of Web pages by assigning certain tasks to members of your Web editing team. You can create a user group for specific tasks and then define permissions for that group. For example, you could create a user group for copy editors, new page editors, image editors, and so on. You define permissions for a group based on the tasks group members will be performing and their experience. For example, if you have a group for copy editors, you can prohibit members of this group from accessing folders or files at the Web server. You can also restrict the styles and fonts they use in order to maintain the look of the other

15

Web pages on the site. If you create a group for new page editors, you can restrict the templates or pages they can use as the basis for a new Web page.

Creating a User Group

You can create a new user group at any time. Creating new user groups enables you to divide the Web editing workflow as your site grows and evolves. To create a new user group, follow these steps:

1. Choose Edit | Administer Websites and select the name of the Web site you want to administer. The Administer Password dialog box appears.

2. Enter your password and then click OK or press ENTER. The Administer Website dialog box shown next appears.

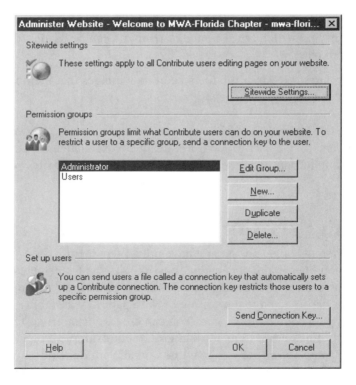

3. Click the New button in the Permission Groups section of the Administer Website dialog box. The Permission Group Name dialog box shown next appears.

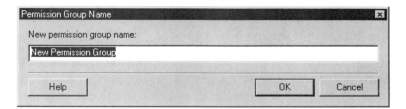

4. Enter a name for the user group. Choose a name that reflects the tasks the user group will perform.

5. Click OK. The new user group is added to the list in the Permission Groups section. After you add a new user group, you can edit it to specify permissions for the group.

6. Click OK to close the Administer Website dialog box. Contribute uploads the changes to your Web server.

Duplicating a User Group

When you need to create a new user group that has almost identical permissions to those permitted to an existing user group, you can save yourself a lot of work by duplicating the applicable group. When you duplicate a group, you can assign a unique name for the duplicated user group and fine-tune the permissions by editing the user group. To duplicate a user group, follow these steps:

1. Choose Edit | Administer Websites and select the name of the Web site you want to duplicate. The Administer Password dialog box appears.

2. Enter your password and then click OK or press ENTER. The Administer Website dialog box appears.

3. In the Permission Groups section, select the name of the user group you want to duplicate.

4. Click the Duplicate button. The Permission Group Name dialog box appears. The name of the original user group appears in the dialog box appended by the next available number. For example, if you are duplicating a user group called Editors, Contribute's default name for the duplicated group is Editors 1.

5. Accept the default name for the duplicated user group, or enter a new name.

6. Click OK. The duplicated user group appears in the Permission Groups section of the Administer Website dialog box. You can edit the duplicate

15

user group by clicking Edit. Editing permissions for a user group is covered in the "Editing a User Group" section.

7. Click OK to exit the Administer Website dialog box. Contribute uploads the changes to your Web server.

Removing a User Group

As your Web site matures, you may find it necessary to remove a user group. When you remove a user group, its members will no longer be able to connect to the Web site and edit pages. To remove a user group, follow these steps:

1. Choose Edit | Administer Websites and select the name of the Web site you want to remove. The Administer Password dialog box appears.

2. Enter your password and then click OK or press ENTER. The Administer Website dialog box appears.

3. In the Permission Groups section, select the user group you want to remove.

4. Click Delete. Contribute displays a warning dialog box asking if you're sure you want to delete the user group.

5. Click Yes to remove the user group. Or, click No to preserve the user group.

6. Click OK to exit the Administer Website dialog box. Contribute uploads the changes to your Web server.

Administering Site Permissions

After you set up your user groups, you can assign different permissions to each group. By modifying each group's permissions, you ensure that your Web pages will have a consistent look and quality. If each group is assigned a specific task, you can tailor the group's permissions to fit the job at hand. If you don't want a group to have access to certain privileges—for example, access to files or folders at the Web server—you deny the group access. If you're working with a smaller editing team that consists of two or three groups, you can create a group of your most trusted and experienced employees and give that group more permission than employees who are just beginning to edit Web pages with Contribute.

Editing a User Group

To assign permissions, you must edit each user group. When you edit a user group, you can specify settings for each of the six permissions sections discussed earlier in this chapter. In the following sections, you'll learn to specify settings for each section of the Permission Group dialog box.

Setting General Permissions

When you set general permissions, you can modify the group description and specify the group's home page. To set general permissions for a user group:

1. Choose Edit | Administer Websites and select the name of the Web site you want to administer. The Administrator Password dialog box appears.

2. Enter your password and then click OK or press ENTER. The Administer Website dialog box appears.

3. Select the name of the user group whose permissions you want to modify. The General section of the Permission Group dialog box appears. The Group Description text is highlighted, as shown in Figure 15-1.

4. Accept the default Group Description, or enter a new one. It's a good idea to give an accurate description of the group's Web editing duties, especially if you're sharing site administrator duties with other colleagues.

NOTE *When you create a new user group, the Group Description field is blank.*

5. Accept the default Group Home Page (the home page of the site), or click the Choose button to open the Choose File On Website dialog box. Select the Web page file that will serve as the user group's home page and then click OK to close the dialog box.

6. Click OK to close the Permission Group dialog box. Or, you can select another permission group to edit.

7. Click OK to close the Administer Website dialog box. Contribute uploads the new settings to your Web server.

15

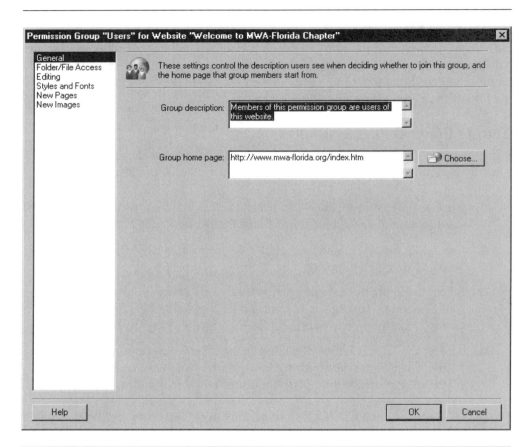

FIGURE 15-1   You can modify a user group's description and home page.

Setting File and Folder Permissions

When you're setting permissions for a group, you can also specify whether the user group has access to files and folders on your Web server. If you decide to give the user group folder access, you can specify the folders to which the group has access. To set folder and file permissions:

1. Choose Edit | Administer Websites and select the name of the Web site you want to administer. The Administrator Password dialog box appears.

2. Enter your password and then click OK or press ENTER. The Administer Website dialog box appears.

3. Select the name of the user group whose permissions you want to modify. The General section of the Permission Group dialog box appears.

4. Click Folder/File Access. The Permission Group dialog box is reconfigured, as shown next.

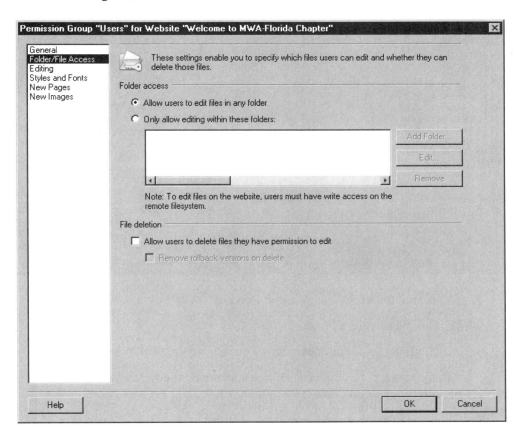

5. In the Folder Access section, do one of the following:

■ Click the Allow Users To Edit Files In Any Folder radio button to give the user group unlimited access to folders on your Web server. If you select this option, proceed to step 9.

■ Click the Only Allow Editing Within These Folders radio button to restrict folder access. To specify which folders you want the group to access, proceed to step 6.

15

6. Click the Add Folder button. The Choose Folder dialog box appears, as shown next.

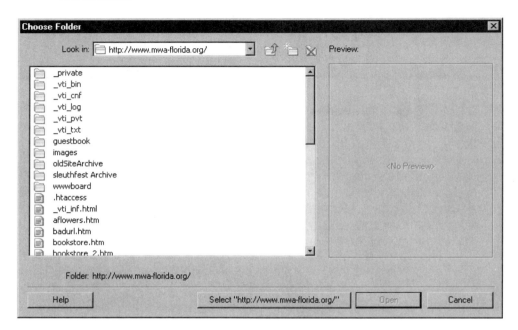

7. To select a folder, do one of the following:

- Double-click the folder.

- Click the folder and then click Open.

After you select the folder, its name appears on the Select button at the bottom of the dialog box.

8. Click the Select button. Contribute adds the folder to the list. To add other folders to the list, repeat steps 6 through 8.

9. In the File Deletion section, click the Allow Users To Delete Files They Have Permission To Edit check box to allow members of this user group to delete files in folders to which you have given them access.

10. In the File Deletion section, click the Remove Rollback Versions On Delete check box; Contribute will then delete rollback versions of files that members of this user group delete. If you choose this option, you will not be able to recover previous versions of deleted files such as Web pages and edited images.

11. Click OK to exit the Permission Group dialog box. Or, select another section to edit.

12. Click OK to exit the Administer Website dialog box. Contribute uploads your revisions to the Web server.

 While editing the Folder/File Access section for a user group, you can remove access to a folder by selecting it and then clicking the Remove button. To modify access to a folder (for example, allowing access to a subfolder), select the folder you want to edit and then click the Edit button.

Defining Editing Permissions

You can also control the amount of editing members of a user group can perform on Web pages, and determine how Contribute handles the creation of new paragraphs and spaces. You can give a user group unlimited editing privileges or limit the group to editing and formatting text. To define editing permissions for a user group, follow these steps:

1. Choose Edit | Administer Websites and select the name of the Web site you want to administer. The Administrator Password dialog box appears.

2. Enter your password and then click OK or press ENTER. The Administer Website dialog box appears.

3. Select the name of the user group whose permissions you want to modify. The General section of the Permission Group dialog box appears.

4. Click Editing. The Group Permissions dialog box is reconfigured, as shown in Figure 15-2.

5. In the Non-Template Pages section, choose one of the following options:

   ■ **Allow unrestricted editing**   Allows members of this user group to edit any page element supported by Contribute, such as inserting tables, images, and so on. If you choose this option, the Protect Scripts And Forms option is enabled by default. Deselect this option to allow members of this user group to delete code tags, form tags, and form elements.

15

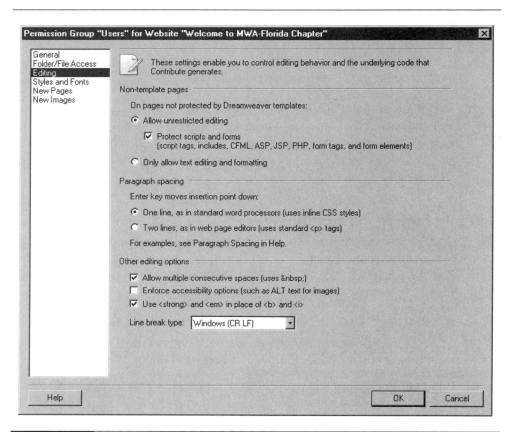

FIGURE 15-2 You can specify editing options for a user group.

CAUTION *It is recommended that you enable the Protect Scripts And Forms option. If a user inadvertently deletes a required tag, the associated Web page may not function properly, and the services of a Web designer will be required to fix the error.*

■ **Only allow text editing**   Allows members of this user group to edit only text elements and apply formatting such as styles, numbered lists, or bulleted lists. If you choose this option, members of this user group will not be able to edit images, tables, links, and so on.

6. In the Paragraph Spacing section, choose one of the following options:

   - **One line, as in standard word processors** Causes paragraphs to be spaced closer together than standard HTML paragraph spacing. If you choose this option, members of this user group can insert standard HTML paragraph spacing by pressing ENTER twice.

   - **Two lines, as in Web page editors** Inserts two spaces after each paragraph, as the standard HTML <p> tag does. When members of this user group press ENTER, Contribute inserts the standard <p> paragraph tag and two spaces appear below the paragraph when the page is displayed in a Web browser.

7. In the Other Editing Options section, choose one of the following options:

   - **Allow multiple consecutive spaces** Allows members of this user group to insert multiple spaces between words. When Web pages are created with this option, and multiple spaces are inserted, Contribute inserts the necessary tag (< >) each time the user presses the spacebar. When the page is displayed in a Web browser, all of the spaces inserted by the page editor will be displayed instead of a single space.

   - **Enforce accessibility options** Causes Contribute to prompt members of this user group to insert accessibility options, such as alternate text that enables visually impaired Web page visitors to view text descriptions of images. This option also allows viewers with text-only browsers to view image descriptions.

   - **Use <strong> and <em> in place of <b> and <i>** Causes Contribute to use the <strong> and <em> tags when members of this user group boldface or italicize text. The latest browsers prefer these tags to the <b> and <i> tags.

8. Click the triangle to the right of the Line Break Type field and choose an option from the drop-down menu. Choose the option that pertains to the operating system used by the Web server hosting your site. For example, accept the default Windows (CR LF) option if your Web hosting service uses a Windows NT machine. If you are unsure as to the type of machine used by your Web hosting service, check with their technical support team.

15

9. Click OK to exit the Permission Group dialog box. Or, select another section to edit.

10. Click OK to exit the Administer Website dialog box. Contribute uploads the changed settings to your Web server.

Specifying Formatting Permissions

When you specify Styles and Fonts permissions, you determine which styles and fonts members of a user group can apply to Web page text. You also determine how Contribute applies fonts. To specify formatting permissions for a user group:

1. Choose Edit | Administer Websites and select the name of the Web site you want to administer. The Administrator Password dialog box appears.

2. Enter your password and then click OK or press ENTER. The Administer Website dialog box appears.

3. Select the name of the user group whose permissions you want to modify. The General section of the Permission Group dialog box appears.

4. Click Styles And Fonts. The Permission Group dialog box is reconfigured, as shown in Figure 15-3.

5. In the Styles section, accept the default Allow Users To Apply Styles option. If you deselect this option, the Styles menu will not be available to members of this user group. If you accept the default option, you can choose one or both of the following options:

   - **Include HTML paragraph and heading styles**   This option displays HTML paragraph and heading styles. When users select one of these styles, Contribute automatically creates the proper tags to display the style in a viewer's Web browser.

   - **Includes CSS styles in the Styles menu**   This option displays any styles that have been defined using a Cascading Style Sheet. The Cascading Style Sheet can be linked to the HTML page or included in the head section of the document.

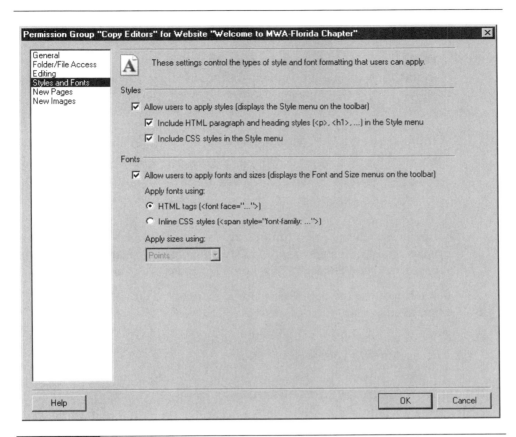

FIGURE 15-3   You can specify which styles and fonts are available to a user group.

6. In the Fonts section, accept the default Allow Users To Apply Fonts And Sizes option. If you deselect this option, the Font and Sizes menus will not be available to members of this user group, and the text will be formatted using the Web page HTML code. If you accept the default option, you can

choose one of the following options to determine how Contribute applies fonts and sizes:

- **HTML tags**   Contribute will format the text using HTML tags. For example, text using the Verdana font face will be coded as follows:

```
<font face="Verdana, Arial, Helvetica, sans-serif">Text to be styled. </font
face>
```

- **Inline CSS styles**   Contribute will use inline CSS tags to apply font styles. For example, text using the Geneva font face will be coded as follows:

```
<span style="font-family: Geneva, Arial, Helvetica, sans-serif"> Text to be
styled.</span>
```

- **Apply sizes using**   Determines which unit of measure Contribute uses when applying a style using CSS styles. Click the triangle to the right of the field and choose Pixels, Points, or Ems.

7. Click OK to close the Permission Group dialog box. Or, select another section to edit.

8. Click OK to close the Administer Website dialog box. Contribute uploads the new settings to your Web server.

Defining New Web Page Permissions

You can maintain a uniform look throughout the Web sites you administer by modifying the New Pages section of the Permission Group dialog box. You can specify how a new Web page is created. You can allow members of a user group to flex their creative muscles by creating a new page from a blank page, or you can specify which pages and templates they can use to create a new page. Choosing the latter option ensures that the site will have a uniform look and feel. To define New Page permissions, follow these steps:

1. Choose Edit | Administer Websites and select the name of the Web site you want to administer. The Administrator Password dialog box appears.

2. Enter your password and then click OK or press ENTER. The Administer Website dialog box appears.

3. Select the name of the user group whose permissions you want to modify. The General section of the Permission Group dialog box appears.

4. Click New Pages. The Permission Group dialog box is reconfigured, as shown in Figure 15-4.

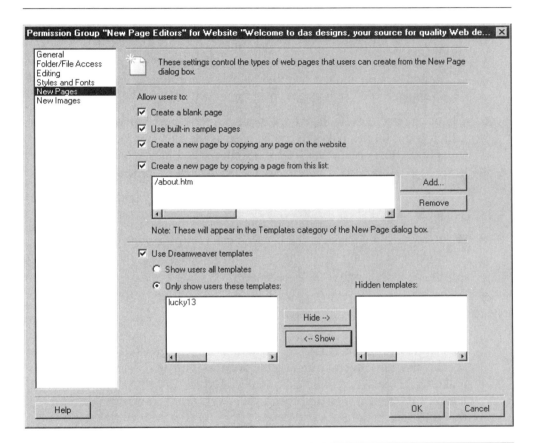

FIGURE 15-4   You can maintain Web page uniformity by specifying which methods can be used to create new Web pages.

5. In the Allow Users To section, choose one or all of the following options:

- **Create a blank page** This default option enables members of this user group to use a blank page as the basis for a new Web page. This is the Contribute equivalent of placing a blank piece of paper in a typewriter—members of the user group are given a blank canvas with which to work.

- **Use built-in sample pages** This default option enables members of this user group to use a Contribute preset page as the basis for a new page.

- **Create a new page by copying any page on the website** This default option enables members of this user group to copy an existing Web page and use it as the basis for a new page.

6. Choose Create A New Page By Copying A Page From This List to specify which pages on the Web site can be used as the basis for a new page. When you choose this option, the Add and Remove buttons become available.

- Click the Add button to open the Choose File On Website dialog box. Select a page to add to the list and then click OK. Contribute adds the page to the list.

- After you add pages to the list, you can remove a page by selecting it and then clicking the Remove button. This removes the page from the list, but does not delete the page from the site.

7. Choose the default Use Dreamweaver Templates option to allow members of this user group to use Dreamweaver templates that have been created by your Web designer and uploaded to your Web server. Dreamweaver templates have editable regions that users can add text or images to, and non-editable regions that have been locked by the creator of the template. When you make Dreamweaver templates available to your Web editing team, you ensure a consistent look and feel for the Web site. You can choose from the following options:

- **Show users all templates** Enables members of this user group to select any Dreamweaver template from the Web site.

- ■ **Only show users these templates** Activates the Show and Hide buttons. To hide a template from members of this user group, select the template you want to hide from the left window and then click the Hide button to add the template to the Hidden Templates window. To make a hidden template available to members of this user group, select the hidden template from the Hidden Templates window and then click the Show button to add the template to the list in the left window.

8. Click OK to close the Permission Group dialog box.

9. Click OK to close the Administer Website dialog box. Contribute uploads the changed settings to your Web server.

TIP *If you don't want your Web site to deviate from the look and feel of what your designer created, don't allow members of any user group to create a new page from a blank Web page or one of the Contribute presets. You can do this by deselecting the first two options in the New Pages section of the Permission Group dialog box.*

Defining New Image Parameters

Images are an important part of any Web site, but so is usability. If a Web page is cluttered with several images that have large file sizes, the page will load slowly into the user's browser, especially if the user is accessing the Internet with a dial-up connection. In this regard, you can limit the maximum file size of images that your Web editing team adds to pages, but not the number of images. Limiting file size is one safeguard against slow-loading Web pages; however, as site administrator you should inform your Web editing team not to overload a page with images. You can limit the maximum file size of images added to pages by following these steps:

1. Choose Edit | Administer Websites and select the name of the Web site you want to administer. The Administrator Password dialog box appears.

2. Enter your password and then click OK or press ENTER. The Administer Website dialog box appears.

15

3. Select the name of the user group whose permissions you want to modify. The General section of the Permission Group dialog box appears.

4. Click New Images. The Permission Group dialog box is reconfigured, as shown in Figure 15-5.

5. Accept the Unlimited option and members of this user group will be able to insert an image no matter how large the file size. I recommend deselecting this option unless your Web pages are being viewed over a corporate intranet with a blindingly fast connection.

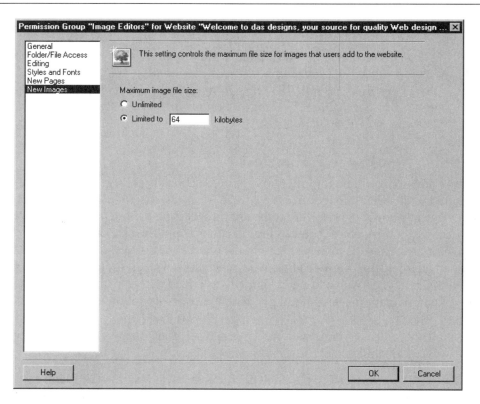

FIGURE 15-5   You can limit the file size of images that are added to Web pages.

6. Click Limited To [ ] Kilobytes. The default size is 64K, but this is still quite large, especially when you consider that members of a user group can insert an unlimited number of images per page. If users with slow connections to the Internet will view your Web pages, you should specify a maximum file size no larger than 40K.

7. Click OK. The Permission Group dialog box closes.

8. Click OK. The Administer Website dialog box closes. Contribute uploads the new settings to your Web server.

Did you know?

You Can Load Images in Stages

Have you ever visited a Web site where the pictures seemed to load in stages? When the page first loads, you see a low resolution (or, as the image editing gurus refer to it, pixelated) image that appears to be very blocky. On the next pass, the image is displayed normally. If the image is a JPEG file, you are viewed a Progressive JPEG. If you're viewing a GIF image, this is an Interlaced GIF.

If any member of your Web-editing team tells you they absolutely have to stack the page with images, tell them to edit the images in a program where they can export the image as an Interlaced GIF file, or a Progressive JPEG file. If you have an experienced image editor on your Web design team, they can export the images in the appropriate format using an image editor such as Firework MX. Fireworks MX lets your image-editing guru display the images side-by-side using different image formats, whereupon your image editor can compare image quality and file size before exporting the image so it loads in stages.

15

Summary

In this chapter, you learned to administer a Web site. You learned to create user groups and specify which items members of a user group can edit. You can also specify which fonts and styles members of user groups can use, as well as what they can use to create new Web pages. You can also limit the maximum file size of images that each user group can add to Web pages. In the next chapter, you'll learn how to send a Web site connection to members of a user group.

Chapter 16

Defining Site Connections and Customizing Contribute

How to...

- ■ Send connections to user groups
- ■ Modify site connections
- ■ Set up a secure site
- ■ Customize Contribute

After you set up user groups and define permissions for user groups, your next task is to send connections to the members of each user group. When you send a connection to members of a user group, they can use it to connect to the Web site and begin editing Web pages. You can send a connection via e-mail or post it to a directory on your network server where your Web editing team can download it. After receiving a connection key, the recipient double-clicks the connection key, which launches Contribute. The recipient then is prompted to enter a password to unlock the key and enter his or her information. After completing the connection, the recipient inherits the permissions of the user group you selected when creating the connection.

When you administer a Web site, you can send a connection key to colleagues you want to have access to the site. The connection key you send is encrypted, which ensures that the information you send is secure and can be accessed only when the recipient double-clicks the key and Contribute launches.

The user group information and permissions are stored at your Web server. Whenever a user makes a connection to the site from within Contribute, the software recognizes the user by his or her e-mail address and allows the permissions you specified for the user group of which the user is a member.

Sending Site Connections to Other Team Members

After you decide which employees will be members of your Web editing team, and which user group each employee will be a member of, send the employee a connection key. You can send the connection key via e-mail or place it in a secure folder on your network server. To send a connection key to members of a user group, follow these steps:

1. Choose Edit | Administer Websites and choose the Web site you want to administer from the submenu. The Administrator dialog box appears.

2. Enter your administrator password and click OK. The Administer Website dialog box appears, as shown next.

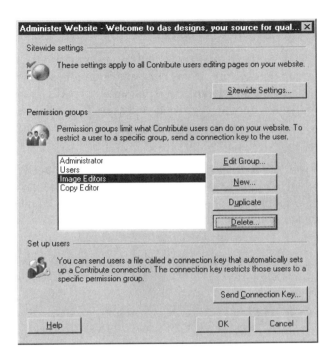

3. Click the Send Connection Key button. The Export Wizard shown next appears.

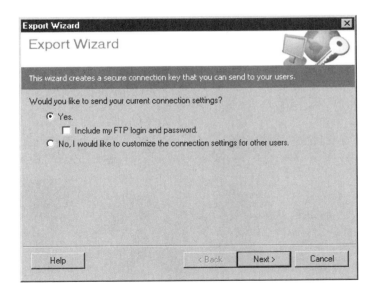

4. Choose one of the following options:

   ■ **Yes** This sends your current connection settings to the members of the user group you specify. If you choose this option, select the Include My FTP Login And Password check box and users will be able to connect to the Web site with your login and password. If you deselect this option, users will be prompted to enter their FTP logins and passwords. If you choose this option, proceed to step 5.

   ■ **No, I would like to customize the connection settings for other users** This option allows you to specify a different path to the server, for example, a directory on your network server where Web files are stored. If you choose this option, refer to the "Customizing a Connection Setting" section.

5. Click the Next button. The Group Information section of the Export Wizard appears, as shown next.

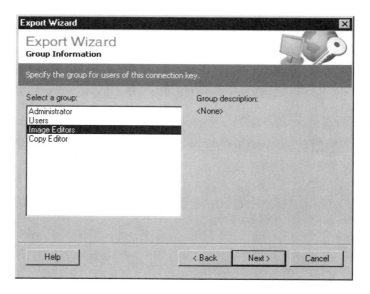

6. Select a user group and then click the Next button. The Connection Key Information section of the Export Wizard appears, as shown next.

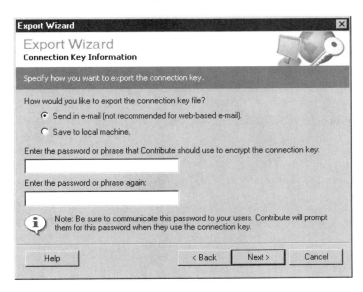

7. Choose one of the following methods for sending the connection key:

■ **Send in e-mail**   This option launches your default e-mail application and allows you to choose recipients for the connection key from your address book or by manually entering e-mail addresses. This option attaches the connection key to the e-mail. Even though the connection key is encrypted, Macromedia recommends that you do not send the connection key through Web-based e-mail.

■ **Save to local machine**   This option allows you to save the connection key to your local machine. If you're on a network, you can save it to any machine in your network to which you have access.

8. Enter a password and confirm it.

16

9. Click the Next button. The Summary section of the Export Wizard appears, as shown next.

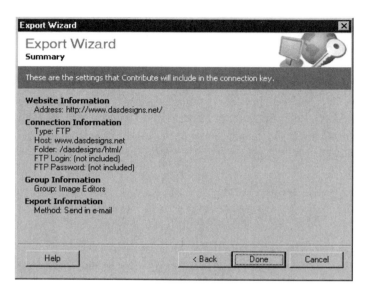

10. Click the Done button. Or, you can change any setting by clicking the Back button to return to the applicable section of the Export Wizard.

■ If you choose the e-mail option in step 7, your default e-mail application opens. Enter the e-mail addresses of the members of this user group to which you want to send the connection.

■ If you choose the Save To Local Machine option in step 7, the Export Connection Key dialog box appears. Navigate to the folder on your machine or to a folder on a machine in your network in which you want to save the connection key and then click the Save button.

If you send the connection key via e-mail, be sure to inform the recipients which password they will need to unlock the connection key. If you save the connection key in a folder on your local machine or network, send a memo to the members of the user group with the path to the connection key, as well as the password to unlock the connection key.

Customizing a Connection Setting

If your Web server has the option of multiple FTP users, you can specify different usernames and passwords for user groups. If your Web server is configured for multiple FTP users, you can create a custom connection setting to reflect the different usernames and passwords. To create a custom connection, follow these steps:

1. Follow steps 1–3 of the preceding section.

2. Choose No, I Want To Customize The Connection Settings For Other Users.

3. Click the Next button. The Connection Information section of the Export Wizard appears, as shown next.

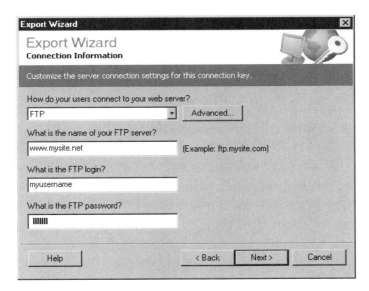

4. Click the triangle to the right of the How Do Your Users Connect To Your Web Server? and choose FTP or Local/Network. If you choose FTP, proceed to step 5; otherwise, proceed to step 10.

5. Enter the name of your FTP server—for example: www.myserver.com.

6. Enter the login name for the FTP server.

7. Enter the password for the FTP server.

16

8. If your company has a firewall, click the Advanced button. The Advanced Connection dialog box shown next opens.

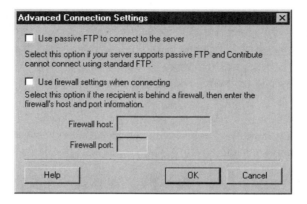

9. Choose one of the following connection options:

- **Use passive FTP to connect to the server**   Choose this option if your server supports passive FTP, and you cannot connect using standard FTP.

- **Use firewall settings when connecting**   Choose this option to create a connection through your company's firewall. If you are unsure of the settings, check with your company's IS or IT department.

10. If you are creating a connection to a local or network server, enter the path to the directory where Web files are stored on your server.

11. Click the Next button. The Group Information section of the Export Wizard opens.

12. Select the user group to which you want to send the connection key and then click the Next button. The Connection Key section of the Export Wizard appears.

13. Choose the method by which you want to send the connection key as outlined in the preceding section.

14. Enter and confirm the password that members of this user group will use to unlock the connection key.

15. Click the Next button. The Summary section of the Export Wizard appears.

16. Review the connection information and click Done. Or, you can change any setting by clicking the Back button to return to the applicable section of the Export Wizard.

NOTE *If you send the connection via Web-based e-mail, you may encounter an error message telling you the file cannot be attached to the message. If this occurs, relaunch the Export Wizard and re-create the connection key. Save the connection key to your hard drive and then send the attachment via your Web-based e-mail application and attach the connection key file to the e-mail. To reiterate, Macromedia recommends not sending a connection via Web-based e-mail, which is a good security measure. Even though the key is encrypted, it could be intercepted by a third party.*

Modifying Site Connections

If your organization moves the Web site you are administering to another server, you'll need to edit your connection and send a new connection key to members of your Web editing team. When you edit site connections, you can specify a new path to a local or network server or specify the URL for a new FTP server. For more information on editing site connections, refer to Chapter 3.

Setting Up a Secure Site

When you use Contribute to edit Web pages, file folders are created at your Web server to store information such as user groups, permissions, and rollback versions of your Web pages. Contribute stores these files in folders that begin with an underscore (_); for example, _mm, _baks, and _notes. The default configuration of most Web server software prevents visitors from viewing anything in a folder that begins with an underscore.

However, some Web server software must be configured to prevent visitors from accessing folders that begin with an underscore. If you are not sure how your server is configured, perform this simple test:

1. Launch Contribute.

2. Enter your site's Web address followed by a forward slash and **_mm**. For example: http://www.mysite.com/__mm.

3. You should see the error message shown in Figure 16-1. This means that visitors won't be able to access directories that begin with an underscore.

If the contents of the directory are listed, contact your Web server's technical support team and ask them how to deny access to these directories. If you are administering an intranet Web site, contact your IS or IT team and ask them how to configure your Web server software to prevent access to these folders.

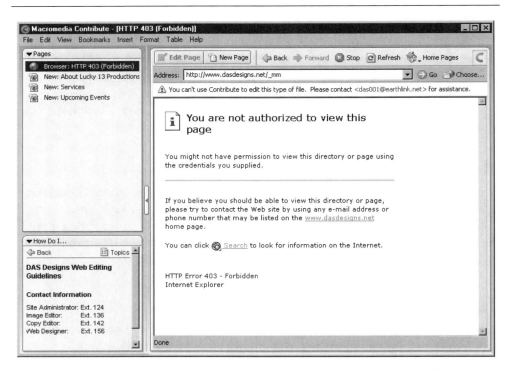

FIGURE 16-1   Visitors to your Web site should receive an error message if they attempt to view folders that begin with an underscore.

Troubleshooting Connection Difficulties

The Connection Wizard makes it possible for you to easily connect to a Web site that you want to edit. The wizard is set up so that you can configure the connection for a Web server or network. However, Web servers can differ, and in this regard, you may encounter problems while making a connection or modifying a connection key for a user group. The following is a list of commonly encountered connection problems and their solutions:

- **The next section of the Connection Wizard does not appear after clicking the Next button**   Make sure you have entered the proper information. For example, if you cannot advance past the Connection Information section, make sure that you have entered the proper username and password for an FTP connection or that you have entered the proper path for a network connection.

■ **Connection Wizard is unable to find the remote folder** Make sure that you have entered the proper URL to your FTP server. In most cases, the URL is the same as the URL to your Web site. If you experience difficulties, check with your Web server's tech support team to make sure that you've entered the proper URL to the FTP server.

> **TIP** *Most Web hosting companies send out an e-mail containing the FTP information when a Web site is initially set up. If this information is still available, it may include the path to the remote folder where Web files are stored.*

■ **Connection Wizard is unable to locate the remote folder on a network server** Contact a member of your IS or IT team to make sure that the folder in which your Web files are stored is shared throughout the network. If the folder is shared, make sure that the folder has read, write, overwrite, and rename privileges.

■ **The My Connections dialog box does not appear when you edit a connection** Make sure that you are working in online mode.

Dealing with Server Issues

Once you establish a connection to a Web site, you and members of your Web editing team can access any page or folder on the site and edit up to the limits of your permission group. However, there may be times when it seems as though you or a member of your Web page editing team cannot access a file or folder you previously edited. When this occurs, you may be confronted with a server issue. If your Web site is on a shared server, the server may have more traffic than it can handle, and you will not be able to connect to your Web site. If this occurs, try editing your pages in a few minutes. If this occurs on a continual basis, contact your Web server's technical support team and report the issue. If they are unable to help you, consider switching to a server that can handle more traffic.

If you are unable to publish a page after editing it, you may also be dealing with a busy server. Contribute depends on an active connection. If the server is busy, try waiting a few minutes before publishing the page. Also check to make sure that you are still connected to the server. If you become disconnected from the server, an error message to that effect is displayed below the Address field, and the Retry Connection button is activated. Wait a minute or so and then click the Retry Connection button to reestablish your connection with the server. If the problem occurs on a regular basis, contact your Web hosting service's technical support team for assistance.

16

Many Web hosting services limit their customers to a maximum amount of disk space in which files can be stored on the server. If you have minimal server disk space, and maintain a large Web site, you may exceed your maximum disk space if you enable a large number of rollbacks. If this becomes an issue, you can either decrease the number of rollbacks you make available to your Web editing team or contact your Web hosting service to procure additional storage space.

About Shared Settings Folders

Contribute creates files that contain information about shared settings. These files are stored in the _mm folder in the root of each Web site to which you have made a connection. Whenever you modify a group's permissions, this information is stored in the shared settings file on your Web server. Whenever members of a user group make a connection to a Web site you are administering, Contribute updates their permissions by reading the shared settings file.

Do not attempt to manually edit any shared settings file by using a text editor such as Notepad. When you need to change a user group's permissions, administer the Web site as outlined in Chapter 15.

About Web Hosting Services

A Web hosting service has a myriad of fast connections to the Internet and several server computers that have their customer's Web pages stored in them. When users enter a URL in their browser address field, they are connected to the computer that stores the pages for the Web site corresponding to the URL. Large organizations that need the utmost reliability generally purchase a dedicated server from the Web hosting service. A dedicated server has its own IP address. Smaller businesses and individuals can still get reliable service at a less expensive rate by purchasing a shared server. A shared server, as the name implies, shares several URLs at the same IP address. The URL of a Web site on a shared server points to a folder within a shared server.

The amount of features offered by a Web hosting company is truly amazing. Of course, the more features the steeper the price tag. Web hosting clients can choose the number of e-mail addresses for their site, the amount of disk storage used from the server, and other features such as a secure site for clients offering online purchasing options.

If you are a Web designer who also administers a Contribute Web site, you can do so from within Dreamweaver MX version 6.1 or greater. For more information on integrating Dreamweaver MX with Contribute, refer to Dreamweaver MX 6.1 or greater Help files, or visit Macromedia's Contribute developer pages at http://www.macromedia.com/desdev/contribute/.

Setting Up Contribute for Screen Readers

If members of your Web editing team are visually impaired, you can set up Contribute to work with screen readers such as JAWS. By default, support for screen readers is disabled because it may interfere with text editing features of Contribute. To enable support for screen readers, follow these steps:

1. Locate the ScreenSupport.htm file. The default location for this file is c:\Program Files\Macromedia\Contribute\Configuration\Startup.

 The location of the Startup directory may differ depending on your installation of Contribute and your operating system. If the files are not in the default location, use the Windows search utility to find the ScreenSupport.htm file.

2. Open the file in an HTML editor such as Dreamweaver or in a text editing utility such as Notepad.

3. Locate the following line of code:

```
var USING_SCREENREADER = false;
```

4. Change the code to read as follows:

```
var USING_SCREENREADER = true;
```

5. Save the file. Contribute should now be configured to work with most screen readers.

Customizing Contribute

As you've learned throughout the course of this book, you and members of your Web editing team can use Contribute to easily update and create new Web pages for your organization's Web site. As site administrator, you will be working with members of your team who have varying levels of skill and knowledge. Members of your Web editing team can use the Contribute How Do I… panel to get information about how to perform certain activities. You can customize the How Do I… panel by adding sections you want to make available to members of your Web editing

16

team, such as contact information or content guidelines for your organization's site. Each section opens an HTML document. A customized How Do I... panel is shown in Figure 16-2.

The individual sections in the How Do I... panel are HTML documents. You or your Web designer can create your own HTML documents for the How Do I... panel, but keep in mind that the panel has a limited amount of space in which to display the document. In this regard, you're better off using one of the existing HTML documents from the How Do I... panel as the basis for your custom page. You can create a custom page for your Web site to provide information for members of your Web editing team, as shown in Figure 16-3.

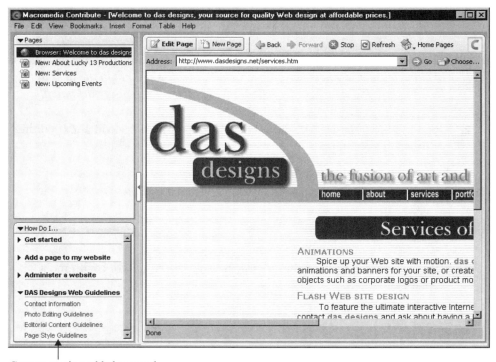

Custom section added to panel

FIGURE 16-2 You can customize the How Do I... panel to add guidelines specific to your organization.

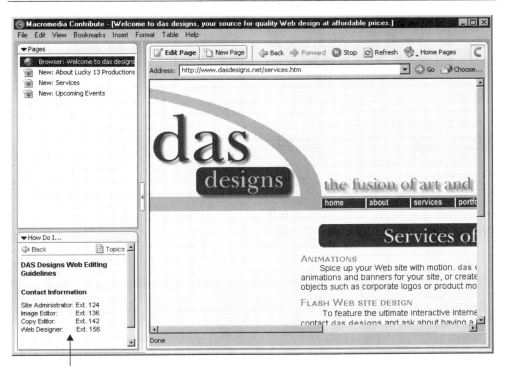

Custom page added to panel

FIGURE 16-3   You can create a custom page for the How Do I... panel.

To create a custom page for the How Do I... panel, follow these steps:

1. Launch an HTML editor such as Dreamweaver or a text editing application such as Notepad.

2. Navigate to the following directory: C:\Program Files\Macromedia\ Contribute\Configuration\Content\Tasks.

   NOTE   *The path to the Tasks folder may be different on your machine, depending on your installation of Contribute.*

3. Select one of the HTML documents. The document appears in your editing application.

16

4. Edit the document to reflect the information you want displayed within the How Do I... panel. Figure 16-4 shows a custom page for the How Do I... panel being edited in Dreamweaver MX. The document in this figure has already been saved with a new filename.

5. Choose File | Save As. Save the document as an HTML file in the Tasks folder, but give it a unique name. Do not put any spaces in the document name.

6. Create other documents as needed for your custom How Do I... panel section.

After you create the custom pages for the How Do I... panel, you're ready to modify the document that displays the headings and submenus in the How Do I... panel. This is an XML document called Tasks.xml. You can edit an XML document

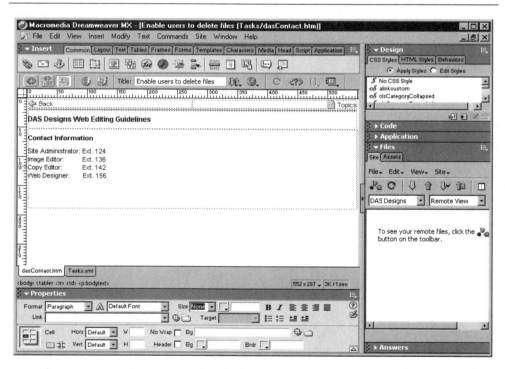

FIGURE 16-4   You can create a custom page by editing an existing page from the Tasks folder.

in a text editing program, or an HTML editor such as Dreamweaver MX. To edit the Tasks.xml document, follow these steps:

1. Launch an HTML editor such as Dreamweaver MX, or a text editing application such as Notepad.

2. Navigate to the following directory: C:\Program Files\Macromedia\ Contribute\Configuration\Content\Tasks.

NOTE *The path to the Tasks folder may be different on your machine, depending on your installation of Contribute.*

3. Select the file named Tasks.xml and open it. Notice that each section of the document is formatted with tags, as shown here:

```
<category name="Administer a website" id="25">
    <task name="Edit permission groups " file="task61.htm" id="26"/>
    <task name="Set up other users" file="task62.htm" id="27"/>
    <task name="Set up page rollback" file="task63.htm" id="28"/>
    <task name="Enable users to delete files" file="task64.htm" id="29"/>
</category>
```

The category name is the main listing for each group. When the category name is clicked, the category group expands to reveal each task name. Notice that the category name and each task name has an ID number. Each task name is linked to an HTML file that opens when the task name is clicked. You will be formatting your additions to the How Do I… panel in the same manner.

4. Scroll to the last category of the document.

5. Begin a new category section by placing your cursor to the right of the last </category> tag and pressing ENTER.

6. Enter your category name and format it as shown in the previous example. Use the next available ID number, as shown in the following example:

```
<category name="DAS Designs Web Guidelines" id="30">
```

7. Create a line of code for each task name as shown in the preceding example. Use the next available ID number for each task and enter the name of the HTML file that will open when the task name is clicked, as shown in the following example:

```
<task name="Contact information" file="dasContact.htm" id="31"/>
```

16

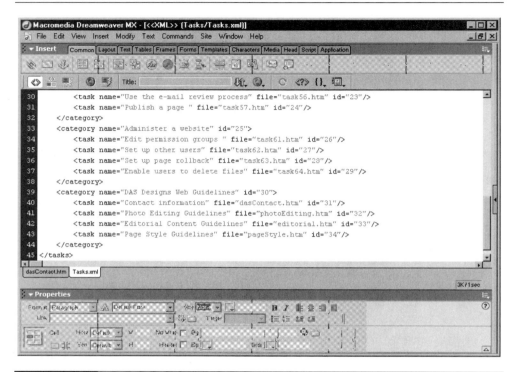

FIGURE 16-5 You edit the Tasks.xml file to add category names and links to the How Do I... panel.

8. After entering the code for each task, create a line of code that reads as follows:

```
</category>
```

9. Save the document. Figure 16-5 shows the Tasks.xml file being edited in Dreamweaver.

Summary

In this chapter, you learned to send connection keys to members of user groups. You also learned to deal with server issues and to set up Contribute for use with screen readers. You also learned how to customize the How Do I... panel. In the upcoming appendices, you'll find useful information about Contribute as well as keyboard shortcuts.

Part VI

Appendixes

Appendix A

Installing Contribute

In order to successfully use Contribute, your computer must meet minimum hardware and software requirements. Before installing Contribute on your machine, make sure your systems meet or exceed these minimum requirements:

- **Operating system** Windows 98, ME, NT (Service pack 3 or later), 2000, XP Home, XP Professional

- **Processor** Pentium ll or equivalent; 300 MHZ or faster

- **Memory** 64 MB of RAM (Random Access Memory)

- **Hard disk space** 275 MB of available disk space

- **Web Browser** Internet Explorer 5 or later

- **Monitor** 800×600 resolution with 256 colors (16- or 32-bit color is recommended for viewing and editing Web pages with JPEG images)

- **CD-ROM Player**

After you have ascertained that your equipment meets the minimum standards, you are ready to install Contribute on your machine. To install Contribute, follow these steps:

- Insert the Contribute installation disk in your CD-ROM drive. The Contribute installer launches.

- Follow the onscreen prompts to choose the directory in which Contribute will reside and enter your serial number.

- After the installation is complete, you can launch Contribute by double-clicking the Contribute icon on your desktop, or by choosing Start | Programs | Macromedia | Contribute.

- After Contribute launches, the Register Now screen appears. Click Register Now to register Contribute.

- You are now ready to create a connection to the Web sites you will be editing.

Appendix B

Contribute Keyboard Shortcuts

You can expedite your workflow in Contribute if you learn the keyboard shortcuts to the commands you use most frequently. You can speed up your work even more if you combine keyboard shortcuts with the context menu.

Command	Keyboard Shortcut
New Page	CTRL-N
Edit Page	CTRL-SHIFT-E
Publish	CTRL-SHIFT-P
Save	CTRL-S
Save for Later	CTRL-SHIFT-L
Preview in Browser	F12
Print	CTRL-P
Exit	CTRL-Q

TABLE B-1   File Menu Command Keyboard Shortcuts

Command	Keyboard Shortcut
Undo	CTRL-Z
Redo	CTRL-Y
Cut	CTRL-X
Copy	CTRL-C
Paste	CTRL-V
Paste Text Only	CTRL-SHIFT-V
Select All	CTRL-A
Find	CTRL-F

TABLE B-2   Edit Menu Command Keyboard Shortcuts

Menu Command	Keyboard Shortcut
Sidebar	F4
Browser	CTRL-SHIFT-B
Back	ALT-LEFT ARROW KEY
Forward	ALT-RIGHT ARROW KEY
Stop	ESC
Refresh	F5
Go to Web Address	CTRL-O
Choose File on Website	CTRL-SHIFT-O

TABLE B-3   View Menu Command Keyboard Shortcuts

Menu Command	Keyboard Shortcut
Image	From My Computer	CTRL-ALT-I
Table	CTRL-ALT-T
Links	Drafts and Recent Pages	CTRL-ALT-L
Section Anchor	CTRL-ALT-A
Line Break	SHIFT-ENTER
Special Characters	Non-breaking space	CTRL-SHIFT-SPACE

TABLE B-4   Insert Menu Command Keyboard Shortcuts

B

Menu Command	Keyboard Shortcut
Check Spelling	F7
Bold	CTRL-B
Italic	CTRL-I
Underline	CTRL-U
Align | Left	CTRL-ALT-SHIFT-L
Align | Center	CTRL-ALT-SHIFT-C
Align | Right	CTRL-ALT-SHIFT-R
Align | Justify	CTRL-ALT-SHIFT-J
Indent	CTRL-ALT-]
Outdent	CTRL-ALT-[
Keywords and Descriptions	CTRL-ALT-K
Page Properties	CTRL-J

TABLE B-5   Format Menu Command Keyboard Shortcuts

Menu Command	Keyboard Shortcut
Select Table	CTRL-T
Insert | Table	CTRL-ALT-T
Insert | Insert Row Above	CTRL-M
Merge Cells	CTRL-ALT-M
Split Cell	CTRL-ALT-S
Table Properties	CTRL-ALT-T

TABLE B-6   Table Menu Command Keyboard Shortcuts

Menu Command	Keyboard Shortcut
Macromedia Contribute Help	F1
Welcome Page	ALT-HOME

TABLE B-7   Help Menu Command Keyboard Shortcuts

Appendix C Contribute Resources

Contribute is a new product. However, Macromedia, a company well known for creating software for the Web, produces it. You won't find many resources for Contribute on the Web; however, you'll find several useful resources at Macromedia's Web site. Listed here are the URLs and descriptions of the most valuable Contribute resources at Macromedia.com.

Contribute Designer Developer Center
http://www.macromedia.com/desdev/contribute/

In this section of Macromedia's Web site, you'll find information devoted exclusively to Contribute. You'll find video tutorials here, information about administering Contribute Web sites, creating content for Contribute Web sites, and much more. You'll also find links to other valuable resources about Macromedia software and Web design.

Contribute Support Center
http://www.macromedia.com/support/contribute/

In the Contribute Support Center, you'll find the latest information about Contribute. You'll find technical notes and an extensive menu on the right side of the page that links to other important support information about Contribute, such as integrating the software with Dreamweaver, the latest updates and downloads, and more. You'll also find links to additional Contribute documentation that you can download and view with Adobe Acrobat Reader.

Contribute Online Forum
http://webforums.macromedia.com/contribute/

In the Contribute Online Forum, you'll be able to post messages about the software. If you've got a design issue, or are having a problem connecting to a Web site, you can post a message here. Chances are you'll receive a prompt response from a Macromedia volunteer or another Contribute user who experienced a similar problem and solved it.

University of Notre Dame, Office of Web Administration
http://web.nd.edu/resources/contribute_deploy.shtml

Here is a site with some excellent tips for Web site designers and administrators on how to structure a Contribute-friendly Web site. You'll find information on setting up folders for a Contribute Web site, working with Dreamweaver templates, and much more.

C

Index

INTERNATIONAL CONTACT INFORMATION

AUSTRALIA
McGraw-Hill Book Company Australia Pty. Ltd.
TEL +61-2-9900-1800
FAX +61-2-9878-8881
http://www.mcgraw-hill.com.au
books-it_sydney@mcgraw-hill.com

CANADA
McGraw-Hill Ryerson Ltd.
TEL +905-430-5000
FAX +905-430-5020
http://www.mcgraw-hill.ca

GREECE, MIDDLE EAST, & AFRICA
(Excluding South Africa)
McGraw-Hill Hellas
TEL +30-210-6560-990
TEL +30-210-6560-993
TEL +30-210-6560-994
FAX +30-210-6545-525

MEXICO (Also serving Latin America)
McGraw-Hill Interamericana Editores S.A. de C.V.
TEL +525-117-1583
FAX +525-117-1589
http://www.mcgraw-hill.com.mx
fernando_castellanos@mcgraw-hill.com

SINGAPORE (Serving Asia)
McGraw-Hill Book Company
TEL +65-863-1580
FAX +65-862-3354
http://www.mcgraw-hill.com.sg
mghasia@mcgraw-hill.com

SOUTH AFRICA
McGraw-Hill South Africa
TEL +27-11-622-7512
FAX +27-11-622-9045
robyn_swanepoel@mcgraw-hill.com

SPAIN
McGraw-Hill/Interamericana de España, S.A.U.
TEL +34-91-180-3000
FAX +34-91-372-8513
http://www.mcgraw-hill.es
professional@mcgraw-hill.es

UNITED KINGDOM, NORTHERN,
EASTERN, & CENTRAL EUROPE
McGraw-Hill Education Europe
TEL +44-1-628-502500
FAX +44-1-628-770224
http://www.mcgraw-hill.co.uk
computing_neurope@mcgraw-hill.com

ALL OTHER INQUIRIES Contact:
Osborne/McGraw-Hill
TEL +1-510-549-6600
FAX +1-510-883-7600
http://www.osborne.com
omg_international@mcgraw-hill.com

New Offerings from Osborne's
How to Do Everything Series

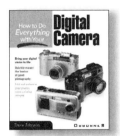

How to Do Everything with Your Digital Camera
ISBN: 0-07-212772-4

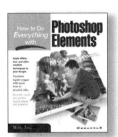

How to Do Everything with Photoshop Elements
ISBN: 0-07-219184-8

How to Do Everything with Photoshop 7
ISBN: 0-07-219554-1

How to Do Everything with Digital Video
ISBN: 0-07-219463-4

How to Do Everything with Your Scanner
ISBN: 0-07-219106-6

How to Do Everything with Your Palm™ Handheld, 2nd Edition
ISBN: 0-07-219100-7

HTDE with Your Pocket PC 2nd Edition
ISBN: 07-219414-6

How to Do Everything with iMovie
ISBN: 0-07-22226-7

How to Do Everything with Your iMac, 3rd Edition
ISBN: 0-07-213172-1

How to Do Everything with Your iPAQ
ISBN: 0-07-222333-2

 O S B O R N E
w w w . o s b o r n e . c o m

Orders: McGraw-Hill Customer Service 1-800-722-4726 fax 1-614-755-5645   For more information: Karolyn_Anderson@mcgraw-hill.com 1-617-472-3555   www.books@mcgraw-hill.com/library/html

Finally!

because technology should
improve your life, not complicate it...

Start!
the *no nonsense* guide to
Mac OS X Jaguar

Click!
the *no nonsense* guide to
Digital Cameras

Start!
the *no nonsense* guide to
Windows XP

Create!
the *no nonsense* guide to
Photoshop Elements 2

The No Nonsense approach
at a no frills price.